FEMALE SEXUAL ABUSE OF CHILDREN

The Ultimate Taboo

Edited by
Michele Elliott

JOHN WILEY & SONS
Chichester · New York · Weinheim · Brisbane · Singapore · Toronto

First published in 1993 by Longman Group UK Ltd
This edition published in 1997 by John Wiley & Sons Ltd,
Baffins Lane, Chichester,
West Sussex PO19 1UD, England

National   01243 779777
International (+44) 1243 779777
e-mail (for orders and customer service enquiries):
cs-books@wiley.co.uk
Visit our Home Page on http://www.wiley.co.uk *or*
http://www.wiley.com

Other Wiley Editorial Offices

John Wiley & Sons, Inc., 605 Third Avenue,
New York, NY 10158-0012, USA

VCH Verlagsgesellschaft mbH, Pappelallee 3,
D-69469 Weinheim, Germany

Jacaranda Wiley Ltd, 33 Park Road, Milton,
Queensland 4064, Australia

John Wiley & Sons (Asia) Pte Ltd, 2 Clementi Loop #02-01,
Jin Xing Distripark, Singapore 129809

John Wiley & Sons (Canada) Ltd, 22 Worcester Road,
Rexdale, Ontario M9W 1L1, Canada

British Library Cataloguing in Publication Data

A catalogue record for this book is available from the British Library

ISBN 0-471-97221-5

Typeset by Anglia Photoset Ltd, Colchester
Printed and bound in Malaysia by TCP

Contents

List of contributors

Michele Elliott is a child psychologist and the founder and Director of the children's protection charity, KIDSCAPE. She has chaired World Health Organisation and Home Office Working Groups on child sexual abuse and was awarded a Winston Churchill Fellowship. She has published numerous books and articles and is a leading expert in the field of child abuse prevention.

Hilary Eldridge is Head of Training and Programme Development at Gracewell Institute. After completing post-graduate training at Leicester University School of Social Work, she worked as a probation officer for thirteen years, specialising in work with sex offenders. She joined Gracewell when it opened in 1988, and was involved in designing and running its residential assessment and treatment programme for male sex offenders. In 1990, she began working with women offenders on a non-residential basis.

Hereward Harrison is the Director of Counselling at ChildLine, and is a qualified social worker and psychotherapist with 25 years' experience. He has worked with a variety of voluntary and public agencies in the UK and USA. He was Principal Social Worker (Teaching) at Guy's Hospital before joining ChildLine.

Kate Hunter trained as a nurse, then worked as a health visitor. She then trained as a counsellor at Bristol University. She is currently working as a counsellor employed by a group of general practitioners in Bath. She also sees some clients on a private basis.

Kathryn Jennings completed both her BA and MA degrees in Criminology at the University of Toronto in Canada. The title of her Master's thesis was 'The Demographic Characteristics of Child Molesters in a Relapse Prevention Programme' and was completed in

September 1990. She is currently working on her Doctorate in Sociology at The Ontario Institute of Studies in Education, The University Of Toronto. Her research interests primarily lie within the area of sexual offenders. The focus of her PhD thesis will be on female child molesters. Miss Jennings has worked with many types of offenders in various occupations and settings such as probation and parole, correctional centres, treatment facilities and group homes. She thoroughly enjoys her work and plans to continue researching and working in this field.

Jane Kinder Matthews, is a Psychologist and Clinical Director of Transition Place, St Paul, Minnesota, which is an outpatient mental health clinic specialising in the treatment and evaluation of child sexual abuse victims and offenders. She has been working with adult female offenders since 1985 and adult male offenders since 1980. She co-authored a study on *Reunification of Sexually Abusive Families*, which has been published in *Family Sexual Abuse, Frontline Research and Evaluation* edited by Michael Quinn Patton. She also co-authored *Female Sexual Offenders: An Exploratory Study*, the first study published which dealt with working therapeutically with female sexual abusers. Jane Kinder Matthews continues to develop important work with female sexual abusers.

Cianne Longdon, psychotherapist and trainer, specialises in working with survivors of female sexual abuse. She is writing a book based on her own experiences as a therapist and survivor for other survivors and professionals working with them. She is currently researching the nature of female sexual abuse in our society, and has set up the first national association (AWARE) aimed at helping both professionals and survivors. She can be contacted through KIDSCAPE.

Nora M. Sargent MA holds a Masters Degree in Counselling in Ministry from Fairfield University, Fairfield, Connecticut and is now a doctoral candidate in Clinical Psychology at the University of Rhode Island. Ms Sargent is also a therapist at New England Clinical Associates in West Hartford, Connecticut, where she has worked extensively with adolescent and adult victims of child sexual abuse, as well as with offenders. Ms Sargent is a contributor to *Vulnerable Populations, Volume 2* published by Lexington Books, 1989 and to the *Revised Handbook of Clinical Intervention in Child Sexual Abuse*, Lexington Books, 1993, edited by Suzanne M. Sgroi.

Suzanne M. Sgroi MD is the Executive Director of New England Clinical Associates, West Hartford, Connecticut, a private office devoted to the treatment of child sexual abuse. She also is the Director of the Saint Joseph College Institute for Child Sexual Abuse Intervention. Dr Sgroi is the author of the two volume work: *Vulnerable Populations, Volume 1, Evaluation and Treatment of Sexually Abused Children and Adult Survivors* and *Volume 2, Sexual Abuse Treatment for Children, Adult Survivors, Offenders and Persons with Mental Retardation,* published by Lexington Books, Lexington, Massachusetts. She is also the author of the pioneering work, *Handbook of Clinical Intervention in Child Sexual Abuse,* published by Lexington Books in 1982, with a Revised Edition published in 1993. This book was awarded the American Journal of Nursing Book of the Year Award in 1983. A strong advocate for specialised treatment for adult survivors, Dr Sgroi has extensive experience with this population. Dr Sgroi is recognised as one of the world experts in evaluating and treating child sexual abuse.

Olive Wolfers was formerly employed by Social Services as Development Officer (Child Sexual Abuse). She gained an MA in Social and Community Work at Bradford University in 1990. Olive has recently joined NSPCC and is working as a trainer and in a direct capacity with adults and young people who are involved in sexually aggressive behaviour. In 1987 Olive and a probation colleague initiated a joint agency Child Sexual Abuse Perpetrators Project, which is now an official alternative to custody. More recently Olive has researched Women–Child Sexual Abusers. Primarily a practitioner, Olive has worked for many years with children and young people, previously subjected to sexual abuse, specialising in assessment and therapeutic work, and it is their influence and experience which is pivotal in all the work she undertakes.

Val Young is a women's psychotherapist, and works in a natural health co-operative practice in North London. Her holistic approach is based on feminist understanding, and she is committed to demystifying therapy. Other work includes training, group facilitation and supervision, and she holds workshops on self-help techniques. In common with other professionals working with adult survivors and in child protection, she feels that there is considerable misunderstanding and denial of the nature and extent of all forms of abuse in Western society, and that in failing to invest in its prevention, society is abusing itself as well as perpetuating the abuse of the children in its care. She says 'We are now seeing the consequences of decades, probaby centuries, of child abuse in the West, and these are far more serious and real than whatever fears or fantasies have held us back from facing the reality of this collective shame.'

Acknowledgements

I am indebted to all those survivors who have had the courage to write and talk about the abuse they suffered as children. Meeting and sharing their experiences has had a profound effect on me and I want to acknowledge them all. Wherever possible, I have let the men and women tell their stories in their own way. At times, I have had to consolidate, rewrite and edit, but this has been done with their help.

I am grateful, as well, to the professionals who have taken valuable time to write about working with survivors. Suzanne Sgroi and Norah Sargent and Kate Hunter provide detailed, practical guidance on how to enable adult survivors to learn to cope and go on with their lives. Cianne Longdon offers a unique perspective from a therapist/survivor's view. Hereward Harrison provides us with the child's voice — what today's children are telling the national helpline, ChildLine. Olive Wolfers and Val Young give the basis for new insights about child sexual abuse and Kathryn Jennings shows how little has been written about female sexual abuse.

I felt it important to include chapters on working with abusers because the majority were themselves victims of child abuse. I do not expect survivors to understand or to deal with the chapters on abusers, but professionals working with women abusers will welcome the advice and guidance that Jane Kinder Matthews and Hilary Eldridge have provided, and I am very grateful that they have contributed to the book.

The professionals and survivors I talked with come from the United States, the United Kingdom, Australia and Canada. I am sure that there are professionals and survivors in other parts of the world who have important contributions to make to this subject and they are welcome to contact me at KIDSCAPE. (KIDSCAPE is a registered charity with the aim of keeping children safe.)

There are many others who have lived through and helped with the conception of this book and I owe them a big vote of thanks: Sue Woods, Jane Kilpatrick, Melanie Penders, Daphne Joiner, Linda

Llewellyn, Frances O'Loughlin and my husband Ed and children
Charles and James.

Michele Elliott
KIDSCAPE, Keeping Kids Safe
152 Buckingham Palace Road
London SW1W 9TR
Tel: (071) 730 3300

1 Introduction

Michele Elliott

'I thought I would die before anyone recognised the pain I was in. My mother and grandmother sexually abused me from the time I was four. I hated going home and spent most of my time figuring out how to get out of the house. I ran away continuously from the age of 6. I begged my aunt to let me live with her. In my life I have taken most drugs, been alcoholic, had a nervous breakdown and have never had a happy relationship with a man or woman. Yet, I have managed to hide the real reason from everyone. I felt that I must be a complete freak of nature for this abuse to have happened to me. *No one* is sexually abused by a woman. I must be crazy.

You have no idea what a relief it is to know that I am not alone, that I am not crazy and that this really did happen. I am a professional person dealing with distressed children. Maybe some day I will be able to deal with the hurt child within me. My colleagues would be amazed if they knew what I had been through. For the moment I must continue to hide what happened. It is still not safe to talk about it.'

Secrecy, distress, anger, controversy and fear surround the issue of female sexual abuse. Secrecy is deemed necessary because of the hostile reaction many have had to the subject of female sexual abuse. As the person above said, it isn't safe yet. The distress and anger come from the survivors, who have not been believed or have been made to feel guilty because they spoke out.

Cianne Longdon says in Chapter 4, 'Because female sexual abuse arouses such strong reactions, particularly in other women, survivors fear being ostracised, receiving anger and criticism or being gossiped about. Some survivors, either from fear of ridicule or from having negative response to disclosing have, in desperation, and from a desire to receive help of any sort, said that their abuser was a man.'

Anger, too, from some who see this issue as being 'anti-female' and being used to get male abusers off the hook. It seems that even talking about female abusers is considered treason by some to the cause of feminism. Yet, in Chapter 9, 'A feminist view', Val Young says, 'Though it is important to respect theories, it is more important, in any discussion about the extent and nature of child abuse, that the focus is on finding ways of stopping abusive behaviour and putting the responsibility firmly onto the perpetrators. We hold men responsible for regulating negative male behaviour, so, in the spirit of feminism, women need to take responsibility for acknowledging negative female behaviour.'

There is controversy because the idea that women might sexually abuse children is new and unproven. Statistics show that it rarely happens and if no one has reported it then it must not happen. Overriding all this is fear from survivors that they won't be supported and from researchers and writers that their work may have to be revised. Fear, too, from many professionals who have established themselves with the accepted knowledge of how and why child sexual abuse happens and who does it. The reality is that we are all still learning about this traumatic area of child abuse. We may find that the sexual abuse by women is rare and thereby confirm our existing theories. If, however, we find that the problem is greater than we first thought, we must then reconsider the possible causes of child sexual abuse. Whatever happens, we have to give support to those who have suffered.

It is no wonder that this book on female sexual abuse took so long to write and to publish. Finding survivors willing to talk was no problem, finding people willing to listen was. *Female Sexual Abuse: The Ultimate Taboo* combines accounts from survivors with input from professionals about working with survivors and with abusers. It is a first step in bringing the subject into the open.

Part 1

Professionals

1 What survivors tell us — an overview

Michele Elliott

In 1968 I was presented with my first case of child sexual abuse. Nothing in my training to become a child psychologist had prepared me for this. Nothing personally had prepared me for this. An eleven year old girl told me she was being sexually abused by her stepfather, who was my bank manager. The only study which had been mentioned in my university courses was one compiled in 1955 by Weinberg (1955) indicating that there might be as many as 'one case of incest per million of the population among English speaking peoples'. So my initial reactions were that I knew the stepfather (and bank managers couldn't do such things), and why was the one in a million walking into *my* office. Over the years, we were all to learn that child sexual abuse is a much greater problem than anyone had imagined. Susan Brownmiller (1975), Florence Rush (1980), Alice Miller (1985), Eileen Bass (Bass and Thornton 1983), Sandra Butler (1979), Judith Herman (1981), Suzanne Sgroi (1982) and countless others wrote about the problem and women started coming forward to talk about the abuse they had suffered at the hands of men. The statistics indicated that the overwhelming majority of victims of sexual abuse were girls sexually abused by their fathers.

We accepted that because we could only go on what people told us. The books and articles concentrated on female victims and male abusers. Then adult men started talking about the abuse they had

suffered as children — again from men. Statistics projected a boy to
girl ratio of victims variously as 1:6, 1:9 and 1:12 (Knopp 1986).
However, Eugene Porter, Flora Colao and Mindy Mitnick, on the
basis of their work, concluded that the ratio of girl to boy victims was
much closer. They indicated that perhaps 40 to 50 per cent of victims
of sexual abuse were boys (Porter 1986). It seemed that boys were
equally or almost equally at risk from sexual abuse by men. Indeed, in
a survey carried out by Mrazek, Lynch and Bentovim (1981) in the
United Kingdom it was found that 98 per cent of the reported abusers
were male.

There has always been another possibility — and one which causes
enormous controversy and distress: women who sexually abuse. It is
thought that even raising the possibility of women abusing would
detract from the much larger and more pervasive problem of male
abuse of children. However, the fact that there are women who
sexually abuse children should not be used to diminish the scale of the
problem of men who sexually abuse children. What it does mean is
that perhaps the accepted knowledge about child sexual abuse needs
to be re-examined.

I remember vividly giving a talk at an RAF base several years ago
and stating that abusers were men. At the end of the talk an officer
came up and, with tears in his eyes, said 'It isn't only men, you know
— my mother did it to me'. He walked away quickly before I could
respond. It made me think that maybe we should *at least* give the
victims of female sexual abuse permission to talk. Then on a local
radio phone-in programme, we raised the issue of child sexual abuse
by women. Philip Hodgson (the presenter) and I talked for a few
minutes before the calls started coming through: 'Finally someone is
willing to open up the subject of female sex abusers and really listen to
us. This is fabulous — a day I thought I would never see. I am a 58
year old man who was sexually abused from the age of 4 to 12 by my
aunt . . .'

A woman said: 'My mind knows it wasn't my fault — that it was
her dirt, her filth, but it's also mine: I grew with it as part of my body,
dressed with it, ate with it, cried with it, slept with it. I can't seem to
separate myself from her. Yet, I felt and feel utterly, utterly alone and
evil to the core. Knowing how she used me hurts beyond all physical
pain. It means the end of the hope that I was really loved by my
mother . . .'

A man in his fifties disagreed that it was abuse: 'Looking back it
seemed no great drama. Even though I was only 7 years old, I knew
how to fondle her and suck her breasts. Oral sex led to full
intercourse with my mother. We had sex until I left home at the age of
18.'

We had more calls that we could deal with and by the time I got back to the KIDSCAPE office, it was apparent that this was an issue which would not go away. The letters started arriving the next day: 'During the war, my brother and I were evacuated to a house in the country. The woman who took care of us made us touch her. She had friends over and we had to engage in all kinds of kinky sex. We were terrified . . .'

'Rubbish — women don't sexually abuse children. It must have been the children misunderstanding motherly love . . .'

'My sister was 4 years older than me and we started having sexual relations when I was 10. This went on throughout our adult life until she moved to New Zealand. It was a wonderful relationship and certainly not abusive. I think there are far more of these relationships happening than anyone dares to admit. I now know that my sister was raped by our father while my mother held her down, which probably contributed to her initiating sex with me. Whatever the reason, we both enjoyed our sexual relationship tremendously.'

'My teenage babysitter began sexually abusing me when I was 6. It went on for about four years. I actually thought that babysitters did that to all the kids until we got another babysitter. When I tried to get her to have oral sex, she told my mother and I got into trouble. Believe me, I kept it all a secret until now. It was bad enough being abused, though some of it I liked. What was worse than the abuse was being in trouble for something I didn't even understand and certainly could not control. To this day I hate all forms of physical contact and the thought of sex makes me physically ill.'

'I am a university lecturer. My twin sister and I were sexually abused by my mother until we both escaped to university. No one ever knew. To this day, my sister and I see our mother and pretend that we had a happy family with no problems. The problems my sister and I have now are not surprising. Neither of us has been able to have a relationship, produce children or find any peace. Although we are both highly successful in our professions, our personal lives are a disaster.'

'When I was seven, one of the nuns who taught us used to put her hand up my skirt and fondle my genitals whenever I was standing next to her desk. I only found out that this happened to the other girls when I grew up and confided in my best friend from school days. It had happened to her and some others. I was so angry that I went back to the school and confronted the nun, who didn't deny it, but said that she did it "out of love" for us and surely I could understand that. Imagine trying to tell an adult that a nun was sexually abusing you — who would believe you? I haven't told my parents to this day, as it would upset them too much.'

'There are some areas of sexual abuse about which people still don't talk. During the 1940s I was sent to a boarding school for

children without fathers. The residential staff were all unmarried
ladies who seemed to enjoy delivering frequent punishments in front
of an audience. For example, if boys misbehaved during a meal, they
were taken across to the girls' tables and had their trousers taken down
and were spanked in front of the girls. Or we would be taken to the
matron's bedroom while she was in bed, and had our bare bottoms
smacked while she and several others watched. The sexual dimension
was always there. There was much talk of bottoms, spankings and
who was doing what to whom. Multiply that by thousands in similar
institutions and you find the *raison d'être* for those specialist magazines
in which dominant ladies subject submissive men to thrashings with a
variety of implements.'

The letters and calls went on and on — from men and women who
were sexually abused by their mothers, relatives, babysitters and
other carers. Most had never told or had not been believed. Many had
been unable to find anyone willing to talk or listen. One 60 year old
man said: 'I tried to tell my therapist when I was 35. She told me that
I was having fantasies about my mother and that I needed more
therapy to deal with it. In reality my mother had physically and
sexually abused me for as long as I could remember. The abuse was
horrific, including beatings and sado-masochistic sex. It took a lot of
courage for me to tell. When she (the therapist) didn't respond, I quit
therapy and spent the next 15 years in hell. I began to think that
maybe I had just imagined it all, but why were the memories so vivid
and in such detail? Just hearing that this has happened to others has
helped to restore my sanity. Maybe now I can find someone who will
listen and believe me. Sixty years is a long time to wait.'

Why has it taken so long to bring out the problem of female sexual
abuse? Female sexual abuse seems to be more of a taboo because:

- Female sexual abuse is more threatening — it undermines
  feelings about how women should relate to children.
- It has taken years for people to accept that children are
  sexually abused, but that sexual abuse has been placed in the
  context of male power and aggression. Women are not
  supposed to be sexually aggressive and the male power theory
  eliminates them as possible abusers, unless they are coerced
  by males. As will be seen in this chapter, Jane Kinder
  Matthew's chapter and in the stories of many of the survivors,
  male coercion was not present in significant numbers of cases.
- People find it difficult to understand exactly *how* a woman
  could sexually abuse a child. Women are not seen to be
  capable of this kind of abuse because they do not have penises.
- When adult survivors of female abuse have told their stories,
  they have often met with the rebuttal that they are fantasising.

A child recently told that her mother had sexually abused her, along with the child's father. The therapeutic team took the view that she was clearly projecting and fantasising. The abuse by the father was never in doubt.

- Current statistics indicate that sexual abuse of children by females is rare. David Finkelhor and Diana Russell in *Child Sexual Abuse* (1984) estimate that 5 per cent of abuse of girls and 20 per cent of abuse of boys is perpetrated by women. Previous statistics indicated that child sexual abuse was rare, even by males. That has since been shown to be untrue. Statistics are based upon what we are told and may give a false picture if some victims are not telling.

After the KIDSCAPE First National Conference on Female Sexual Abuse, the television programme 'This Morning' opened up a hotline for callers to talk about abuse by women. In the course of one day, they had over 1000 telephone calls. 90 per cent of the callers had never told anyone about their abuse before that programme. It is possible that books like this will unleash a flood of stories and change our perception of the role of women in child sexual abuse, or we may confirm that abuse by women is rare. There are many questions we need to ask:

- How many of the victims of female sexual abuse are boys. How many are girls? Of those who have contacted me, approximately 33 per cent were men; 67 per cent were women.

- Do victims of female abuse suffer in similar ways to victims of male abuse? The men and women I have dealt with say that, like the victims of male abuse, their lives have been dramatically affected. They have:

  - turned to drugs, alcohol, solvents;
  - often attempted suicide;
  - gender identity problems (One man, made to dress in girl's underwear by his abusers, has continued this behaviour into adult life and has difficulty with relationships. A disturbing aspect of some of the cases is the hatred of and violence towards women and girls that some of the men are admitting to feeling.);
  - difficulties maintaining relationships;
  - unresolved anger, shame and guilt;
  - self-mutilated;
  - been anorexic or bulimic;
  - suffered chronic depression;
  - become agoraphobic;

— been chronic run-aways when they were children;
— in some cases, sexually abused children (see Chapters 5 and 6);
— been fearful of touching their own children.

● How has abuse by mothers affected the adult survivors? Those who were sexually abused by their mothers seem to have an overpowering need to find a bonding mother-love. Many of the survivors say that, though they hate their mothers for what they did, they still want to be loved by their mothers and would not confront them — as one woman said 'with flowers, let alone with the abuse that she perpetrated on me'.

● Has the abuse always been perceived as negative? A minority of the male survivors say that the sexual relationships with their mothers and other female members of the family have been wholly beneficial and natural, as far as they were concerned. A few men said that the relationships carried on into adult life and some are currently in sexual relationships with mothers, aunts and sisters.

The attitude of the older women 'initiating the boy' into the joys of sex is often the subject of jokes. One Canadian man related how a female relative had 'acted out her sexual anxiety on me when I was 12. I was supposed to like it, but I have found women repulsive ever since'. This myth of the boy enjoying sex with older women is just as harmful as the myth that girls 'ask for sex from older males'.

None of the women who contacted me has felt that the abuse was in any way beneficial, though some have said that the abuse sometimes felt good. This has caused them considerable pain and confusion.

● Is the female abuser usually coerced by a male? It is often assumed that, if a female has sexually abused a child, it must have been done either with a male partner or under the influence of a male partner. Yet, more than three-quarters of the women and men who have contacted me say the female abusers acted alone — often there was no man in the family or he was gone. However, the number of cases I am concerned with is small, 127 people. It would be wrong to generalise their experiences without proper representative research.

● Do victims of both male and female abuse feel differently towards the abusers? One woman, abused by both her mother and father, said 'There's something about a mother. When you're small, she should be the first person you go to if you're hurt; the first person to cuddle, who gives you love and care. So when she abuses you, it leads to an even greater sense of despair than when your father does it. In my dreams I castrate my father and suffocate him. But I can't attack my mother. I'm torn between love and hate.'

• How do the female abusers see themselves? Jane Kinder Matthews deals with this issue in Chapter 5, but one woman I know is haunted not only by the memories of children she has abused but by her present fantasies of abusing and killing children. 'When these thoughts come into my head, I want to kill myself.' She has attempted suicide many times and is given to prolonged bouts of depression.

Another woman was sexually abused by her mother and subsequently sexually abused her daughter. She has undergone extensive therapy, as has her daughter. The woman feels guilt and shame for what she did, though she understands why it happened. She and her daughter are now friends and the one thing that has made her happy is that her grandchildren will not suffer. She says, 'At least we have broken the cycle and that is something to be grateful for. I will never forgive myself for what happened, but I have hope for the future.'

This woman and her daughter were more fortunate than most because they are resolving the effects of the abuse. Most survivors never hear their abusers admit their guilt or hear them apologise. Unless the abusers do go through this process of taking responsibility, it is impossible for them to successfully go through therapy (see also Chapter 6).

• What do the survivors tell us? The 127 people in this chapter present an important insight into female sexual abuse. This is not a statistical analysis; more a compilation of what they were willing to say. I did not press for details, so we will not know in every case the exact age at which abuse started or the precise number of abusers. Tables 1.1 to 1.5 reflect what the survivors have told me.

Table 1.1   Who were the abusers?

Female survivors disclosed:	
Female abuser only	
Mother	42
Stepmother	5
Aunt	3
Grandmother	5
Babysitter	9
Teacher	3
Nun	1
Dual female abusers	
Mother and grandmother	4
Mother and aunt	2

Table 1.1 *continued*

Dual abusers male and female

Father and mother	10
Male and mother	7
Brother and mother	3
Babysitter and male	1
Total	95

Male survivors disclose:

Female abuser only

Mother	22
Stepmother	1

Dual female abusers

Mother and sister	1

Dual abusers male and female

Mother and grandfather	1
Mother and male	2
Stepmother and father	2
Babysitter and male	1
Couple (friends)	2
Total	32
Total number	127

Table 1.2   Did any survivors abuse children?

Survivors who admit to sexually abusing children:

Females	7
Males	7

Because the numbers of male survivors was less than the number of female survivors, the percentages of self-reported abusers were:

07% female
22% males

Table 1.3   Kinds of abuse reported

The kind of abuse reported by the survivors included:

Fingering
Oral sex
Penetration with objects
Sucking
Forced mutual masturbation
Intercourse
Combination of physical and sexual abuse

Table 1.4   When and where did abuse begin?

The abuse started	In bed		In the bath	
	Women	16	Women	41
	Men	18	Men	3
Abuse began	Under 5	Over 5		Under 15
Female	53	10		1
Male	17	11		3

Table 1.5   Did the abuse cause distress?

The abuse caused distress to	Women	Men
	100%	88%
Four men said it caused no harm		

The survivors are beginning to provide us with some sketchy details, which may help us to understand better what they went through. 96 per cent of all of those people who were brave enough to come forward said the abuse they suffered dramatically adversely affected their lives. That is not surprising. 78 per cent of the survivors said they could find no one willing to help or believe. That is profoundly disturbing. One woman was told that the abuser must have been male and was offered help to deal with the 'real' abuser.

Uncovering cases of female sexual abuse has been traumatic. There is a strongly held view that the issue of female sexual abuse should not be raised publicly, but should be dealt with in private. A journalist in a recent article in a national newspaper insisted that it was wrong to give all this attention to female sexual abuse and that a conference held about the issue was 'political'.

Political? Listening to and trying to understand the pain that people have suffered, whether at the hands of males or females should not be termed political. All this attention? There has been little attention paid to female sexual abuse. There are few books to help us understand how to deal with even the small number of cases of female abuse so far reported. Kathy Evert (Evert and Bijkerk 1987) was the first survivor to tell her story in *When You're Ready*, a book which has been of enormous help to other survivors. Estela Welldon (1988) in *Mother, Madonna, Whore* devotes considerable space to the issue of incest and Mathews, Matthews and Spelz (1989) have published the first study of female abusers. Craig Allen (1991) has also published a comparative analysis of *Women and Men who Sexually Abuse Children*. The literature review by Kathryn Jennings at the end of this book confirms the paucity of materials available.

The concern is still that any attention paid to female sexual abuse will detract from the major problem of abuse by males. However, there is no question that abuse by males is still statistically the largest reported problem. What is disturbing is the idea that suppressing discussion and acknowledgement of female sexual abuse has prevented people disclosing for fear of going against established opinion.

The sad fact is that, if various factions are fighting each other over terminology and 'political' gender issues, children will continue to be abused because we have decided to listen to them only in an established framework.

Perhaps we will eventually confirm the statistics that 95 per cent of sexual abusers of children are men or perhaps we will have to re-evaluate the whole issue of sexual abuse. Whichever happens, we owe it to the survivors to talk about it. In 1968, a little girl told me about her stepfather. I thought she was one in a million. Let's not make the same mistake now.

References

Allen, Craig (1991) *Women and Men who Sexually Abuse Children: a Comparative Analysis* The Safer Society Press.

Bass, Ellen and Thorton, Louise (eds) (1983) *I Never Told Anyone. Writings by Women Survivors of Child Sexual Abuse* Harper, Colophon Books.

Brownmiller, Susan (1975) *Against Our Will* Penguin Books.

Butler, Sandra (1979) *Conspiracy of Silence: The Trauma of Incest* Bantam Books.

Evert, Kathy and Bijkerk, Inie (1987) *When You're Ready. A Woman's Healing from Childhood Physical and Sexual Abuse by her Mother* Launch Press.

Finkelhor, David and Russell, Diana (1984) 'Women as perpetrators' in Finkelhor, David (Ed) *Child Sexual Abuse, New Theory and Research* Free Press.

Herman, Judith Lewis (1981) *Father–Daughter Incest* Harvard University Press.

Knopp, Fay Honey (1986) in Porter, Eugene *Treating the Young Male Victim of Sexual Assault* The Safer Society Press.

Mathews, Ruth, Matthews, Jane Kinder and Speltz, Kathleen (1989) *Female Sexual Offenders, An Exploratory Study* The Safer Society Press.

Miller, Alice (1985) *Thou Shalt Not Be Aware, Society's Betrayal of the Child* Pluto.

Mrazek, Patricia Beezley, Lynch, Margaret and Bentovim, Arnon (1981) 'Recognition of child sexual abuse in the United Kingdom', in Mrazek, Patricia Beezley and Kempe, C Henry *Sexually Abused Children and their Families* Pergamon Press.

Porter, Eugene *Treating the Young Male Victim of Sexual Assault* The Safer Society Press.

Rush, Florence (1980) *The Best Kept Secret: Sexual Abuse of Children* Prentice-Hall.

Sgroi, Suzanne (1982) *Handbook of Clinical Intervention in Child Sexual Abuse* Lexington Books.

Weinberg, K. (1955) *Incest Behaviour* Citadel.

Welldon, Estela (1988) *Mother, Madonna, Whore. The Idealization and Denigration of Motherhood* The Guilford Press.

2 Impact and treatment issues for victims of childhood sexual abuse by female perpetrators

Suzanne M. Sgroi and Norah M. Sargent

The true dimensions of childhood sexual abuse by female perpetrators are unknown and undefined. There is a growing awareness that adolescent and adult females do abuse children sexually as well as physically and emotionally, and that little girls, like little boys, sometimes exhibit sexually reactive behaviours that include victimisation of more vulnerable children. Today, however, fewer cases involving sexual abuse of children by female perpetrators have been reported and less has been written about impact and treatment issues for their victims.

Finkelhor's and Russell's (1984) analysis of the American Humane Association's National Study on Child Abuse and Neglect Reporting isolated economic, social and ethnic differences between perpetrators who were mothers and those who were fathers, i.e. the mothers were typically poor, single and Afro-American. He also noted that mother–child sexual abuse more often involved physical abuse and abuse of younger children. One also must wonder how much the characteristics of the female perpetrator identified in that study highlighted society's resistance to the truth that 'even' economically secure women and women who reflected the majority of female clinicians at the time, i.e. white women also sexually abuse their children.

In fact, when studying decision-making factors utilised by reporters of child sexual abuse, Zellman (1992) noted that family socioeconomic status weighted reporters' judgements, i.e. they were more likely to report suspected abuse if the case involved poor families.

So strong is the resistance to the reality of child sexual abuse by females that one author cited a case example in which a boy was abused by his mother and later included this apparent disclaimer: 'The examples of mothers sexually abusing their own children, which have been mentioned in previous chapters, can be safely interpreted as aberrations, having little or no significance for the training of professionals in working with child sexual abuse' (O'Hagan 1989, p. 113). Dolan (1991), on the other hand, suggests from her personal therapeutic caseload that abuse by females is not the rarity it was once thought to be. Sanderson (1990) aptly sums up the dilemma by acknowledging that, while sexual abuse of children by females is less frequent than that by males, it 'is likely that abuse by females is still relatively under-reported, as is abuse directed at male children, which may account for a bias in these findings' (p. 75). Under-reporting of child sexual abuse by females as a cultural bias is suggested by numerous authors (Allen 1991, Banning 1989, Baron, Burgess and Kao 1991, Krug 1989, Mathews, Matthews and Speltz 1991). As late as 1991, reports on longitudinal studies of sexual offender treatment were obliged to delete findings on female sexual offenders because the treatment of this population was too new to interpret responsibly (Maletzky 1991, p. 12–13).

A history of childhood abuse by a female abuser tends to be disclosed later rather than earlier by victims and survivors. That is, a person who discloses childhood sexual abuse by a male abuser as a presenting issue or during a clinical assessment, may wait until later in the treatment relationship before bringing up a suspicion or a memory of abuse by a female perpetrator. Goodwin and DiVasto (1979) cite two cases in which clients initially presented with a complaint of aftereffects of sexual abuse by males and only after the clients had developed sufficient trust in the therapeutic relationship did they reveal that they actually were abused by their mothers. This may be because the person feels safer and more confident that she or he will be believed by the clinician after a trust relationship has been established within the framework of addressing other sexual victimisation issues. Often, however, the client reports that memories of childhood sexual abuse by a female perpetrator had not emerged in the earlier phases of the therapy. Sometimes, the clinician's failure to probe for such a history conveyed an implicit message that such a disclosure from the client would not be acceptable. In the absence of a direct question or invitation to disclose, it is not unusual for adolescent or adult survivors to assume they do not have the clinician's permission to share highly charged or embarrassing experiences or material which they may view as shameful. Fearing a negative response, they often choose not to take risks in the area of self-disclosure. Courtois (1988) suggests that female victims may 'feel additional shame and stigma when their incest experience is "out of the ordinary"', i.e. when they are sexually abused by females (p. 68).

It follows, therefore, that clinicians should ask, periodically throughout treatment, 'Are there other times that you can remember when someone had sexual contact of any kind with you during childhood?' Perhaps the clinician might add, 'So far, we've only talked about sexual abuse by males. Was there ever a time when a female had any type of sexual contact with you?' Although the immediate response may be negative, such probes establish a climate in which the client has permission to disclose such experiences later, or when she or he is ready to do so.

Apparently, this disinclination to reveal abuse by females extends to the female offender as well as to the female victim. In a study of 75 males and 65 females who had been substantiated by child protective services, female offenders were more reluctant to admit to sexually abusive acts with children regardless of legal substantiation, but more frequently report being sexually abused in childhood than do their male counterparts (Allen 1991). The author of the study suggests that the differences in acknowledging offence behaviour could be explained in any of three ways: (i) men more frequently are perpetrators of sexual abuse than are women and less frequently the victims of childhood sexual victimisation; (ii) because of societal mores, men may be more reluctant to talk about their own history as victims and better able to talk about their assaultive or abusive behaviours meted out to others; or (iii) that 'sexual abuse may be perceived as a more deviant act for a woman than for a man, and therefore more difficult for a female offender to acknowledge' (p. 59). It is particularly salient to this discussion to note that Allen also found that female offenders were more likely than males to be sceptical that child sexual abusers could change their behaviours.

In this chapter, we will address these and other issues from the perspective of working with a small but memorable cohort of cases of child sexual abuse by female perpetrators. Nearly all of our cases were characterised by scenarios in which a male partner was described as the instigator and the female perpetrator seemed to be a co-abuser. This pattern resembles that of the male-accompanied or male-coerced and later self-initiated category described by Finkelhor and Russell (1984) and Mathews, Matthews and Speltz (1989, p. 14) as well as the co-offender pattern described by McCarty (1986). It was usual for our clients to retrieve memories of abuse by the male perpetrator first and, later, to report participation in the abuse by the female perpetrator.

Still later, these clients sometimes reported incidents when the female perpetrator committed the sexual abuse by herself. By contrast, a few of our clients reported sexual abuse initiated independently by female perpetrators, without any prior connection to male initiated abuse. This pattern is similar to the Independent Female Offender category described by McCarty (1986) and the Woman Acting Alone pattern described by Finkelhor and Russell (1984) and Mathews, Matthews and Speltz (1989). To date, we have seen only four cases in which the female perpetrator fits the entirely male-coerced pattern described by all of the above authors (i.e. the female perpetrator always functioned as an accomplice to a male perpetrator and never initiated sexual contact with the child independently). None of our cases involved female perpetrators who fit the Teacher/Lover offender pattern also described by Mathews, Matthews and Speltz (1991).

Table 2.1 describes characteristics of 10 cases (8 female victims and 2 males) of childhood sexual abuse by female perpetrators from the caseload we discuss in this chapter. Two of the children (cases 2 and 3) were sexually abused by the same perpetrator, their mother. One child (case 1) was sexually abused by two female perpetrators at the same time. Thus, Table 2.1 also reflects abuse by a total of 10 female perpetrators.

Table 2.1   Characteristics of cases of child sexual abuse by female offenders

Case Number	Sex of Victim	Age of Victim	Abuser's Relationship to Victim	Pattern of Abuse	Type of Sexual Abuse by Female Abuser[1]	History of Physical/ Emotional by Same Abuser
1[2]	M	8 yrs	unrelated	independent	F, OS	No/No
2[3]	M	<5 yrs	mother	male-coerced	B, E, F, I, OS, P, W	No/No
3	F	<5 yrs	mother	male-coerced	B, E, F, OS, P, W	No/
4	F	<5 yrs	mother	male/coerced	F	Yes/Yes
5	F	<5 yrs	mother	male-coerced	E, F, W	No/No
6	F	<5 yrs	mother	male-coerced/ independent	F, P	Yes/Yes
7	F	<5 yrs	mother	male-coerced/ independent	F, P	Yes/Yes
8	F	<5 yrs	mother	male-coerced/ independent	A, B, F, OS, P, W	Yes/Yes
9	F	<5 yrs	mother	independent	E, W	No/No
10	F	9 yrs	sister	independent	F, S	No/Yes

Notes

1 A sexual acts with animals; B bondage; E enemas; F fondling; I intercourse (vaginal and/or anal); OS oral sex; P penetration with objects; S sucking nipples; W witnessing sexual interactors.

2 Abusers were two neighbourhood adolescent girls.

3 Cases 2 and 3 are siblings.

Case 1 involved a male victim who was sexually fondled at age 8 years by two unrelated adolescent girls who also performed oral sex on him. This boy was unable to report his victimisation to anyone during childhood. It is interesting to note that throughout his childhood his mother was physically and emotionally abusive towards him while his father was emotionally neglectful and psychologically absent. The adolescent female perpetrators were not relatives or babysitters; instead, they gained access to the boy by befriending him while he was playing in a park nearby his home. These female perpetrators acted independently without male coercion to commit the sexual abuse. They did not physically abuse the victim.

The second male victim (case 2) was sexually abused by his mother at the instigation of his father who was intermittently psychotic and who also sexually and physically abused the son. In this case, the abuse by the mother included bondage, mutual sexual fondling, reciprocal oral sex, reciprocal administration of enemas and sexual penetration with other objects. The mother performed all of the sexual behaviours with her son in response to coercion by her husband who also physically and sexually abused her. In addition, the son was coerced by the father to have vaginal intercourse with his mother and his older sister while the father watched. The sexual abuse of this boy by both parents was initiated before he was five years old and persisted until age 14 years, when he was removed from the parents' home.

One of the female victims (case 3) was the older sibling of the second male victim (case 2). Her sexual abuse by the mother also included bondage, mutual sexual fondling, reciprocal oral sex, reciprocal administration of enemas and sexual penetration with other objects. Both siblings were also forced to witness their parents having sexual intercourse with each other. The sister was subjected to vaginal and anal intercourse by her father as well as by her brother; sometimes her mother was present and sometimes only her father was present. Her sexual abuse by both parents began before she reached age 5 years and persisted until she reached age 16 years, after which the abuse was disclosed and she was removed from the home.

Neither sibling reported physical abuse by their mother but both reported physical abuse by their father. It is noteworthy that both of these siblings required psychiatric hospitalisations soon after they were removed from their parents' home.

Two other female victims (cases 4 and 5) were sexually abused by mothers who were male-coerced and did not initiate sexual contact independently thereafter. In both of these cases, the sexual abuse by the mothers began when the victims were less than 5 years old; the abuse consisted of fondling at the father's direction followed by sexual acts performed on the victims by the male abusers with the mothers in attendance. A history of extensive physical and emotional abuse by the mother was present in case 4 but not in case 5. However, the female victim in case 5 also was subjected to enemas performed by the mother at the father's direction, and was a witness to abusive acts performed on her younger brother, including genital fondling and enemas by the mother and beatings by the father.

The next three cases (6, 7 and 8) all involved female victims whose mothers were initially coerced by their husbands to perform sexual acts upon the daughters; later, however, the mothers sexually abused the girls independently. All of these girls were physically and emotionally abused by their mothers and sexually abused by their fathers. In each of these cases, the physical, sexual and emotional abuse all began when the girls were under 5 years of age. In cases 6 and 7, the sexual abuse by the mothers was limited to genital fondling and penetration of vaginal and anal openings with objects. Neither subject reported that the sexual abuse by the mother continued after they reached school age (approximately 6 years old); however, physical and emotional abuse by these mothers persisted until the subjects were much older.

In case 8, the sexual abuse was instigated, initially, by the girl's father and was carried out by the mother at his direction; later, the mother often instigated the father's participation in the abuse or performed the sexual abuse on her daughter independently. This victim's sexual abuse by the mother included bondage, genital fondling, oral sex, penetration with objects, being subjected to sexual contact with animals, and witnessing sexual interactions between her parents. The father modelled all of the abusive acts first and directed the mother to perform them also. In addition the girl was subjected to anal and vaginal intercourse and impregnated by her father. The physical and sexual abuse by the mother stopped after the girl reached mid-adolescence. Emotional abuse by both parents and physical and sexual abuse by the father persisted well into this victim's adulthood.

In case 9, the female victim received comparatively little physical care from her mother during her early childhood. However, before age 5 years, the mother began to subject the child to enemas on a daily basis, allegedly to relieve constipation. This pattern persisted until the girl left home to attend college when she was approximately 18 years old. The enemas by the mother were resumed when the girl returned home for vacations and it was 'necessary' for the mother to administer a final enema on the daughter's wedding day. When this girl reached pre-adolescence, her mother began to expose her to adult sexual interactions by arranging for bedroom doors to be left open so that the child could witness the mother's sexual relationships with various boyfriends. Although being exposed to her mother's sexual liaisons was embarrassing and disruptive for the child, this victim did not view her mother's behaviour as abuse ('I thought all families were like that and I knew I had a terrible problem with constipation!') until after she herself reached her thirties.

In case 10, the perpetrator was a sister who was five years older than the victim and who acted independently. This victim was emotionally abused by her mother, who frequently yelled at her and belittled her intelligence and her competency to perform everyday tasks. The victim received some nurturing from her older sister, who nevertheless belittled her in much the same fashion as their mother had done. When the younger girl was nine years old, the 14 year old sister coerced her into fondling the sister's breasts and sucking her nipples. The older girl masturbated herself while her younger sister stimulated her breasts. When the victim was reluctant to repeat this scenario, the older sibling threatened to tell their mother that the younger girl had initiated the sexual behaviour and, therefore, was to blame. The victim believed she would be punished severely if her older sister lied to their mother and co-operated with the sexual behaviour several more times in response to her sister's threats and demands. Although there was no known history of physical or sexual abuse by either parent, this victim reported feeling unsupported and without allies in her family.

It is noteworthy that none of the cases of child sexual abuse by female perpetrators listed in Table 2.1 was reported by the victims during childhood. The abuse of the siblings in cases 2 and 3 was discovered accidentally; these were the only cases in which the children were removed from the home at a time when sexual abuse was on-going. Only case 1 involved a one-time incident of sexual abuse by extra-family perpetrators. Eight of the ten victims were sexually abused by their fathers, who initially coerced the mothers into performing sexual acts with the children. In all but one of the male-coerced cases (case 5), the fathers were described as physically abusive as well as sexually abusive toward the victims. In three of the male-coerced cases (2, 3, 5) the mothers were described as passive women who were dominated totally by their husbands.

For the purpose of clarification, we defined emotional abuse as verbal abuse of the child: yelling at the child for a variety of reasons and employing name-calling, belittling of the child's personal characteristics and/or performance, and/or undermining the child's efforts. However, we did not define the emotionally abusive components of being coerced to perform sexual acts or being forced to witness sexual interactions between others as emotional abuse *per se*. Likewise, we defined physical abuse as physically assaultive behaviour toward children that occurred separately from any physical coercion that might have been a component of the sexual abuse. Thus, the column in Table 2.1 that identifies physical or emotional abuse of child victims by female perpetrators is intended to document physical or emotional abuse that took place independent of the sexual abuse. It is interesting to note, therefore, that four of the female perpetrators (cases 4, 6, 7, 8) also physically and emotionally abused their victims on occasions separate from the incidents of sexual abuse. One of these four women abusers (case 4) was classified solely as a male-coerced perpetrator of sexual abuse who did not commit sexually abusive acts with her victim independently. However, the other three female perpetrators who also physically and emotionally abused their victims (cases 6, 7, 8) fit the male-coerced/independent classification: these women did commit child sexual abuse on their own as well as physical and emotional abuse.

On the other hand, three of the four independent abusers (the two adolescent abusers in case 1 and the adult abuser in case 9) were not described as physically or emotionally abusive toward their child victims. one of the independent abusers (case 10) was emotionally abusive toward the child victim. Three of the four independent abusers (cases 1 (2 abusers) and 10) were adolescents at the time when they sexually abused their victims. The female perpetrators in case 1 were the only extra-family perpetrators.

All of the cases in this sample involved Caucasian families and Caucasian perpetrators. All of the families were working class, middle class or upper class in regard to socioeconomic status. None of the female or male perpetrators had criminal records or criminal life-styles.

Clinical observations

This cohort of cases of sexual abuse of children by female perpetrators is a small sample acquired over a 15 year period. Only two cases (2 and 3) involved victims who were less than 18 years of age when we saw them clinically. These were the only two cases that afforded an opportunity to evaluate the female abuser directly and to obtain independent corroboration that the reported sexual abuse had taken place. All of the other cases involved adult survivors of childhood sexual abuse whose histories could not be corroborated independently by us as clinicians. Thus, in the majority of cases, we are sharing our observations of the psychic or subjective reality of the impact of childhood sexual abuse by a female perpetrator. Since the sample is small, it is impossible to determine whether our observations and conclusions about these clinical subjects are applicable to others. Within this context, we are sharing our impressions of common themes and therapeutic issues that appeared to be pertinent for our clients.

Isolated impact of sexual abuse by a female perpetrator

It was not possible to isolate or differentiate the impact of childhood sexual abuse by a female perpetrator for any of the victims with whom we worked. All but two of the victims (cases 1 and 10) had been sexually abused in childhood by at least one male perpetrator as well. Seven of the victims also had been physically abused by their fathers. Five of the victims had histories of physical and emotional abuse by their mothers, one other child was emotionally (but not physically) abused by her mother.

It seems reasonable to anticipate interactive and cumulative effects when multiple types of childhood trauma occur for the same person. Within a multi-trauma milieu, it was difficult for us as clinicians to isolate singular effects of sexual abuse by a female perpetrator for any of these clients. Nevertheless, all seven of the adult female clients reported a perception that sexual abuse by a first degree female relative (mother or sister) was the most shameful and damaging form of childhood victimisation they had suffered. All of the women adult survivors had repressed their memories of sexual abuse by their mother or sister and all found it more difficult to disclose this type of abuse than their other victimisations. Moreover, all of these women reported that it was harder for them to sustain the belief that they had been sexually abused by a female relative than to acknowledge that they had been physically and/or emotionally abused by their mothers and sexually and/or physically abused by their fathers.

Barriers to disclosure

Acknowledging the reality of childhood sexual abuse is an important recovery task for all adult survivors, irrespective of the gender of the abuser (Sgroi 1989, p. 112). We have several hypotheses for why it was harder for the women in this sample to sustain the belief that their mothers had sexually abused them. First, to believe that a woman would sexually abuse her own child requires a person to challenge powerful stereotypes about motherhood and mother–child relationships that are dearly held, even cherished by our society. It is hard to relinquish the stereotype of a benevolent and nurturing mother–child relationship, even when one's personal experiences were in sharp contrast to the ideal. Thus, it simply may generate too much cognitive dissonance for an adult survivor to acknowledge to self or to others that she or he was sexually abused by her or his mother. In other words, to view oneself as so powerful a sexual object that 'My own mother succumbed to the temptation to have sexual contact with me', may be a belief that is too threatening and overwhelming for the child to integrate and absorb.

It is possible, also, that when girls are victimised by female perpetrators, confusion and conflict about the meaning of same-sex sexual abuse may magnify the traumatic impact of the experience. Girls who are sexually abused by other females may fear that a same-sex victimisation experience happened to them because they looked more like boys than like girls. Or they may fear that early same-sex victimisation will determine their sexual orientation thereafter. If they are unable to disclose the abuse or if it was necessary for them to repress the memory of what occurred, it is probable that these fears and fantasies about the meaning of the same-sex victimisation experience will remain and be amplified or elaborated later on. When memories do return, such victims may be ashamed to disclose the nature of the abuse and dread rejection or censure if or when they do disclose.

How do children who are being traumatised by childhood sexual abuse deal with the cognitive dissonance that accompanies a growing awareness that they are, in fact, engaging in behaviours that are proscribed by society? Some deal with the dissonance by denial, distancing, dissociation and repression; others develop severe symptom or acting-out behaviours; others become adept at parentified and caretaking behaviours; still others do all of the above or some combination thereof (Sgroi and Bunk 1988). All of these coping mechanisms assist the traumatised child to hide from self and others. It is possible, then, to keep childhood sexual abuse a secret from oneself as well as from others. Also, it is possible that sociocultural stereotypes about idealised mother–child relationships and confusion and fears associated with same-sex victimisation amplify and reinforce cognitive dissonance in a way that makes repression and delayed disclosure of this type of abuse even more likely.

Differentiation of self

An important clinical issue for the women who were sexually abused by female perpetrators was that of differentiation of self. It is, of course, a normal developmental task of early childhood to learn to differentiate one's own body from the bodies of parents and caretakers. Establishment of personal physical boundaries is probably an important step in developing personal psychological boundaries also. For young children, learning to tolerate and celebrate physical and psychological autonomy are critical development milestones that may serve as a foundation for the more socially mediated process of separation from parents and family later during adolescence. As might be expected, the women who had been sexually abused by both parents seemed to have even greater difficulty with self-differentiation and establishment of personal identity. This issue is poignantly illustrated in a teaching videotape about a female adult survivor of maternal sexual abuse (Groth and Rosemary 1990). The client, Rosemary, explained that her mother had told her that it was all right for the mother to fondle Rosemary's genitals because, 'Your body is my body'. Later, Rosemary's father gave her the same message when he sexually abused her also. In this case, the message by both parents was explicit as well as implicit: 'We own you. Your body belongs to us, not to you. We can do whatever we want with/to you'. Most child victims of parental sexual abuse receive this message implicitly. When the child's mother communicates so powerfully that there is no differentiation between the mother's body and the child's body, achieving autonomy can seem immensely difficult, even impossible to the child.

It was not surprising, therefore, that all of our women clients who had been sexually abused by their mothers reported fears that they would become like their mothers. One commonly reported fear was that they would become as dependent on male partners as they perceived their mothers had been. Another concern expressed by these clients was the fear that they, too, would become abusive toward others as their mothers had been abusive toward them. Still another fear was that they would be susceptible to control or even to abuse by their mothers throughout their adulthood.

We saw numerous examples of coping strategies created to address these fears. The women whose mothers were still alive at the 'time of the clients' therapy, often found it necessary to distance themselves from their mothers, visting them infrequently if at all. These women often imposed extensive constraints on contacts or interactions with their mothers and sometimes created elaborate structures in order to tolerate whatever contacts did take place. For example, one client refused to speak to her mother on the telephone if the mother initiated the call; instead, she would listen while her mother left a message on the answering machine. The client would then call the mother later when she felt better prepared for the interaction and had been able to plan her response to her mother's anticipated questions or requests. This plan, by necessity, prevented the client from ever spontaneously answering her telephone since she never could guess correctly when her mother might call. Another woman routinely arranged for her partner to be present in the room whenever she spoke to her mother on the telephone. It was not unusual for any of these clients to make detailed plans, including safety and exit manoeuvres, for how they would conduct themselves during a visit with their mothers. In general, these women felt unable to individuate successfully from their mothers and, in fact, seemed to believe that such separation and real independence would be forever beyond them.

Fear of their mothers and feeling controlled by their mothers were issues also for those clients whose mothers were deceased when treatment began. These women tended to ruminate on the maternal relationship and reported that they still felt dominated by their mothers and unable to control their own lives. It was not unusual for these clients to report that they felt cheated by their mothers' deaths since they believed that it was no longer possible for them to come to terms with their relationships with their mothers.

Establishment of personal identity

The tremendous difficulty experienced by these women in separating themselves from their mothers, was linked to the issue of personal identity. The pervasive theme was: Who am I — as an autonomous self, as a woman, as a partner, as a mother, or for those who did not have children, as a potential mother? For some, being a woman was an identity that seemed fraught with danger. They could not 'simply' avoid people of the other gender as some victims of child sexual abuse by males have done. Being the same gender as their abuser seemed to impart a contradictory message: to be a woman is to be at once the vulnerable victim and the powerful abuser. These women often reported that they saw themselves and all other women as potential victims and abusers.

Meiselman (1990, p. 35), points to the socialisation of girls as nurturant and empathic towards children as one explanation of why maternal-perpetrated incest is less frequent than paternal. Burkhart and Fromuth (1991) suggest that not only is sexual coercion (the behaviour, for example, of the child molester of both genders as opposed to the child rapist) common, but that it is covertly supported by the roles of women and children as dictated by society. What then are the personality correlates of the girl/woman who violates this role and how does the female child who is sexually exploited by her mother interpret this behaviour in the light of societal messages that mothers are nurturing and benevolent?

Some dealt with this issue on an interpersonal basis by avoiding close relationships with other women, preferring instead to meet their relational needs with men: 'With men I was going to get something back that was to my benefit . . . I saw men as my allies even when the relationship wasn't sexual . . . Women were nurturers and attackers' (Groth and Rosemary 1990). Others spent most of their time in groups of women; thus, they had little or no contact with men, but neither did they have intimate (either sexual or non-sexual) contact with individual women. This latter group nevertheless reported on-going mistrust of women in general, perceiving them as untrustworthy and domineering. The exception came with those clients who had sought and found female mentors (outside the family) during their childhood. These women reported less difficulty in relating to other women and to be fearful of women or to perceive other women as potential victimisers.

Committed relationships, marriage and sexual functioning

Of the eight adult clients (one male and seven females) with a history of childhood sexual abuse by a female perpetrator, all but one had difficulties in committed relationships and/or marriages at the time they began therapy. Three of the women had never married; one woman married a man who was emotionally abusive toward her and who subsequently sexually abused their daughter; two other women married, had children and subsequently were divorced from their husbands (one of these women was physically and emotionally abused by her first husband); the last woman entered into a marriage of convenience which she left shortly after the wedding. The male client was divorced after his wife learned that he had sexually abused a friend's child (they had no children of their own). Of the three who never married, one had entered several ill-fated partnerships with other women. None of these women clients had histories of physically or sexually abusing children.

The above histories suggest that the relational difficulties that one might expect in this population were certainly present for these clients. All four of the women who had been married reported difficulties becoming sexually aroused and having orgasms when they had sexual relations with their partners. Two of the single women had avoided sexual relationships during adulthood. The other woman, a lesbian, reported that she had satisfactory sexual arousal and orgasms during her lesbian relationships but was unable to tolerate a long-term relationship with a female partner, despite her expressed wish to do so.

The adult male client in this sample had a heterosexual lifestyle and, after extensive treatment for sexual offence behaviour and chronic substance abuse, eventually reported that he was able to establish close friendships with women and to have satisfying sexual relationships with women. Prior to his treatment, this man had a history of feeling inadequate and undermined in his marriage. Some men who are victims of childhood sexual abuse by female perpetrators report sexual dysfunctions in their relationships with women; this man did not. He attributed his later positive experiences in relating to women to improved self-esteem and better interpersonal and communications skills. However, despite these successes, he had not maintained a committed relationship with any of his partners.

Although many hypotheses can be made about the relational difficulties exhibited by these clients, it is extremely difficult (if not impossible) to attribute them to the impact of childhood sexual abuse by female perpetrators without also taking the other elements of their traumatic histories into consideration. In any event, a larger sample size and comparison with control groups would be required for responsible interpretations to be made.

We wondered if there was a homophobic basis for the fear of other women expressed by most of the adult female clients in this sample. As we mentioned earlier in this chapter, same-sex sexual abuse tends to cause confusion and fears about homosexuality for many child victims. Two of the women in this sample expressed fear that establishing a nurturing and supportive relationship with another woman could be 'unsafe', i.e. they were concerned that closeness with another woman would inevitably lead to sexual interaction. These two women also expressed some confusion about their own sexual orientations and had avoided intimate relationships with either males or females. It is possible that some of these clients may also have feared that other women might feel sexually aroused by them when this was not consciously intended on their part. This reflects the clients' fears that they were somehow responsible for their own childhood sexual abuse by a female relative: 'I was and continue to be so powerful a sexual object that others could not avoid becoming sexually attracted to me'. Or, as Rosemary explains in the previously cited teaching videotape: 'I thought of myself as tempting to everyone!' (Groth and Rosemary 1990).

In light of this, it becomes particularly important that the female clinician acknowledges the transference and countertransference issues which might arise when a female victim or adult survivor of abuse by a woman, seeks treatment with a female therapist. As noted by Dolan (1991), this therapeutic milieu may be a strong force in providing a corrective emotional experience wherein the female client can re-evaluate representatives of her gender (including herself) as 'safe', strong and healing. Dolan also points out that lesbian therapists working with lesbian clients of sexual abuse by females, may help their clients to explore their sexual identification apart from their trauma histories and 'the therapist's positive role modelling may also be helpful for the client in establishing a healthy sense of identity as a lesbian' (pp. 209–210).

Parenting and relationships with children

Only three of the adult female clients had children; the other four adult women expressed fears of parenting. Although none of the adult female clients was identified as a sexual abuser of children, all but two of the women (cases 9 and 10) reported fears that they might become sexually aroused by children or might, somehow, feel compelled to abuse them. The four women who did not have children had dealt with this issue quite directly by avoiding parenting altogether. Three of these women (cases 4, 6, 7) seemed phobic toward children; they avoided proximity to children or situations in which they might be asked to care for children. The other female client (case 8) who was not a parent did not avoid children; instead, she worked with children professionally while having little contact with them in her personal life.

We speculate that avoidance of parenting and avoidance of close contact with children may be related to the self-talk employed by the clients to explain their own child sexual abuse by female perpetrators. Perhaps these women told themselves during childhood that they represented an irresistible attraction that their abusers had been unable to overcome. In other words, they may have distorted reality by viewing themselves as so powerful that they were in control of their abusers and brought sexual victimisation upon themselves. The utility of such a cognitive distortion is in its capacity to help a vulnerable child to feel empowered: If I am responsible for my abuse, I am in control of it and of my own destiny. On the other hand, viewing oneself as a powerful and sexually irresistible child has numerous disadvantages. These include amplification of negative feelings about oneself and the tendency to view oneself as damaged or contaminated. In addition, this distortion about oneself might be generalised to others: i.e. all children are powerful and contaminated in the same way. Safety considerations might dictate, therefore, that children are dangerous to unwary adults and should be avoided.

Another possibility is that the women who feared they would become sexually aroused by children simply believed that they were so damaged and so eroticised that an innocent child would become a desirable sex object for them. Such women might become very confused if they noticed themselves admiring or becoming interested in children. The danger, of course, would be to confuse a normal interest in or attraction toward children, with erotic interest in them. Females daily encounter a variety of sociocultural messages that children are cute and lovable and that 'normal' women ought to be attracted to children and want to parent and care for them. The dilemma for the woman who was sexually abused by a female perpetrator (especially by a mother or mother-figure) is that her life experiences have imparted different messages: Children are dangerous, being a mother is dangerous, I am a high-risk mother, or I would be an unfit mother.

Although not reported by any of these clients, some women who are adult survivors of childhood sexual abuse, report confusion and anxiety about certain aspects of the maternal–child relationship. For example, it is not unusual for some women to experience sexual arousal while they are breastfeeding their children. The mechanical stimulation of the baby's sucking and pulling on the nipples normally evokes both a hormonal and physiological arousal response in the mother. Unfortunately, the woman whose life experiences have predisposed her to fear that she might abuse her child is likely to become terrified by this normal phenomenon. Worse, she may view it as a sign that she is sexually attracted to her own child. It is difficult for women who do not have histories of childhood trauma to disclose a sexual arousal response to a baby's suckling. For an adult survivor of childhood sexual abuse, disclosure of this phenomenon (and alleviation of her fears by a competent professional) may be all but impossible.

In the teaching videotape, Rosemary disclosed that she became sexually aroused when she spanked her child (Groth and Rosemary 1990). The little girl had run out into the street and narrowly escaped being struck by a car. Rosemary's fear for her child's safety quickly turned to anger and she spanked the little girl on her buttocks with a hairbrush. Her sexual arousal and subsequent orgasm were terrifying to Rosemary. She reported on the videotape that it was a long time before she could disclose this experience to a therapist and process its meaning and the associated effects, and come to terms with the event in its entirety. Small wonder!

Therapeutic implications

It is obvious that all of the foregoing observations have significant implications for the clinical stance of the therapist, the therapist–client relationship, and the types of therapeutic interventions that are likely to be helpful.

Clinical stance of the therapist

The clinician's theoretical framework for therapy, her or his past experiences of mother–child relationships, and contemporary status of resolution of conflicts about mothers, mothering and women in general are all important factors. Simply stated, we think that clinicians need to believe it is possible for a woman to be a 'good-enough' mother or for children to receive 'good-enough' parenting in order to work successfully with clients who were traumatised by sexual abuse by female perpetrators. When this is not the case, the clinician's outrage about inadequate or abusive mothering can be a toxic influence on the therapeutic relationship. An important therapeutic task for the clients will be to come to terms with their relationships with their female abusers (Sgroi and Bunk 1988, p. 174). This may include working through levels of fear, betrayal, anger and rage, especially when the abuser was a mother or a mother figure. It is likely also to include processing and resolving confusion and conflicts about female attributes, roles and functions in today's society. Ultimately, it will be important for persons who were sexually traumatised by women to be able to view their abusers as multi-dimensional human beings rather than as monsters or as saintly (if misunderstood) figures. That is to say, the abuser attains a life-sized perspective (rather than a larger-than-life status) in the client's eyes. Thus, the female abuser eventually can be viewed as a person with strengths and weaknesses and positive and negative attributes; a person who made serious errors and committed serious transgressions but who was not all-powerful or demonic.

We believe that clinicians must have the capacity to view female sexual offenders in this way in order to assist clients to attain such a perspective. This does not mean that it is the clinician's task to encourage the client to forgive the woman who sexually abused her or him during childhood. Forgiveness should not be viewed as the *sine qua non* of coming to terms with the relationship with the abuser; feeling forgiving toward one's abuser may be a long way off for many adult survivors (Sargent 1989, p. 177). It does mean that the clinician must be able to separate her or his own feelings and possible conflicts regarding females, mothers and mother–child relationships from those of the client. As well, it means that the clinician needs to give the client permission and freedom to process these issues for herself or himself without being negatively influenced or burdened by the clinician's unresolved conflicts in the same arena. Our experience has been that many clinicians have not addressed these issues satisfactorily for themselves in regard to their own mother–child relationships and/or relationships with women in general. We think, therefore, that clinical stance in regard to these issues may be more relevant and more problematic for clients who were sexually abused by females during childhood than for those who were sexually abused by males. For clinicians who work with this population, it will be necessary to do some self-examination and, perhaps, work on some of their own unresolved issues before or during (but apart from) their work with clients.

Therapist–client relationship

It follows, logically, that the therapist's capacity to model a non-judgemental, accepting attitude toward persons who were sexually abused by female perpetrators is critical. We have already suggested that clinicians should be prepared for the possibility that disclosures of sexual abuse by male perpetrators may occur first, and that it often is necessary to ask specifically about abuse by female perpetrators. Clinicians can help clients by being familiar with all of the issues discussed in the preceding section of this chapter (difficulties in self-differentiation, problems with establishing a personal identity, fear of parenting and the like). An important difference in working with male versus female clients who were sexually abused by female perpetrators should be remembered. Male clients are more likely to seek treatment because of the impact of sexual dysfunction on their marital or intimate relationships. Female clients, on the other hand, may have a broader range of relational difficulties, including such issues as homophobia, intense self-loathing, phobic avoidance of children and the like.

Regardless of how clients present, we cannot emphasise strongly enough the importance of the therapist's capacity to communicate non-judgemental acceptance while also modelling consistency, nur-turing, limit-setting and maintenance of appropriate personal bound-aries. This is the key to all good therapeutic relationships and for therapy with survivors of many types of childhood trauma. It is pertinent to mention this familiar issue in this chapter, nevertheless, because there is greater likelihood that lack of familiarity and experience in working with clients who were sexually abused by female perpetrators may be disorienting for many clinicians. It could, of course, be devastating for clinicians to allow such disorientation and its consequent pitfalls to influence negatively the therapeutic relationship.

Helpful therapeutic interventions

In this section, we will discuss some therapeutic interventions that seemed helpful for our clients. We have found that a peer group therapy experience with other adolescent or adult survivors of childhood sexual abuse amplifies and enriches individual therapy (Sgroi and Bunk 1988, Sgroi 1989, Sargent 1989). It is highly unlikely, however, that many clinicians can offer peer group therapy limited to persons who were sexually abused by female perpetrators. If a client is the single group member to have been sexually abused by a female perpetrator, she or he may find it particularly hard to disclose the gender of the abuser and the circumstances of the abuse. Our experience is limited to working with female clients in all-female groups. Females who were sexually abused by same-sex perpetrators may experience themselves as different from other group members. Some are able to tell their clinicians, 'I feel strange about telling this about myself in the group'. This probably reflects an underlying fear that they are 'particularly damaged' — not just members of the population who were sexually abused in childhood, but also members of a rarely mentioned group who were sexually abused by mothers, sisters, aunts, grandmothers, female babysitters, female religious or the like.

Group therapists should be aware, then, that such clients are likely to reveal childhood histories of sexual abuse by males long before they reveal sexual abuse by female perpetrators within the group. These clients probably are observing and monitoring responses of group members to 'safer' topics before they feel emboldened to reveal what they believe to be the 'worst' taboo: sexual abuse by female perpetrators, especially when the abusers were mothers or female authority figures. Their reluctance to disclose probably includes the fear that other group members will be repelled by them.

When it is possible to take abuse histories into account in determining which clients are in which group, it is desirable to put at least two clients with a history of sexual abuse by a female perpetrator in the same group. If this is impossible given the client pool available, we have found commonalities in therapeutic issues for female victims of sexual abuse by female perpetrators and those who were physically abused by females. In fact, one member's disclosure of physical abuse by a female perpetrator may facilitate disclosure of another member's disclosure of sexual abuse by a female perpetrator and vice versa. We believe this is because group members tend to gain confidence that their own disclosures will be accepted and affirmed when they see this process occurring (and contribute to the process) for the other members.

A common belief among clinicians is that victims of trauma will be more comfortable, less fearful and better able to work on therapeutic issues in a peer grouping with other members of the same gender. Although this is true for survivors of many types of childhood trauma, clinicians should remember that women abused in childhood by female perpetrators may fear being in a therapy group with other women. For them, the experience may feel like an amplification of their childhood experience of feeling vulnerable with a woman and being victimised by her. Their initial peer group therapy experience with other women group members and female co-therapists may be akin to feeling surrounded by victimisers! As one client said, 'There are a lot of breasts in this room! I'm not sure I'm going to be safe'.

Group therapy interventions

We believe in a co-therapy model and prefer to conduct therapy in time-limited cycles. Peer group therapy for female adult survivors is conducted with two female co-therapists and group membership of

8–10 female clients. The office sponsors three time-limited cycles of these groups each year, with each cycle consisting of 12–15 weekly 90 minute sessions. The clients all know at the beginning of each cycle that there will be an agreed-upon number of weekly sessions that will end on an announced date. After a four or five week hiatus, another time-limited cycle will begin at the office. Membership in each cycle is determined by mutual agreement between the office and the client. After initiating this model in 1985, we now find that each group cycle has 7–8 members with previous experience of working in our groups and 2–3 members who are 'new' to this therapy modality. Some women participate in one cycle only; others participate in successive cycles for one to three years; still others 'hopscotch' their participation in cycles over a several year time period.

We conduct 3–4 screening/evaluation sessions with each prospective member before she enters the group for the first time. All of the group members are encouraged to be in individual therapy during the cycle as well as participating in the group. Some are seen weekly in individual therapy; some bi-weekly; some monthly, depending on their individual needs. The individual sessions are necessary for members to process more fully the issues evoked by group participation. Thus individual and group therapy are not separate and compartmentalised therapeutic interventions. The individual and group therapists are allowed to share information because permission to share information is a prerequisite for membership in the group. This allows group members to receive encouragement from their individual therapists to bring up certain issues or ask for particular types of help in the group. On the other hand, the group therapists have a greater understanding of each member's recovery process as viewed by the individual therapists. A more complete description of this model has been presented in detail (Sgroi 1989). With the modifications described earlier in this chapter, we have found it to be very helpful for women survivors of childhood sexual abuse by female perpetrators.

The following group therapy interventions are especially pertinent for this population.

Demonstration and modelling of support and nurturing by adult women (other group members and therapists) without strings attached

After victims of sexual abuse by female perpetrators disclose this aspect of their trauma histories, they are likely to anticipate censure or withdrawal responses by the other women in the room. Repeated demonstrations of affirmation, acceptance and support for the survivor's subjective reality ('I feel as if I was spawned by a monster instead of raised by a mother!') are powerful interventions. Gradually most of our clients have responded with more confidence, less shame and a greater willingness to trust women in the group and women in general.

Gentle challenge of distortions of reality

At the same time as support and affirmation are being offered, group members can challenge the common distortions of reality voiced by this population. This message to the woman who was physically and/or sexually abused by her mother, sister or a significant female abuser is repeated over and over: We do not think you are bad or evil or damaged. You have the right to feel however you wish to feel about yourself. Our feedback to you is that we experience you differently. You are not repellent, loathsome or fearful. We are glad that you are here and respectful of your feelings. We are glad that you could share all of this with us. There is no need to flee or drop out. You can stay in the group and proceed at your own pace. There is no requirement that you trust anyone until you are ready.

Mutuality and reciprocity of member-to-member interactions

In well-run peer group therapy, the female survivor of childhood sexual abuse by a female abuser will have opportunities to extend affirmation and support as well as receive them. Also, she will have chances to challenge the cognitive distortions of others without being punitive or blaming. The mutuality and reciprocity of member-to-member interactions demonstrates to these clients that they can have nurturing, supportive and non-abusive interactions with other women as well as receive help safely from other women.

Role-playing

This intervention can be a very effective way for clients to identify and process all of their thoughts and feelings about a relationship or prepare for upcoming meetings or contacts with persons with whom they feel vulnerable or disadvantaged. Many group members are reluctant to participate in role-plays that involve themselves directly. In the group, a woman may be invited to ask two other members to do the role-play for her initially. She can ask one person to role-play herself, for example, and another to role-play her female abuser. The member who is the subject of the role-play would give the other women background information and answer their questions about the respective roles. (Anyone who wishes to refuse to be the 'surrogate client' or 'surrogate female abuser' may refuse.) After the first role-play, the entire group can process the experience. In a second stage of role-playing, the member now role-plays herself with another group member role-playing her female abuser. In a third stage, the member asks another women to role-play herself while she role-plays her female abuser.

This staged approach to role-playing allows the member some much needed distance from the interaction in the beginning. However, it can also help her to feel empowered when she role-plays herself and to experience receiving an apology or explanation from the surrogate female abuser. By role-playing her own abuser, she can come closer to viewing this person as a multi-dimensional human being.

Therapeutic use of metaphor

This powerful intervention is used by the therapists for assisting members to process many issues. It requires a capacity enabled by experience and training to identify metaphors that are introduced by clients and tell stories that can be woven into the group interactions. For example, one woman who had been sexually abused by her mother came to the group 30 minutes late for a session. Apologetically, she explained that she had a strong urge to purchase a car seat for her infant son on the way to the session and the delay had made her late. This same woman described herself as 'up in the air' most of the time. When she returned to her car with the newly purchased car seat, she discovered that there were two other car seats in the back of the car; she had 'forgotten' that she had purchased these car seats earlier in the week. The woman disclosed that she was terribly concerned for her son's safety, but not sure why. She looked terrified as she said this.

One of the therapists asked her, 'Why is a raven like a writing desk?' As she puzzled over this famous quotation from *Alice in Wonderland*, the therapist asked another group member, 'How is a car seat like a parachute?' A lively discussion ensued among the group members. The woman's fear that she would injure her own child through neglect or abuse in unconscious mimicry of her own mother's abusive behaviours was uncovered gradually. She herself could participate in the discussion and gradual uncovering without feeling overwhelmed by the associated affects. The metaphors enabled her to see that she was taking extra precautions for her son in order to feel safer in regard to her own abusive experiences. The group could congratulate her on how well she was taking care of herself and her son (with three car seats, she and her husband had one for each car plus an extra), but also point out that she had the skills and capacity to work more directly on her relationship with her own mother. The client's mother, the group learned, lived nearby and kept offering to babysit for her grandson. The woman was terrified to allow her mother to babysit for her son but unaware of the connection between her fear that her son would become injured in a car accident and her fear that he would be abused by his grandmother. Once aware of the connection, she was able to borrow strength from the group to set the needed limits about babysitting with her mother and to role-play how to do it. The thought-provoking question, 'Why is a raven like a writing desk?' was repeated by group members and therapists throughout the rest of the cycle whenever anyone in the group shared a current behaviour she found puzzling or annoying.

In conclusion, we believe that group and individual therapy offer multiple opportunities for healing and recovery for adult survivors of childhood sexual abuse by female perpetrators. In this chapter, we have presented clinical observations on a small cohort of clients. We do not see this population as untreatable or 'particularly damaged'. We hope that our experiences and observations may be helpful to other clinicians and encourage others to work directly with this client population and share their ideas and experiences as well.

References

Allen, C. (1991) *Women and Men who Sexually Abuse Children: A Comparative Analysis* The Safer Society Press.

Banning, Anne (1989) 'Mother–son incest: confronting a prejudice' *Child Abuse and Neglect* 13 (4) pp. 563–570.

Baron, Robert S., Burgess, Mary L. and Kao, Chuan Feng (1991) 'Detecting and labeling prejudice: Do female perpetrators go undetected?' *Personality and Social Psychology Bulletin* 17 (2) pp. 115–123.

Burkhart, Barry and Fromuth, Mary Ellen (1991) 'Individual psychological understandings of sexual coercion' in Grauerholz, Elizabeth and Koralewski, Mary A. (Eds) *Sexual Coercion: A Sourcebook on Its Nature, Causes and Prevention* Lexington, MA: Lexington Books.

Courtois, Christine A. (1988) *Healing the Incest Wound: Adult Survivors in Therapy* London: W. W. Norton & Co.

Dolan, Yvonne M. (1991) *Resolving Sexual Abuse: Solution-Focussed Therapy and Ericksonian Hypnosis for Adult Survivors* New York: W. W. Norton & Co.

Finkelhor, D. and Russell, D. (1984) 'Women as perpetrators' in Finkelhor, D. (Ed.) *Child Sexual Abuse, New Theory and Research* New York: The Free Press.

Goodwin, Gean and Di Vasto, P. (1979) 'Mother–daughter incest' *Child Abuse and Neglect* 3 pp. 953–957.

Groth, A. Nicholas and Rosemary (1990) *Rosemary: Beyond Survival* A videotape interview produced by Forensic Mental Health Associates, Orlando, Florida.

Krug, Ronald S. (1989) 'Adult male report of childhood sexual abuse by mothers: Case descriptions, motivations and long-term consequences' *Child Abuse and Neglect* 13 (1) pp. 111–119.

Maletzky, Barry M. (1991) *Treating the Sexual Offender* London: Sage Publications.

Mathews, Ruth, Matthews, Jane Kinder and Speltz, Kathleen (1989) *Female Sexual Offenders* Orwell, Vermont: The Safer Society Press.

Mathews, Ruth, Matthews, Jane Kinder and Speltz, Kathleen (1991) 'Female sexual offenders: A typology' in Michael Quinn Patton (Ed.) *Family Sexual Abuse: Frontline Research and Evaluation* London: Sage Publications.

McCarty, Loretta M. (1986) 'Mother–child incest: Characteristics of the offender' *Child Welfare* 65 (5) pp. 447–458.

Meiselman, Karin (1990) *Resolving the Trauma of Incest: Reintegration Therapy with Survivors* Oxford: Jossey-Bass.

O'Hagen, Kieran (1989) *Working with Child Sexual Abuse* Milton Keynes: Open University Press.

Sanderson, Christiane (1990) *Counselling Adult Survivors of Child Sexual Abuse* London: Jessica Kingsley.

Sargent, Norah (1989) 'Spirituality and adult survivors of child sexual abuse: some treatment issues' in Suzanne M. Sgroi (Ed.) *Vulnerable Populations, 2: Sexual Abuse Treatment for Children, Adult Survivors, Offenders and Persons With Mental Retardation* New York: Lexington Books of Macmillan Freepress.

Sgroi, Suzanne (1989) 'Healing together: peer group therapy for adult survivors of child sexual abuse' in Suzanne M. Sgroi (Ed.) *Vulnerable Populations, 2: Sexual A buse Treatment for Children, Adult Survivors, Offenders and Persons with Mental Retardation* New York: Lexington Books of Macmillan Freepress.

Sgroi, Suzanne and Bunk, Barbara (1988) 'A clinical approach to adult survivors' in Suzanne M. Sgroi (Ed.) *Vulnerable Populations, 1: Evaluation and Treatment of Sexually Abused Children and Adult Survivors* New York: Lexington Books of Macmillan Freepress.

Zellman, Gail (1992) 'The impact of case characteristics on child abuse reporting decisions' *Child Abuse and Neglect* 16 (1) pp. 57–74.

3 Helping survivors through counselling

Kate Hunter

The aim of this chapter is to help survivors understand generally what happens in counselling, not to go into the counselling process in depth.

Lucy and I work together in therapy. She has generously agreed that I may write about some of my experiences of working with her as a counsellor. I also work with others who have been sexually abused in childhood by women, as well as with many individuals sexually abused by men. Lucy, like others, has been very damaged by these experiences and yet never fails to amaze me with her resilience and strength in having survived her abuse. Lucy visited her general practitioner in a very anxious state. She was in the process of divorcing her alcoholic husband, she was sleeping badly and generally feeling very stressed and tearful. She felt she could no longer put on a 'brave face'. Her doctor suggested to her that she meet me, the counsellor employed by the practice, and Lucy agreed.

We met on four occasions over a period of four months. Lucy used this time to express her anger about her husband and her concern for her present relationship. She was experiencing outbursts of anger and sudden desperate tears; all of which was very confusing for her and her partner. I felt puzzled by the strength of her anger when, in fact, her divorce was well under way. My notes from that time remind me of the outpouring from Lucy in these early sessions. There was a sense of chaos and crisis which Lucy was finding quite overwhelming.

Lucy was obviously a very capable woman, having survived an abusive relationship with her husband whilst caring for her two sons. She had established a new relationship with a very supportive; caring man (who she subsequently married), a new home for herself and her sons and was cutting the ties with her husband who had tormented her for years. My puzzlement concerning the strength of Lucy's feelings, reflects my experience of working with other survivors of sexual abuse. There is a sense that something is missing in what they have told me. The feelings being expressed seem stronger than the present situation warrants.

This is a common experience for any counsellor in their work, as a present-day life experience will often trigger feelings from the past. With survivors of sexual abuse who are not able to talk of their experiences, or who are in the early stages of therapy, there is a gap between expressed feelings and present events, which seems particularly strong and acute. Now I am much more likely to ask clients early on whether they were ever sexually abused. This can help individuals to speak of their experiences and know that I am willing to listen.

In these early sessions we addressed issues like the difficulty Lucy had in taking time from work and also what counselling might offer her. I learnt that Lucy's mother was schizophrenic, having been admitted to a mental institution several times before her final admission when Lucy was about twelve years old. As far as she knew her mother was still a patient there. Her parents had separated when she was eighteen months old, her mother having sole custody of Lucy until her final admission to hospital. Lucy had over the years been cared for by various relatives.

She talked of how coming to see me 'churned' things up and that she felt that this could help her rid herself emotionally of her husband and in particular of the anger she still felt towards him. There was a great sense of violation and injustice when she spoke of him.

We met on an irregular basis which is unusual to my way of working; however, it felt appropriate to respect Lucy's choice in meeting me less often. I expressed concern that she was obviously experiencing deep distress, and that my preference would have been to meet on a weekly basis.

Lucy reached a crisis point when her husband started work in the same office as her. He had been violent to her in their marriage and she felt deep outrage at the way he seemed to be trying to haunt her. He had also been using their children as a means to continuing his relationship with Lucy, resulting in her feeling that she would never be free of him. As I later learnt, this was a direct reflection of some of Lucy's earliest experiences and feelings.

She was taking sick leave as she felt unable to return to work while her husband was working in the same office. We agreed to meet in future on a weekly basis and Lucy dealt very capably with her work situation which resulted in her husband being transferred to another office and Lucy returning to work.

Soon after this, Lucy told me she had been sexually abused by her mother from the age of two. Her parents had separated when she was eighteen months old and never lived together again. They divorced when she was nine. Lucy lived with her mother and some relatives. Her father lived alone over thirty miles away and seldom visited.

The sexual abuse continued until Lucy was twelve. It involved vaginal penetration with sharp objects, being forced to sexually stimulate her mother and, on one occasion, being abused by a boyfriend of her mother. Lucy suspected that her relatives knew of the abuse.

Her mother frequently tried to commit suicide. Lucy recounted that, when she was only four months old, her father had found his wife collapsed with Lucy in her arms. She had attempted to kill herself. Lucy was blue with cold and had developed pneumonia, which nearly caused her death. Her mother was again admitted for psychiatric care.

The trauma of recalling these memories and new memories as time passed, was deeply distressing for Lucy. Her present relationships and family life became, at times, very unsettled and needed attention in counselling sessions. Lucy had kept her memories buried for many years enabling her to cope with her day-to-day life. As memories emerged in therapy and between our meetings, Lucy had to deal with immense pain.

Lucy often experienced herself thrown back into feeling like a very young child and of feeling the associated terror. She has regressed in our meetings and an argument with her partner could lead her back to experiencing herself as a young child. Her partner had to share her journey with her in order to make sense of their current relationship.

Our work now alternates between talking of the present and of experiencing the pain of her past. She is expressing her outrage and anger about the abuse from her mother and from others who betrayed her trust or refused to acknowledge the fact of her abuse. She is also grieving for all the experiences she has missed in her childhood and adulthood.

Her family were dealing with painful memories of their own. One of her sons started talking about abusive experiences he had suffered at the hands of his father. Lucy spoke of our meetings at this time as a lifeline. A group for survivors of sexual abuse was starting and Lucy was keen to become involved. Unfortunately she was unable to pursue this, due to the timing of the group.

Lucy has been through times of denial. The horror of her memories has sometimes been too great for her. As when working with any survivor of sexual abuse, I have always confirmed my belief in her experiences whilst acknowledging the pain involved in facing these memories. It is crucial to confirm a client's experiences. Individuals abused by women have an extra hurdle in believing that their memories of abuse by women are less readily believed by others and even by themselves. It is difficult and painful to hear stories of sexual abuse. As a woman, it is sometimes uncomfortable to listen to a male client recalling a catalogue of abuse by many different women, often professional women. The abuse can easily verge on the unbelievable. Facing the horrifying reality that both male and female adults abuse, rape and torture children is an issue for all of us working in the field of child abuse.

It has been impossible for me ever to doubt Lucy's memories in the face of her extreme pain, and this has been her own means of confirmation when she disbelieves herself. She felt an acute sense of greater shame and guilt that she had been abused by a woman, and worse still by her mother. She felt that, if her abuse had been perpetrated by a man, this would somehow be more acceptable to herself and others, or at least less shaming. Generally, Lucy feels that life is worth fighting for and that she is able to heal herself. At times of absolute despair, death feels like the only escape, although she has decided that this is not an option for her.

Working with people who have been sexually abused has meant witnessing agonising pain, which clients describe as a violation and destruction of their very essence. One incident with Lucy highlighted the need to contain this pain in a safe environment. Lucy has, in the past, been admitted for psychiatric care when she had post-natal depression following the birth of both her children. This has left her with a fear of being contained by psychiatric services, which she experienced as abusive and very confusing. At this particular session Lucy regressed and reached a stage (possibly pre-verbal or per-haps re-experiencing her mother silencing her whilst she abused her) when she was unable to speak and felt she could not breathe. This was obviously terrifying for Lucy, and I held her emotionally through this experience and suggested possible reasons for this happening.

I have purposely not included many details of Lucy's story as she will give a much more accurate account of these than I. She has taught me a great deal in the course of her counselling. I have found myself developing an added dimension — a deeper understanding and insight into the effects that childhood sexual abuse has on the survivors. Many feel their very core has been violated, and reclaiming their sense of self in adulthood is a long and tortuous journey. How many individuals with severe psychiatric illness who have lived in mental institutions for years as a result of child sexual abuse have become too distant for any therapy? To reclaim a healthy view of self when it was so violated in infancy is a tough task for anyone and for those involved in their recovery.

Lucy has experienced this very deep violation of herself. Many damaging experiences have happened as a result of her sense of worthlessness. In her child's mind she feels she must have been essentially bad for this abuse to happen and, at times, she feels this still. Only now when she can validate her right to her feelings in the present can she heal that little girl. As she is able to behave and feel differently in her present life situations she can recover a sense of herself.

The counsellor's task, as I see it, is to enable people to mourn the loss of their childhood, to bring out their feelings and to allow the individual a safe place so their stories can emerge. This may be a painful and slow process, whether the abuse was by a male or by a female. Counsellors also need safe places and support to help themselves cope with the pain they are hearing.

I have included a few of the issues which come to the fore in my work with survivors of child sexual abuse. Trust or lack of it is an important issue. They have learnt that adults are untrustworthy. They have often experienced coercion and abuse of trust. Trust in any individual does not just happen, it is a living process. A counsellor can expect to be continually tested and re-tested as therapy evolves. Safe boundaries are essential and often need to be stated clearly. Trust may come and go perhaps having little to do with the individual counsellor, but more likely a replay of the client's confusion about having been involved with untrustworthy adults. A client will probably long to feel safe and secure, and yet be terrified by the possibility that someone may have been found offering this. They will be familiar with being abandoned by adults they may have hoped they could trust. I offer open contracts with clients if I agree to work with them.

I have also found that a catalogue of abuse and of many different abusers is not uncommon. A child who feels a lack of self-worth, feels it doesn't deserve love and care from adults and is unable to tell any adult what is happening, has a deep sense of being bad. This can lead to later forms of abuse for these people, both in childhood and later in adulthood. Some individuals remember enjoying the sexual abuse, which makes them feel that they are to blame. Sexually abusing a child is a criminal act, no child is ever to blame for sexual abuse. This fact needs to be stated to survivors and will need continual reinforcement throughout therapy.

It is essential never to have any sexual contact with these clients either whilst they remain clients or after the ending of therapy. This would be a replication of the initial abuse and seriously damage the trust established in counselling. If a client has never been given control or the right to control physical contact with adults whilst a child they will be unfamiliar and uncomfortable with physical contact of a safe nature. If counsellors have any confusion about touching clients, they should not do so. Touching could give mixed messages and might be damaging and confusing for the clients.

People who have been sexually abused will, in the process of counselling, believe that they cannot be healed. My experience with sexual abuse survivors has led me to believe that these individuals can heal and are capable of creating satisfying lives for themselves. The ability and the motivation clients have to recover from their experiences never ceases to amaze me.

As with any client, the individual is the expert on what is needed. When I have questioned the validity of helping a person face these painful memories, I have checked with the client. I have sometimes wondered whether I am being abusive in encouraging an individual to face memories, yet each client has told me that they wish to continue with psychotherapy. This has reassured me that this painful process is healing and not abusive. I have had to explore my own experiences which came closest to feelings of sexual abuse. This I have done with friends I trust, in my own therapy and sometimes after supervision sessions. I have learnt to control my caseload in terms of who I am able to work with, otherwise I am threatened with being overwhelmed by the number of people seeking help concerning their experiences of sexual abuse. I may have to refer clients to other therapists, which, of course, can be done in a caring, supportive way.

Supervision has been enormously helpful and supportive in terms of receiving information, acknowledging both my own feelings and the difficulties of this type of work and in reassuring me about the healing process. I have learnt that people will need, at any one time, different aspects of the healing process. Disclosure may be as far as one person wishes to go. Present difficulties may be so immediate that these are the focus of the work.

As a woman working with individuals who have been sexually abused by women I have had to examine my own feelings in a different way as compared to working with survivors of abuse perpetrated by men.

Everything I read by survivors and counsellors, from the processes I am involved in and the individuals who share their experiences with me, confirms my belief that therapy is helpful, wanted and needed by survivors of sexual abuse.

I am grateful to the many individuals who have shared their experiences with me either directly as clients or by writing about their recovery from the effects of child sexual abuse. They have taught me a great deal. I am also grateful for the support of my supervisor and the general practitioners who have made my work with Lucy and many other courageous people possible.

Lucy Jenner's story

My mother began sexually abusing me long before my third birthday. Unfortunately the abuse was not an isolated incident. Indeed it continued with unflinching regularity throughout my childhood until I was 13 years old. As I write this more than 30 years later, I still bear the anger, guilt and desolation it created within me. With the help of my therapist Kate, my sons and my friends, I have now found the courage to relate some of those memories that still haunt me today. While the pain of the past will never completely leave me, I have at last made progress towards a brighter future. A future I had always believed I would never have.

I was 16 years old before I remembered anything clearly about the sexual abuse. I had blocked out any cohesive, conscious memory in order to survive and protect my sanity.

It was a cold winter afternoon and I sat by the fire with my stepmother at the old house in the Midlands. I liked and admired my stepmother a great deal and over the months I had lived with her, my father and their children, I had often relaxed in her company. She was a kind intuitive soul and she made me feel almost confident in her presence. We were chatting about children and the amusing things they sometimes say and do. So it was on this day, during a lighthearted chat that I first broke my silence about the abuse.

I began by saying that when I was small I remembered thinking that all women were really men dressed up to look like women. My stepmother looked confused and asked me why I had thought that.

Everything seemed to go quiet. I could feel my breathing getting heavier and my heart pounding in my ears. It felt like I was travelling extremely fast down a helter-skelter and I felt very sick. I felt the sensation of choking and my throat ached. Somewhere very far away I could hear my stepmother's voice calling to me. She was asking again why I had thought that all women were really men. I could sense that words were spewing from my mouth but I couldn't grasp their meaning. It was like I was babbling away in a foreign language, but I had little control over what was being uttered. The floodgates had opened and the flow was unstoppable.

Much later I felt numb and my stepmother's voice was no longer a far away whisper. She was relating to me what I had told her. I had described an incident where my mother had sexually abused me when I was very young. My stepmother told me most emphatically that whenever I felt unsure that the abuse had really taken place, I was to recall my actions at this particular moment. I was rocking to and fro, sucking my thumb — something I had not done since I was a small child. My stepmother hugged me until I stopped sobbing.

A tremendous sense of relief washed over me. Someone else actually knew my secret and there was no ridicule or dismissal. I had always known that I had a secret, a deep, dark secret. I knew because I was different from everyone else — I didn't love my own mother. The secret came in my nightmares, in vague shadows of inexplicable horror, but I had never known their true meaning. The revelation explained so much. Most times I could hardly bear anyone to touch or hug me. My stomach would turn over in revulsion because, on reflection, it would trigger off a blurred recognition. I especially dreaded school sports, when friends would hug each other after a hockey or netball victory. I would hide in the loo to escape the jubilant hugs. Such behaviour always confused me and I felt guilty for acting differently. Perhaps deep down inside I was really a boy dressed-up like a girl.

I rarely trusted anyone. I believed that if someone was nice to me, they wanted something more, and eventually they would hurt or betray me. I could never seem to strike a healthy balance. I see-sawed between total distrust and unconditional faith in anyone I met. I had such a complete lack of self-esteem and experienced terrific mood swings — from chatterbox to mouse, sometimes several times in one day. I was very awkward and, as far back as I could remember, felt a distinct and overwhelming apology for my very existence. I just knew that my mother didn't really love me, but I couldn't quite put my finger on why. She just made me feel dirty and uncomfortable.

Above all with this first recollection, there was an explanation for my fear and loathing for my mother. I was terrified of her and despised her, which made me feel confused, wicked and ungrateful. I still experience that terror — it has always shadowed my life. I tried desperately to bury these feelings and to love and respect her. Everyone told me that I should love her, 'you only have one mother'.

My stepmother never told my father about the sexual abuse, although she led me to believe otherwise. However, she did relate to him that I had experienced a difficult and disturbed childhood. When I was growing up, my father was in infrequent visitor and I viewed him as a stranger. Yet, here he was shouting obscenities at my absent mother. What he failed to do was to comfort me or tell me that he loved me.

An only child, I was born in 1955 in an English Northern town. I was the baby who would heal the rift in my parent's marriage. Such was the enormity of the task placed upon me that failure was only to be expected. When my parents separated, my mother was granted sole custody.

I lived with her in my grandmother's house. I shared a room and a bed with my mother. One side of the bed was pushed against the wall. I had the space between the wall and my mother. The door was kept locked and she had the only key. Escape was impossible — incarceration was complete.

My mother was a young attractive woman with auburn hair. She was a dominant personality known for her quick and fiery temper. She had friends and boyfriends and held down a part-time job. She was the baby of the family and no one refused her anything. Her word was law and she had absolute power in my upbringing. I was never allowed out of her sight except to go to school and was actively discouraged from making any close relationships so I was completely dependent on her. Even today I am completely terrified of her and would never confront her with flowers, let alone with the memories of the incest. (I have recently confronted my mother, however as a result of my therapy.)

When I was a child most nights, after pleading with my nana to stay with her, I was hauled off to bed by my mother. At my mother's whim I was woken when she came to bed. I tried to pretend to sleep to no avail. She would cuddle me from behind — this she called a 'chair' and she would demand that I said I loved her. She would then produce various items to insert into my vagina or anus. Sometimes she used only her fingers. I was forced to have oral sex with her and to stimulate her. At the time of the abuse I would fix my eyes on the rose-patterned wallpaper and concentrate on something else and detach myself from what was happening. Survivors call this 'splitting' and it was this that saved me from insanity. I could see myself below, as I floated out of my body, trying hard to escape in my mind and forget entirely what was taking place.

I never argued or complained. Struggling had ceased long ago, some time in my third year. My mother had taken me to my grandmother's room, where there was a large, brass bed. I liked my nan's bed because it smelt of her and she was always kind to me. Nana was in hospital and my aunt and cousin were away. My mother put me on the bed and locked the door. She had been sexually abusing me some time before this, but I would stiffen and struggle and she hated that. It seemed that my mother had decided that, not only was I supposed to endure this torment, but that I was going to pretend to enjoy it. At the very least I was to be obedient and co-operative. She asked me to stimulate her, but I would not. She told me to smile and I refused. She told me to stop crying, but I couldn't. I started screaming, 'I want out! I want out!' over and over. She put her hand over my mouth and I bit her finger. She put both hands over my mouth and I could smell the stale odour of tobacco on them. Her nails were long and scratched my face, but I would not stop struggling. She was frightening and hurting me. Exasperated, she put my arms down at my sides and held them fast with her arm across them. With her knees, she pinned down my kicking legs. Her free hand reached for the pillow beside me, putting it over my face. She pressed harder until I could hardly breathe. She told me I was a wicked, evil girl because I would not be good for her. She kept shouting and then everything went dark.

I woke up on the floor at the side of the bed. My mother was stripping the eiderdown because I had wet the bed. She didn't seem bothered whether I was dead or alive. I remember thinking that I must have been a very naughty girl for this to happen. She stepped over me to unlock the door. As she took the green eiderdown with her, it slid coldly over my face. I didn't move or make a sound. My grandfather slept next door, but I was too frightened and weak to call him. Besides he was always very angry if anyone disturbed his rest and he didn't much care for me anyway. I was very thirsty and my throat hurt. My mother returned and dragged me into a sitting position. She told me that in future I would do exactly as she said, that I was a wicked girl and that I was never to tell anyone or she would punish me again with the pillow. I didn't care any more what happened to me, so I didn't cry. All the fight was gone. She had beaten me into submission. If only she would at least cuddle me, but she didn't soften in her resolve to punish me. My mother was triumphant.

There have been many ways that my traumatic childhood has affected me. The sexual abuse that I suffered at the hands of my mother has left profound and long lasting emotional and spiritual scars. During my adolescence, my feelings of insecurity and the longing to be loved were overwhelming. I became pregnant, aged 15. The child, a boy, was given up for adoption. The only relief in this agonising time was that I was indeed a female and could function in a heterosexual relationship.

At eighteen, I was consumed with guilt about the memory of the incest and the adoption of the baby, so I planned to die by taking a massive overdose. Thwarted in this, within the space of three months, I met and married a man by whom I was immediately pregnant. He was a heavy drinker, aggressive at times. He knew about the incest and used my resultant low self-esteem as a way to dominate myself and my sons.

Therapy has been a lifeline for me. Kate, my therapist, has helped me to clarify past feelings and to gain a perspective. I can remember the first time I told her of the incest. The relief was intense — she believed me straight away without hesitation. My first therapist was dismissive and negative in her response to my 'confession'. She simply found it too disturbing and quite outside her capability as a therapist. I wonder if she knew the despair and desperation she plunged me into simply because she could not cope or believe me. I wanted to talk —

she made me a cup of tea and changed the subject.

I take one day at a time now. I have a job, have a steady relationship and two lovely sons. My hopes for the future are endless. I want to put my past behind me and live a full and carefree life. I don't want to wake up each morning to face the horror again. Although at times the abuse haunts me awake or sleeping. I wish that none of the abuse had ever taken place and that I had had a loving caring mother. The grief is always there. I have daydreams of who my parents could have been and these dreams are not for wealth or grand beginnings — just for warmth, love and happiness. I remember playing games as a child and always picking happiness as my hope for the future. It still is.

4 A survivor's and therapist's viewpoint

Cianne Longdon

There are a lot of myths and prejudices in society concerning female sexual abuse. It is therefore important to examine our own myths and beliefs before we can effectively work with survivors or make it easier for children to disclose.

Let us examine some of the myths surrounding female sexual abuse:

(i)   Females do not sexually abuse.

(ii)   Females only abuse if coerced or accompanied by a man.

(iii)   If females sexually abuse it is gentle, loving, or misguided 'motherly' love.

(iv)   Females only abuse boys.

(v)   If you are female and you were abused by a female then you will be lesbian; if male — gay or misogynist.

(vi)   If you were sexually abused as a child you will abuse as an adult.

(vii)   People who say they were abused by a female are fantasising or lying. If you are male you are having sexual fantasies, and if the perpetrator was your mother, you are having incestuous wishes. If you are female you are muddled and it was a man who really abused you.

(viii) Women only sexually abuse adolescents.

(ix)   If a 30 year old woman were to seduce a 14 year old boy it would not be sexual abuse, but if a 30 year old man were to seduce a 14 year old girl then it would undoubtedly be so.

(x)   If a mother has an incestuous relationship with her son in his late teens/early twenties it is sex between two consent-ing adults and not sexual abuse.

(xi)   It is worse to be sexually abused by a woman than by a man.

This is a personal exploration of the realities of female sexual abuse as seen from my possibly unique vantage point of being both a survivor and also a therapist working with other survivors.

My definition of sexual abuse is when a child is forced, coerced or manipulated into either doing, or having things done, to their body by a person, male or female, who is in a position of control, care or power over that child. I include the child being made/asked to watch other people engaging in sexual acts whether by force or agreement, or being exposed in any way to sexual activity, talk, pictures, etc., which are way beyond the child's sexual and psychological development.

A great deal is heard these days about sexual abuse and how it is far more widespread than used to be believed. Its occurrence is now generally accepted, both by the public and professionals. With this apparently widespread acceptance, it is important to remember that not very many years ago the mention of sexual abuse was taboo; as far as society was concerned it simply didn't happen.

Another point to remember is that, as far as most of society is concerned, all sexual abuse is perpetrated by men, or, if women are involved, it is only when coerced by men. After all we all know women don't abuse. A consequence of this attitude within society is that, for people like myself who have survived being sexually abused by a woman, we suffer intolerable alienation and little recognition or support from the public or professionals alike.

The long-term effects of any sexual abuse, irrespective of the gender of the perpetrator are devastating enough. When this is coupled with the knowledge that what happened to us simply is not acknowledged as being real or taken seriously by society, the damage done to the survivor is compounded.

It is from the feelings that all survivors of female sexual abuse face, of desperation, isolation and loneliness, that I shall start my explora-tion.

I am a survivor of female sexual abuse which occurred for most of my childhood. My experiences are intensely personal, private and at times still extremely painful. I am at present writing a book for survivors and professionals in which I share my experiences in greater depth. The single most important thing you, or anyone can do for me, and other survivors, is to believe.

Women can and do sexually abuse not only when coerced by men but independently. That they do not, or are literally incapable of doing so, is just one of the myths. Only when these myths with their roots in our traditional perception of women as nurturers and carers, are dispelled, will half the battle be won. One consequence of this disbelief is that, even after disclosure, others may attempt to attribute the abuse to men, thus reinforcing the myth that women do not sexually abuse.

Disclosing that you have been sexually abused by a woman is difficult enough. It is doubly so if you are a woman because it can feel like a betrayal of your own sex to say that they are capable of such appalling acts.

Because female sexual abuse arouses such strong reactions, particularly in other women, survivors fear being ostracised, receiving anger and criticism or being gossiped about. Unfortunately some survivors who have disclosed have received exactly this treatment from other women. In one survivor's words: 'When I first told that my aunt had sexually abused me for years, my family was blown apart. They accused me, amongst other things, of making it up, of being evil, insane and just wanting attention. What hurt the most is that it was the female members of my family who were the most venomous and vindictive.'

Other survivors have told me how, either from fear of ridicule or from having previously received negative responses upon disclosure, they have in desperation, and from a desire to receive help of any sort, said that their abuser was a man. In every case the change of gender within these disclosures was a result not of fantasy or imagination but of the parochial attitude of society and professionals.

I understand the pressures placed on survivors to conform to this need to deny that women sexually abuse. My first attempt at disclosure was met with shock and disbelief. This, combined with my counsellor's attempt to convince me that it must have been a man and not a woman who sexually abused me, left me feeling bruised, battered and wondering if I was crazy.

It took two more attempts before I found a therapist who believed one hundred per cent that I had been abused by the woman I said, and that it was not I who was crazy but those who refused to believe!

The responses other survivors have received range from incredulity to outright denial, for example,

'Do women really do that?'
'Are you sure it wasn't your father?'
'It's a ridiculous idea! How would they do it?'

Before we can begin to change the conspiracy of silence which surrounds female sexual abuse, we need to understand why it exists.

Why is it such a shocking idea to believe that women can, and do, sexually abuse?

One of the reasons for this, I believe is that for so long now we have accepted that women are sexually safe with small children. We do not want to acknowledge that this may not be so, as it creates insecurity and fear. It raises the question 'is there no one, or nowhere, that is safe for our children?' The acceptance that women are in fact not as safe as we would believe attacks the very heart of traditional family values. Today's families are still mainly centred around the mother as provider of all needs. Throughout society women still hold the traditional role of carer, e.g. nurses, teachers, etc.

Whatever the reasons for this denial, let me be clear on one thing. The longer the denial continues, the longer we are potentially putting our children at risk. An example of this frightening lack of awareness came from a head teacher who said, while we were talking about female sexual abuse, 'I had no idea, no idea at all that women did such things'. This is from someone whose school is staffed almost entirely by women, and to whom we entrust the care of our children.

I have looked at some of the difficulties I, and other survivors, have faced as a result of society's attitude. Before I go on to discuss how I work with adult survivors of female sexual abuse, I feel it is important that I give a brief outline of the nature of female sexual abuse. This will be based on my own experience and of those I have worked or talked with.

There is no obvious type of woman who is more likely to sexually abuse. Survivors have experienced abuse from, amongst others, nuns, mothers, aunts, teachers, residential social workers, babysitters and nursery school teachers. It appears that most abusers tend to be close relatives, a high proportion were mothers, however, this may be due to opportunity and accessibility.

There seems to be an idea that, if women do abuse, they only abuse boys. This is not the case, girls are just as likely to be abused. There appears to be no class distinction, and the age at which the abuse starts can be, and has been with some of the survivors I have known, as young as 6 months or even earlier.

From this information it appears that, as with male sexual abuse, female sexual abuse is totally democratic, taking no account of age, gender or social status. Apart from the fact that females do not have a penis, the type of sexual abuse inflicted upon children appears to be the same as that inflicted by men. Another idea that arises from the image of women as gentle carers is that, if women do sexually abuse, it is gentle, unaggressive cuddling, fondling or kissing. Again this is not always so, many of the survivors I have worked with have been brutally sexually abused by a woman acting alone.

The sorts of abuse include anal and vaginal penetration with

objects causing severe tearing and scarring. Boys have had their
penises roughly and brutally handled whilst their abuser was trying to
get them to erect. A female survivor I worked with was 'gang raped'
many times from the age of 13 years by her mother and her mother's
female friends. The rapes included acts of severe degradation and
humiliation with the use of objects such as bottles and candles. This
happened to this woman nearly 30 years ago yet the memories still
haunt her. She says: 'A day barely passes when I do not feel the pain of
my mother and her friends raping my body and soul. I still cannot
handle objects that remind me of the way they were used when I was
young.'

Sexual abuse perpetrated by women includes oral sex and
masturbation of the child, and the child being forced to reciprocate. It
also includes acts of sado-masochism and bestiality. Not all sexual
abuse is as overt, with children being forced to watch the abuser
having sex with male or female partners; sexual acts with family pets;
pornography and acting out of sexual scenes.

These acts are not necessarily carried out in isolation, and are often
accompanied by physical and emotional abuse of varying severity.
The child may be threatened with severe punishment, including
death threats to them, a loved one or family pet. These threats are
used both during the abuse and to get them to participate.

They are often coerced into these sexual acts under the guise of
protecting their siblings or friends. Sometimes the abuser keeps to the
'bargain' and no other child is involved. Other abusers may retract the
promise of protection with the excuse that the child was 'not good
enough', or naughty, then abuses their siblings or friends. If the
perpetrator is the mother or main caretaker then the threat of loss of
love and abandonment may also be used.

Many of the people I have worked or spoken with were subjected
to systematic long-term sexual abuse by a woman. However, for those
who do not disclose long-term abuse, it is important to be aware of two
factors. Firstly, the survivor may have blocked other memories
(because of the trauma), secondly, if it was just one incident it is vital
not to minimise the magnitude of the abuse. Even one experience of
sexual abuse as a child can be traumatic leaving permanent emotional
scarring for life.

Clients frequently minimise their own experiences:

'Oh I'm sure others have had far worse things happen to them.'
'I can't understand why I still feel so bad. After all it was only once
and it was a long time ago.'

The after-effects that survivors of female sexual abuse experience
seem not to differ greatly from those of survivors of male sexual abuse.
They are just as severe and have long-term consequences for both the

survivor and for those involved with them, either personally or professionally.

The long-term effects include substance abuse, self-mutilation, eating disorders, suicide attempts, debilitating depression, relationship difficulties (abusive, or difficulties with intimacy) and many others. The one difference between survivors of male and female sexual abuse appears to be that the dynamics of how they relate to women may differ. People have asked me whether children abused by a woman are likely to be gay as adults? As far as I'm aware there seems to be, as with survivors of male sexual abuse, little, if any, correlation between homosexuality and sexual abuse.

Another question I am often asked is whether it is worse being sexually abused by a woman than by a man? The answer is I don't know. How can we measure and compare the devastating effects of sexual abuse, whether perpetrated by a man or a woman? All I do know is that, because of the reaction of society and professionals today, it is certainly far worse to disclose having been abused by a woman.

Some of the ways I work with survivors of female sexual abuse, I have found useful in my own healing. I believe there is no one therapeutic approach that will be useful to all survivors. After all, we are all individuals and therefore have our own unique ways of dealing with our experiences. I believe it is important that the person working with the survivor should have acquired several skills and theoretical models.

When working with survivors of female sexual abuse, as with survivors of male sexual abuse, it seems to me that there are some important factors that need to be taken into consideration. They may be broken down very simplistically into Do's and Don'ts.

The Do's include: making the survivor feel safe and in control; encouraging the use of other support and resources; examining the dynamics of the survivor/helper relationship; being sensitive to the use of touch and ensuring that the therapists have adequate support themselves.

In creating an environment in which the survivor can begin to explore and heal from their abuse they need to feel safe and in control of the therapeutic process. In order for this to happen, we must listen and believe, and accept their experiences. I believe we should respect that the survivor often knows what is best for them and that we as 'professionals' may not. As John Bowlby once said 'you know, you tell'. It is therefore important to work at the survivor's own pace, not ours.

The survivor may present with various symptoms which include substance abuse, eating disorders, etc. It is therefore important to make sure that the client is aware of sources of support other than the therapist. Even if they appear to have no other obvious symptoms (substance abuse, etc.) it is important to help the survivor to utilise other resources (friends, etc.). This is to prevent recreating the 'specialness' and 'isolation' experienced in the child–abuser dependency relationship.

Survivors commonly believe that in some way they were to blame for their abuse. We may need to reassure them over and over again that they were not to blame, that what happened to them was not their fault but rather that of the abuser. In the words of a survivor: 'Why, why, did she do it? What was it about me that made her hate me so much that she could hurt me so badly?'

The dynamics of the relationship between survivor and helper needs to be addressed. This is not the forum to go into transference and counter-transference; however, I believe it is important to be aware of, and work with, transference/counter transference issues. If the helper is a woman then the survivor may have great difficulty with trust, but they may also find it a great benefit in terms of the healing process.

Be aware and sensitive to the use of touch. It is enormously powerful and therefore we should only touch survivors with their permission. This may be especially important to remember if you are a female helper, as touching may evoke powerful and painful memories of the survivor's abuse.

Finally, working with survivors of female sexual abuse can be very painful and exhausting for both them and for the therapist. It is therefore essential for the well-being and safety of the therapist, and that of the survivor, to ensure that the therapist has adequate support or supervision.

The Don'ts include: a helper/counsellor having a sexual relationship with a survivor; re-abusing the survivor; denying the survivor the reality of their sexual abuse by a woman; pushing the survivor to disclose 'intimate' details; working at the therapist's pace rather than that of the survivor.

I believe it is unacceptable for the therapist to have a sexual relationship of any sort with a survivor he or she is helping therapeutically. To do so is to recreate the power imbalance that survivors experienced as children and that results in re-abuse. For most survivors starting out on their journey of healing, to be respected, valued and cared for may feel very threatening. They are not used to being treated so and feel far more comfortable being misused or abused. After all this may be all they have ever known. I believe therefore that it is vital that we should be aware of our own potential to re-abuse survivors, however inadvertently.

As mentioned above, it is important that we work at the survivor's own pace. In our eagerness to 'help' we must avoid pushing the survivor to disclose at a pace that is inappropriate or abusive.

We need to be continually aware that survivors of female sexual abuse are faced with mass denial of their experiences. Therefore, it is critical not to deny what has happened to them or imply that they are mistaken and that they must have been abused by a male.

As mentioned earlier it is vitally important to be aware of the possibility of re-abusing or retraumatising survivors. We can do this either with malice or by our 'good intent' to help. If we have no real understanding or insight at all of what is really going on for the survivor we may very easily damage them further. One way this can happen is if we, as professionals, refuse to acknowledge and accept that the survivor has been sexually abused by a woman.

Another is to focus on the intimate details of the actual abuse. It is unnecessary for us to know explicit details, it is sufficient to know that they have been sexually abused. It is only constructive if the client wishes to tell. Otherwise I believe it is very abusive and intrusive. A survivors says: 'When my therapist kept pressing me for more and more details it felt like I was being raped.'

Some may find it difficult to accept that professionals could re-abuse their clients in this way. Unfortunately, I have personally experienced this feeling of being abused, yet again. In this case it was by a male therapist.

To begin with he seemed supportive and understanding of my distress at having been sexually abused by a woman. However, as time went on he pressed me for more and more explicit details which made me feel extremely uncomfortable. He justified this by telling me it was necessary for my healing, to verbalise in detail exactly how I had been sexually abused. I soon began to realise he was getting a vicarious experience.

This intense pressure to 'reveal' all is totally unacceptable. Is it not traumatic enough to have been sexually abused and to live the rest of your life with the devastating after-effects? To then have someone getting some sort of 'kick' or pleasure out of your incredible pain is insulting, offensive, and most of all abusive.

In working with survivors of female sexual abuse, to help them find ways of living with the terrible effects of their abuse, I adopt a holistic approach. It is important to remember both that the consequences of being abused pervade the whole of a survivor's life, and also that being abused may well not be the only trauma the survivor has faced.

As I have already explained I believe that no one therapeutic approach is the 'answer'. There are no miracle cures, recovery is a long slow haul and at times an excruciatingly painful journey for both the survivor and their therapist. In my opinion there is essentially very little difference between working with survivors of female and male sexual abuse.

I found in my own journey to healing that my needs changed, and at different times along the way different approaches were useful. This, in my experience, seems to be true for other survivors as well.

To begin with, it may simply be enough, and sometimes more than enough, for survivors just to talk of what has happened to them, to have their experiences heard and believed. Others may not even be able to verbalise their trauma. I have worked with survivors who were, to begin with, unable to verbalise their terrifying abuse. Each time they attempted to tell of their experiences they became as terrified as they were when they were little. One survivor describes these feelings: 'I felt just as I did as a child when she was abusing me and threatening me with violence and death if I told. Her power was so great that somewhere inside me I still believed this to be true. It was only after spending many hours not talking, just shaking, and eventually being held and rocked, that I was able finally to speak of what had happened. It was only then my past began to lose its power.'

She goes on to say: 'Today I still have some difficulty talking of what happened to me, after all it's not pleasant to say that as a child you were sexually abused and violated by a woman, particularly if that woman was your mother. I still feel the pain of it at times. However, I am glad that I persisted, that my therapist had so much patience and compassion. If I hadn't got help, then God only knows what would have happened to me. I'd probably be dead now.'

The overall aim of the therapeutic process has to be to facilitate the survivor to express the varied emotions that may have been repressed or blocked for many years. They need to go through the mourning process and to grieve for their many losses. The loss of their childhood, the loss of their body, their feelings and much more. They need to feel safe enough to express the emotions of anger, fear, sadness, etc., that they well may have held inside for many years. They need to know that their feelings are valid and real, that they have every right to feel the way they do.

Very often survivors will actually re-experience the physical sensations and pain they had whilst being sexually abused. They need great support whilst going through this sometimes terrifying and confusing ordeal.

I, and some of the survivors I work with, have found that bodywork can be extremely useful. This approach was particularly helpful for me as at times I was unable to express what I was feeling any other way than through my body. Powerful feelings that have been repressed for many years may also be unlocked. However, bodywork should be used cautiously by someone who knows what they are doing and only with the permission and understanding of the survivor. Some clients cannot bear to be touched and this must be respected and honoured.

Other approaches that I have found particularly helpful are

psychodrama, visualisation, letter writing, role-play, chair work. Overall though I feel it is essential to be flexible and to be able to work at the pace of the survivor and with whatever is happening to them at that moment.

Once survivors begin to unleash the pain of their sexual abuse, they may feel overwhelmed by the process. It is vital, I believe, that at these times we encourage them to live one day at a time. What they need is a strategy for living today; they may feel they can barely get through another moment, let alone a lifetime. We need to help them find ways to deal with their pain day by day, sometimes hour by hour, or even minute by minute.

Day to day, moment to moment, our feelings and perception of the world can change. No matter how long you have been 'working' on your abuse, or how you may feel that at last you can live your life rather than just exist, there are times when you can be overwhelmed quite unexpectedly with painful feelings and memories of your abuse. The 'trigger' can be a smell, a sound, a memory apparently from nowhere. Of this, one survivor says: 'One day, one moment, you can believe that you are all right, that the world and the people in it are all right, and the next be right back down there in the pit of despair.'

I work with survivors of female sexual abuse individually and in groups. Both ways have benefits and disadvantages for both the survivors and the therapist. Survivors who have kept their experiences to themselves for many years may find the idea of joining a group too threatening, and need a period of individual therapy first.

Being in a group of other survivors can help reduce the feelings of isolation experienced by many survivors. Unfortunately, some women, if faced with an all-female group, find such proximity to other women, understandably, incredibly threatening. This is true, as well, for men who may find themselves in a predominantly female group. In view of this I always see someone who wants to join a group before they first go, to explore the benefits and disadvantages with them.

In my experience, the dynamics of a group of survivors of female sexual abuse is not that different than from that in a group of survivors of male sexual abuse. Facilitators used to working with groups of survivors of male sexual abuse however, should be aware that there are some differences, and therefore not make assumptions based on their previous experience.

I believe that in order to positively help survivors of female sexual abuse we need to facilitate their taking charge of their own lives. We need to help them empower themselves so they may step out of the victim role to which they were subjected as a child. My role, as I see it, is to guide and support using the knowledge I have gained from my own experiences and those of other survivors of female sexual abuse. No matter how hurt we have been as children we have to take responsibility for our own recovery and healing process. If we defer responsibility for this to someone else then we are reliving the power imbalance of our childhood. It is important not to hand over our power to others and in the process depower ourselves.

In conclusion, I would like to reiterate some of the most important points to remember when considering the issue of female sexual abuse. Above all else, women do sexually abuse children on their own. Attempts always to implicate men, are misguided and potentially very dangerous. At best, they divert attention away from women abusers, at worst they deny survivors the reality of their abuse.

Once we have accepted that women can, and do, sexually abuse, we have to consider how best to protect children from abuse and how to help the survivors. As someone who works primarily with adult survivors, I have talked almost exclusively about helping survivors. This is not because I attach secondary importance to protection, but simply because I do not feel qualified to discuss how best to do this.

I am so glad that the KIDSCAPE conference has happened and I shall continue to fight to get society and professionals to acknowledge and accept that female sexual abuse does occur. That is why I will stand up against all who presumably have not suffered being sexually abused by a woman yet continue to say that it does not exist. I have said many times that it is not my intention to detract from the fact that men sexually abuse. Of course they do (I work with these survivors too) but so do women. I know because it happened to me and to the many survivors that I have worked with.

Finally, I would like to say something about survivors as people. Most of us have an incredible inner strength which despite sometimes overwhelming odds helps us to go on living when many would have gone under. That is why we are called survivors and not victims.

All quotes from survivors have been given with their express permission.

5 Working with female sexual abusers

Jane Kinder Matthews

I would like to share with you information about 36 women who have been in therapy with me over the past 6 years. I plan to give you information about the backgrounds of these women and help you understand the subtle and not so subtle dynamics that led to their abusive behaviour. I wish to convince you in some cases that what they did was, indeed, abusive, and I want to suggest ways that the criminal justice system and the child protection system can be utilised in order to ensure the most effective outcomes for these women and their victims.

My primary goal, however, is to convince you that they are human; they are not monsters; they can change; they can develop empathy for their victims; they can lead positive lives; they are salvageable and they are worth salvaging. I need to say that I care deeply about these women, and I am very protective of them. I do not minimise what they have done, but I have always been impressed with their strength, their courage, and, in spite of what they have done, their humanity.

I also want to say before I go any further that, if you are a survivor of female sexual abuse, it is completely up to you whether you want to understand abusers. If you are at a place in your healing process that requires you to be angry with every female sex abuser in the world, then be angry. Be livid or hurt or confused. Express the pain that you need to express in regard to being abused. Your job is to take care of yourself and allow others to respond to the needs of the abusers.

I never planned to work with female sexual abusers just the same as I never planned to work with male sexual abusers. I became intrigued with the whole subject when I was going through an employment interview. I believed what I had been taught by the latest psychology textbook that people with anti-social behaviour had no interest in changing and therefore could not be helped. Towards the end of the interview I asked the director of the programme what sort of success rate they had and was told that they had graduated almost five hundred people over a 10 year period and had never had one of their clients re-offend. At that point I decided that I really wanted that job, because they seemed to be doing at that agency what was supposed to be impossible. I was lucky enough to get the job. I have been working with adult male sex offenders ever since.

In 1985 Ruth Matthews and I were asked to develop a programme for female sexual offenders. Genesis II, a day treatment agency for women in Minneapolis, Minnesota had received requests from probation officers who had female offenders on their caseloads and had no resources for them. We were asked to perform this task based on my work with adult male offenders and Ruth's work with adolescent male offenders.

We found some similarities and differences immediately. The following may be an unfair comparison since I've worked with about 800 male offenders over the past 11 years and with 36 women over the past 6 years. In all cases I'll tell you what we know, with the understanding that this may change as we gather more information and gain more experience.

There are general similarities. Both male and female offenders come from chaotic, abusive backgrounds. Non-nurturing homes are the norm, and verbal, emotional, physical or sexual abuse is a part of their experiences. They tend to be low status members of their peer groups and feel that they do not belong anywhere. They are often friendless and willing to do almost anything for acceptance. Some of the abusive acts that they commit are similar, and they often use some of the same arguments or tricks to gain the co-operation of the victims.

There are, however, differences in the abuse they commit and their response to therapy. Before setting out these differences, I need to give you a very arbitrary definition of shame and guilt:

Guilt is an honest acknowledgement of what has taken place. It makes no moral judgement about the person who committed the act. Shame is a negative judgement of the person and assigns a label of evil or worthless to the person who has committed the act.

Differences in Abuse Patterns

1 None of the women we have worked with has coerced others into being their accomplices.

2 Women use force or violence in the committing of their crimes far less often than men. When they do use physical force it is of a lesser degree than males.
3 Fewer women initially deny the abuse and they are more willing to take responsibility for their behaviour.
4 Men tend to start sexually abusing at an earlier age, i.e. in adolescence. Only 2 of the 36 of our women acted out as teenagers.
5 Women tend to use fewer threats in an attempt to keep their victims silent.
6 Women tend to act out on themselves via self-punishment and self-destructive behaviour, such as: starving and cutting themselves, prostitution and placing themselves in very dangerous situations before they act out on others.

In responding to therapy

1 Men tend to forgive themselves more quickly than the women.
2 Men tend to get out of shame and into guilt faster, therefore they give themselves permission to heal sooner.
3 Women's anger toward themselves tends to be more deeply entrenched.
4 Men tend to develop empathy for the victim later in the course of their therapy, but even after women have developed empathy they tend to shame themselves for their abusive behaviour.
5 The sexual abuse dynamic that is most similar between the two genders is the adult sexual contact with an adolescent. In the case of the female, this indicates the abuser with the least pathology. In the case of the male, it indicates a great deal of pathology. The women in this category take the least time in therapy but the men take as long as their counterparts who have committed different types of crimes.

Typologies

We set up 3 typologies based on our assessment of the women's level of responsibility for the abuse. We assigned 100 per cent of the responsibility for the abuse to the teacher/lover category. They initiated and carried out the abuse. They were the adults and took advantage of their position of power. The pre-disposed category of offenders initiated and carried out the abuse, but the abuse in their own background certainly had a mitigating effect. The last category and least responsible is the male-coerced offender. The male-coerced offender was under the influence of, or forced by, a male to abuse to a child.

We then looked at the negative childhood, adolescent and adult experiences of the different typologies. Tables 5.1, 5.2 and 5.3 indicate some of the common experiences of these women and help us to better understand their behaviours.

Table 5.1   Childhood experiences

	Teacher/ lover %	Predisposed %	Male coerced %
Victim of sex abuse within family	9	100	58
Victim of sex abuse outside family	0	23	50
Victim of physical abuse	42	47	50
Victim of verbal/emotional abuse	71	76	91
Low status in peer group	14	41	83
Low status in the family	71	58	83
Poor school performance	57	35	66

Table 5.2   Adolescent experiences

	Teacher/ lover %	Predisposed %	Male coerced %
Victim of sexual abuse within family	0	64	41
Victim of sexual abuse outside family	85	47	58
Victim of physical abuse	57	85	16
Promiscuity	57	85	75
Onset of drug and alcohol abuse	71	41	58
Feelings of inferiority	100	100	100

Table 5.3   Adult experiences

	Teacher/ lover %	Predisposed %	Male coerced %
Victim of sexual abuse	28	18	66
Victim of rape	55	23	75
Mental health problems	28	29	8
Drug/alcohol addiction	55	29	33
Compulsive over/undereating	71	64	66
Positive work history	55	23	41
Non-assertive with men	85	100	100
Coerced into sexual abuse of others	0	0	100
Initiated sexual abuse of others	100	100	41

Therapy

Before setting out the therapeutic goals of our programme, it might be useful to give a brief summary of the traits or behaviours that we have found in adults who sexually abuse children:

- shame;
- anger — and the two underlying components of anger, pain and fear;
- low self-esteem;
- impaired empathy;
- misinterpretation of the victim's needs;
- misinterpretation of what the victim is communicating.

When you fuse shame and anger with sexuality and add in the other ingredients, you have abuse waiting to happen. Thus, the expression of anger, disappointment, sadness, low self-esteem or just about any other emotion becomes a sexual expression. If the person is hurt and wants to lash out, she is likely to act out sexually, because that is the way she knows how to hurt. Therapeutically our goal is to intervene in this acting-out process.

Each typology presents a different set of challenges to the therapist, but there are basic therapeutic standards which all the women must meet.

1   They must acknowledge the above traits or behaviours in themselves.
2   They must take responsibility for the abuse.
3   They must each do a written life story and present it to the group.
4   They must present their crime story or abuse story to the group.
5   They must prepare and present to the group a collage of themselves.
6   From life story, crime story and collage, their own therapeutic issues will be identified with the therapist.
7   Resolution of these issues, such as dependency, abuse, shame, difficulties with intimacy, parenting problems, communication problems, etc. then becomes a part of each womans' programme.
8   Resolution of abuse through family therapy or couples' therapy will be required.
9   Each woman is also expected to make amends, whether she makes them directly to the victim or not.
10 Each woman must meet the individual exit criteria devised by the therapists for her.

In addition to the above therapeutic intervention we also provide educational components on shame and guilt, sex education, birth control, healthy sexuality, the impact of abuse on victims, and effective processing of deviant sexual fantasies.

We'll start with the treatment of teacher/lover offenders. The case study that illustrates this typology is Judy. Of course, all names have been changed.

Typology of a teacher/lover offender

Judy is one of four children born to a drug addicted mother in Chicago. She spent the first six months of her life in the hospital. This was only partially because of the physical problems associated with her mother's addiction. Her mother was sent to a drug treatment programme almost as soon as Judy was born, with the understanding that she would be reunited with Judy and her three other children when she completed treatment. Unfortunately her mother failed drug treatment and Judy was placed in foster care. Her foster mother was an older woman who had cared for many children in her career. She was about to retire as a foster parent but was convinced to re-open her home just for Judy. Knowing this was to be the last foster child and that it would be a long-term placement, she lavished love and · attention on Judy. Judy responded positively, and grew to love her · foster parents. She describes her time with them as, 'Just like living a · fairy tale. I was treated like a princess.' She interacted mostly with · adults and did not have to develop the necessary negotiating skills.

When she was 13 her mother contacted the State of Illinois requesting that she be allowed to see her daughter. In her petition she stated that she was drug free and was responsibly running a small farmstead in her native Haiti. She had already been reunified with Judy's other sisters and expected her son to join the family soon. She stated that she only wanted the girl to visit and knew that she had no rights to custody based on her abandonment of her daughter. The welfare department consented to the visit, and at age 14, Judy was flown to Haiti for the visit. Once there, her mother refused to return her.

Not only was it emotionally wrenching to Judy to be ripped away from the family she loved, but she was forced to work long hours on the farm. She and her sisters were practically slaves, working in the fields by day and working as cooks and waitresses in their mother's cantina at night.

She met her older brother for the first time when he was released from prison and joined the family. As the oldest child and as the only male, he had more status in his mother's eyes. He soon became his mother's lieutenant and the girls were expected to follow his orders.

He took advantage of Judy's naïveté and manipulated her into being sexual with him. Later, when she resisted his advances, he raped her. At age 15 she became pregnant with his child. When she told him she was pregnant he used his influence to convince their mother that Judy needed a break. She allowed them to fly to Chicago where Judy had an abortion. Her brother returned to Haiti but Judy took the opportunity to escape and return to her foster home.

At 17 Judy met a man who was much older than she was. He asked her to marry him and she consented, believing that it would be the only offer of marriage she would ever receive.

Her husband had seven children by three previous wives, and, at 18, Judy was stepmother to children who were almost as old as she was. Judy had three children of her own within five years, but was constantly required to respond to the needs of her stepchildren. Their lives were in constant turmoil. Her husband had various jobs and various shady money-making schemes but still managed to have his wife and children receive aid for dependent children. After a fire destroyed their apartment, Judy and the children were moved into a 'welfare hotel' as temporary housing. Conditions were intolerable. There was overcrowding and violence — 'temporary' stretched on and on. Judy had a friend in Minnesota who told her that there was better housing available and more employment opportunities in Minnesota. Judy gave her husband an ultimatum and they packed up and moved to Minneapolis.

Her husband hated trying to adjust to a new city and went back to Chicago within a month, leaving Judy and the three children there. Judy applied for assistance and housing and started trying to make a new life for herself and her children.

As word spread among her stepchildren of Judy's stable home more and more of them decided to join her in Minneapolis. As she said, 'The problems arrived one by one.' She was expected to welcome them, share her home with them and stretch her meagre dependent children's grant to cover expenses and provide food. It never occurred to her that she had the right to negotiate with her husband or step-children.

He dictated from afar and set up tremendous double standards. He fathered another child with another woman but expected Judy to ask nothing more in life than to feed, clothe and support his children. Whenever he was upset with her he threatened to inform the authorities that she was receiving supplemental financial support from him, thus making her liable for charges of welfare fraud.

Chaos and stress were the hallmarks of her life as more and more stepchildren arrived demanding more and more of her financial and emotional resources. Two of his children were using drugs, two had fathered children and expected Judy to provide temporary financial aid for them from time to time, and there was interpersonal violence that she was expected to handle. She believed she 'had to' do everything. She tried to hold everything together, denying most of her needs in the process — constantly feeling more and more stress and more and more anger.

One night her husband was particularly brutal in his telephone conversation with her. He refused to listen to anything that she had to say and was giving her impossible orders about what needed to be done. She was furious and in tears when she hung up. Her 16 year old stepson was there and sought to comfort her. Their interaction led to sexual intercourse, and she apologised immediately, stating that the behaviour was 'sick'. Both tried to forget the contact and pretend that everything was all right. Later, her stepson threatened suicide and she decided that she needed to get help for herself and him. She contacted child protection authorities and turned herself in. Police decided not to file criminal charges mainly because her stepson stated that he would not provide testimony at a trial.

Judy appeared at therapy stating that she did not believe she needed professional help. 'I know what I did was wrong, and I'll never do it again.' Later on she was also angry that her stepson was 'getting off scot-free,' referring to the fact that he refused to be actively involved in a therapy group. He was eventually convinced to get the help he needed and deserved.

After her initial resistance Judy blossomed in therapy. She developed social skills, increased her self-confidence and self-esteem, learned to be assertive and think for herself, and most importantly, learned to identify and express her anger.

She completed treatment in about 10 months and made many positive life changes. She is now involved in a 'jobs training programme' and has strictly limited the kinds of things that she is willing to do for her children and stepchildren.

Therapeutically the teacher/lover is very easy to deal with. The main goal in therapy is to convince her that her behaviour is abusive. She needs to understand that someone got hurt because of her sexuality. When she understands that the adolescent was harmed emotionally by her behaviour, her work is basically done.

The anger in her acting-out is not aimed at her victim. It is usually an expression of her anger towards a specific adult or adult sexual partners in general. She may see the sexual contact with an adolescent as an 'affair', and to her that is a viable way of expressing her sexuality. She may initially hold the adolescent as responsible as her for the sexual contact, especially if the adolescent seemed to enjoy the act or if he/she approached the adult for sex. It is very important to emphasise to these women that the adolescent is still a child and that often they are vulnerable because they may desperately want human contact, not necessarily sexual contact. They may be too embarrassed to admit that they are sexually naïve and the abuse consists of pushing them into adult sexual practice before they are ready. Because the women often feel psychologically vulnerable themselves, they may tend to see in their victims stability and sophistication that is not there. These women tend to have the most positive backgrounds and the most skills at their disposal, so they can dash through therapy at a very fast pace. It is not unusual for them to come to their first group with written life stories completed and eager for more assignments.

Typology of a predisposed offender

Helen is a 31 year old mother of one, who acknowledged to her therapist that she had sexually abused seven children.

Helen's life has been one of abuse, panic, shame and desperation. She is the fourth of five children who was sexually abused by her stepfather, mother and others from a very early age.

Initially there were 'cult parties' hosted by her mother and stepfather. Capitalising on her innocence and childish desire to please, they manipulated her by urging her to interact in a seductive manner with their guests, using her as entertainment and rewarding her for her responses. The abuse started with subtle sexual overtones and, step by step, progressed to profound and devastating abuse.

At first they taught her to parrot sexual comments with instructions such as, 'Go ask Fred about that bulge in his pants,' 'Tell Estelle that she would not be such a bitch if she spent more time in bed,' or 'Ask Joe if he would like to have sex with a movie star.' When she did as she was told people laughed, and she liked the laughter even though she had no idea what she was saying. At subsequent parties, remembering the attention she had received, she initiated the sex talk herself. Some of the adults assumed that, because she was saying the words, she was expressing her own interests. They responded with more sex talk, which she parroted to other people. At first Helen was eager for the parties and looked forward to the attention and interaction. Eventually she was asked to do more than just make outrageous sexual statements. She was coaxed into touching and being touched. When she said that she didn't like it she was told, 'Of course you do, we're having fun'. She then, of course, stated that it was fun.

It was an easy step for the adults to start dressing her in a seductive manner and teaching her to flirt with the guests. She did what she thought the adults wanted her to do and they interpreted her 'promiscuous' behaviour as totally her own, generated by her own sexual desires. She was rewarded for acting sexually and being sexual. When she rebelled or resisted, she was punished harshly and severely. One of the more dreaded punishments was the ant hill. After she was thrown on the ant hill once and bitten and scared by the insects, just the mention of 'ant pile' ensured her obedience.

By the time she was 7 some of the people had widened the circle of abuse to include other children. At age 9 she was no longer the object of abuse but had a more insidious task to perform. It was her job to get the victims quieted down by persuading them to drink Kool-Aid laced with tranquillisers. She suffered tremendous guilt and panic because she knew what was going to happen to them. She wanted desperately to save them or warn them, and thought that she should be able to figure out a way to do it, but she dared not for fear of punishment. One of her fantasies was to gather all the children and lead them to safety and take care of them.

Helen was sometimes so frightened that the sexual abuse would begin again that she left her home as soon as the Kool-Aid had been administered and ran headlong into the woods, sleeping all night on the dirt floor of a hunter's shelter. She had no light and was terrified of running on the rough path, through the cobwebs and branches, but being at home was more terrifying.

School was a nightmare for Helen. It was very difficult for her to concentrate on academic subjects, and her outrageous behaviour alienated her from her peers. She often dressed in the same provocative manner that gained approval from the abusive adults, but teachers and students reacted quite differently, labelling her stupid and strange. Here, her explicit sexual comments won her reprimands and punishment. In the mid- to late 1960s no one seemed to understand that this child, who dressed and talked like a prostitute was giving off numerous signals of sexual abuse.

As a teenager Helen acted out in several ways. She was involved in truancy, theft, vandalism and self-destructive behaviour. Drugs, alcohol, suicide attempts and sexual promiscuity were a part of her life. She was defiant, verbally abusive and headstrong. She was adjudicated delinquent and became a part of the juvenile justice system. She refused to comply with their requirements, lashing out at even those who tried to help her. Her involvement with juvenile justice ended when she turned 18.

She married young and was physically and sexually abused by her husband. She conceived a son who lived only a few hours. Helen was devastated, because she believed that a baby would give her the love that she had never had. The death of her son proved to be a pivotal point in Helen's life. All the anger and anguish of her past life came to the surface and was magnified in the process. She wanted to lash out and punish others for all her suffering. She knew, from her own experience, how to inflict pain. She also knew, from her own experience, how awful it was to be hurt. This was the beginning of the conflict of fantasy and shame which plagues Helen to this day. The pairing of sex with anger had been a life-long experience for her, and when she became angry, fantasies of sexually abusing children cropped up. She fought the impulses, shamed and hated herself for having the thoughts, felt the fantasies come back, heaped more hatred and shame on herself and finally acted on the impulses. She repeated this cycle six times over the next five years. One child revealed the abuse and an investigation was conducted. Helen steadfastly denied the abuse and no charges were brought.

The last victim was her own daughter, and, at that point, Helen confessed everything to her husband, from whom she was separated, and gave him custody of the child so she would not hurt her again. She volunteered for treatment and has been involved in the female sex offender programme for almost three years. She has made very good progress, but, because of the massive emotional damage that she suffered, there have been many hurdles to overcome. Her trust level was very low, and both group and therapists have been tested by her. She pushes the limits with passive–aggressive behaviour in order to have us prove that we care about her. She expects to be rejected and interprets the most innocuous statements as criticism. Criticism equals attack in her mind, so she is easily devastated. She hates herself and finds it difficult to understand why we 'put up with her'. Doing therapeutic work often brings up a flood of emotions and she immediately thinks about killing herself because she is so bad.

Sexual abuse fantasies still come when she feels angry, but she has managed to devise a method for processing them, diminishing their power. She is also working on more effective ways of expressing her anger in a more direct and honest manner.

The most important therapeutic goal for the predisposed offender is to voice her own childhood pain. Remember, she has the most devastating background of any of the women, so it is absolutely essential that the wounded child within her is allowed to express what she never got to express. She must voice the sadness, pain, abandonment, rejection that she endured, and she must do more than just relate the narrative story. Feelings and emotions are absolutely necessary. Some of the methods that have been helpful in this endeavour are journaling, writing unsent letters to the people who abused her and writing stories or poems about her pain. Again, the emphasis is on feelings. It's not enough for her to say, 'when my mother slapped me'. She needs to express how it affected her. For example, 'When my mother slapped me and ridiculed me in front of my friends I felt horrible. It was supposed to be a wonderful time. It was my birthday party, and she embarrassed me to the point that I did not want to face those kids. I pretended to be sick so I didn't have to go to school. After that I was always afraid everybody hated me.'

The women in this category need to develop a social network. They have never felt as though they belonged to any group, and, unless they can feel connected to others, they will slip back into isolation, which is a dangerous place for them to be.

As with all our clients, it is also important for the pre-disposed offender to move from shame to guilt. This is a very tall order for these women, since most of their lives have been spent in shame. The more they can be objective about what they've done without judging themselves as horrible or evil, the more likely they will be able to reduce the amount of shame they put on themselves.

Self-abusive and suicidal behaviour are strong elements in these women's make-up, and they are always issues to contend with. Whenever anything, however slight, goes wrong, they are likely to see suicide as the only way out. They also tend to want to punish themselves, and quite often they don't know why. They experience urges to cut themself or to engage in other self-mutilating behaviour even when things are going relatively well in their life.

The women in this category have more deviant sexual fantasies, and developing a way to deal with them is a very important therapeutic issue. The deviant fantasies cause them a great deal of shame and chagrin. They believe that the sexual thoughts automatically make them evil people and quite often they do not wish to acknowledge them, even to themselves. They want to run away from the fantasies as a way of protecting themselves from anguish. One of the ways that we teach them to deal with the fantasies is to honestly acknowledge that acting out sexually would, indeed, give them some good feelings. However, we do not want them to stop the fantasies at this high point of power and importance, because that's what got them into difficulty in the first place. We want them to go on and honestly face the aftermath of their actions. We want them to experience in their mind the fear and apprehension that they might feel; the fear of being caught questioned and/or convicted, and the embarrassment that they might feel at the public disclosure of their actions. We are actively involved in helping the women develop a fantasy process because, left on their own, they are likely to devise a process that would involve them being hacked apart or burned alive. That is what they think they deserve, but it is basically unrealistic and ineffective in controlling the fantasies.

For some women, fantasy alteration or interruption is effective and we do not set up one single approved way of dealing with the fantasies, but the most important goal is to help them to lessen the fear they have of the fantasies and increase their confidence in dealing with them.

To say that these women have low self-esteem is a gross understatement. They hate themselves and believe that they were born evil. It is very difficult to convince them that they have value, but it is absolutely vital that we do. They will never give up their destructive behaviour until they can believe that they are not evil. You can bet that progress in this area will be spotty. They will gain confidence and self-esteem only to have it dashed by some setback which may seem slight to you and me but seems insurmountable to them.

Trust or the lack of trust is an important issue for these women during the entire course of their therapy.

They want to trust, but, because betrayal has been such a big part of their lives, they find it next to impossible. They constantly test in order that we prove that we care for them, but, I'm glad to report that in most instances, they do come to trust us, and we work hard to help them generalise that trust.

Typology of a male coerced offender

Gwen is a 34 year old mother of five who was convicted of aiding and abetting sexual abuse.

Her oldest child, a daughter, was born when Gwen was 16. The father of the child deserted her and she lived with her family part of the time and sometimes on public assistance. When Gwen was 17 she met and married a man with whom she later had four more children.

Gwen's background is one of abject chaos and deprivation. She was the fifth of seven children born to a working class Minneapolis family. Her biological father left the family when she was quite young, and her mother established a long-term relationship with another man.

One consistent rule in the family was that the children's needs were always secondary to the adults'. Her mother always bought clothes for herself but the children often wore tatters. Money went for alcohol, even if there was little or no money for food, and even when food was available there was no guarantee that the children would get their share.

The adults drank heavily and there were many fights. The children were expected to have competence and judgement well beyond their years. They were often blamed for things they did not do and were expected to know things they had no way of knowing. It was a grim atmosphere, with very little warmth and minimal positive human interaction.

The day-to-day care of the younger children was the responsibility of one of the older children, a sister named Janet. Janet assumed the role of mother, preparing the meals, cleaning the house, protecting the younger children from neighbourhood bullies and attempting to shield them from verbal and physical abuse at the hands of their mother and her boyfriend.

When Gwen was seven years old Janet died in a house fire. Gwen was in school and heard the firetrucks go by. She knew instinctively that the fire was at her house and that something horrible had happened to Janet. She describes this as the time when her life fell apart. With her older sister gone there was no one in Gwen's life to encourage, sustain or nurture her. Family members grieved Janet's death, each in his or her own way, but usually silently and alone. Gwen was merely told that she would have to go on in life without Janet and she was never given the opportunity to voice the pain and desolation that she felt as the result of her sister's death. She thought that she was weak and stupid because she felt the pain so acutely.

The family situation did not improve. No one felt obliged to step in and take Janet's place. The barren family atmosphere grew even more bleak. Gwen was desperately alone and yearned for a place to belong. She was also desperate for respite from the constant fighting at home. She escaped whenever she could by leaving the house and roaming the streets with her older siblings. Her mother and stepfather never seemed to notice the absence of the children.

At 14 Gwen was raped by an acquaintance of her brother. She told no one and blamed herself, since she had willingly gone to the party with her brother.

She did fairly well academically but, in adolescence, she felt more and more like an outsider at school. She was alone most of the time, had no money for extracurricular activities, was not encouraged to develop interests of any kind and trusted very few people. She had no one to confide in and felt as though no one cared.

At 16 she met a boy she liked and they started dating. It felt very good to her to have someone in her life, and she wanted to make sure that he stayed around. She looked to him for her sense of value and, as long as he was in her life, felt validated as a human being. She was not particularly interested in sex but feared she would lose him if she did not give in. She also had a very hard time believing that she had a right to set boundaries. She became sexually involved with the boy, became pregnant and was devastated when he deserted her.

Shortly after her first child was born she met Roger. They were married a year later in spite of Gwen's reluctance. She knew it was a mistake and did not want to get married, but she did not have the skills nor the strength to get out of it. Roger was jealous, arbitrary and domineering. He also had a large extended family and these relatives made keeping Gwen in line their own personal concern. Her own family became more and more fragmented and distant and her social support network, which was meagre at best, shrank even more. When

Roger was angry or drinking he beat her, always blaming her for the beatings. She believed that she was responsible for provoking him and tried very hard to anticipate his moods, mostly unsuccessfully. The beatings went on for years, and eventually Roger started blaming her because he was sexually dissatisfied. He raped her on several occasions, and the violence that permeated other aspects of their relationship now became a part of their sexual life as well. She tried to leave the relationship several times, but never quite managed it. She always returned to their home, partly because Roger constantly promised to alter his behaviour and also because he and his family threatened to harm her and the children if she left.

When Gwen's oldest daughter was 13, Roger began sexually abusing her. His stated goal to Gwen was that he wanted to teach the child how to enjoy herself sexually and not be the 'frigid bitch' her mother was. When Gwen resisted she was beaten, and eventually she complied with her husband's demands. Her part in the sexual abuse consisted of bringing the child to her husband when ordered to do so. As the abuse continued, Gwen's empathy for the girl diminished. In her words, 'If he was being sexual with her, he was leaving me alone. At least he was kind and gentle with her.'

Gwen knew that something had to be done about the situation. After a particularly brutal beating she contacted the authorities and confessed to her part in the sexual abuse of her daughter. Her husband denied all the charges and eventually spent four years in prison. Her children were placed with her husband's relatives, she entered a plea of guilty and served a brief sentence in country jail. The court ordered her to enter the day treatment programme at Genesis II for women, which was designed to address her personal problems as well as the sexual abuse issues.

She initially did well at the treatment programme. Her daughter was also in therapy, and the four younger children were seen in family therapy. Gwen decided to divorce her husband in spite of threats by his family. She had made enough progress at Genesis II to be allowed to work. Her children were still in foster care, but a plan was in place to reunite the family. She had moved from a supervised living situation and was in her own apartment. All factors indicated a positive outcome to her case. When she was just on the verge of success Gwen failed. She decided to have a party at her apartment, inviting several male friends. This was in violation of her therapeutic case plan, as she had a long history of non-assertive behaviour with men. During the course of the evening she gave one of the men present permission to have sex with her daughter, who was now 15. Another Genesis II client was at the party and reported the activity to the therapists. The abuse was reported, Gwen's probation was revoked, and she was sent to prison, where she served a term of 11 months.

After serving her sentence Gwen was placed on parole, and her parole officer requested that she re-enter the sexual offenders' programme. She was accepted into the programme and has been participating for about six months. She is doing well. She has been reunited with her oldest daughter and family therapy is under way with the four younger children. She is working again and has her own apartment. She is just at the point in her progress where she had difficulties before, so the therapist, probation officer and social worker are very much alert for warning signs. We are going more slowly in the reunification process in order not to have Gwen overwhelmed by changes in her life. She seems to be doing much better with her major issue of male-dependency and demonstrates a lot of empathy for her children. She understands that all of her children were traumatised by the family violence and the sexual abuse. The children unanimously express a desire to be reunited with their mother and work very hard in family therapy with that goal in mind.

These women tend to have the following psychological profile:

- a very dependent person;
- male dependent;
- non-assertive;
- low self-esteem;
- does not feel loved or loveable;
- expects to be rejected but desperately needs to be accepted;
- desperately alone – yearns to be taken care of by a male;
- feels powerless and ineffective in relationships;
- stays in abusive relationships because she doesn't believe anyone else will have her;
- when sexual abuse is introduced by her partner she goes along even though she knows it's wrong;
- in order to go on she initiates sexual abuse herself.

The primary therapeutic goal is to help decrease their male dependency. We cannot control the kind of men they get involved with, but, if we know they are strong and more assertive, we can have more confidence that they will not be re-involved in sexual abuse.

We try to teach these women to voice their own opinion, even if they fear that people will disagree with them. We try to help them understand that they cannot please everybody and that it is OK if people get mad at them. Because domestic violence has been such a part of their lives they get panicky when they feel someone getting angry with them. They generally try to avoid trouble at all costs and this tends to lead to very non-assertive behaviour. It is a revelation to these women when we insist that they have rights.

It is also important that these women redevelop a sense of empathy, for they have so often had to deaden their own feelings as a way of witnessing and participating in the abuse.

We feel that we've been quite successful in working with these women. So far none of the women has re-offended or re-abused after completing treatment. However, I do want to include what I consider to be our failures.

We have had two women who have not completed the programme and I have some profound fears that they will eventually re-abuse. We expelled one of the women and the other drifted away from the programme after the court mandates for her attendance were removed.

These women had a lot in common and I'll tell you some of the warning signals to watch for. I would classify them as super-narcissistic personalities. They were extremely self-centred and constantly wanted to have their therapeutic issues addressed by the group. Both of them disclosed the abuse themselves in a very dramatic manner and, because they seemed so sincere in their confessions, they were not prosecuted. They both vounteered for treatment and initially seemed to do well.

The first warning signal came in the intake interview. They both spoke of former therapists who were not very understanding and certainly not as understanding as we were. They spoke of feeling judged and rejected by other therapists when they shared information about their abuse perpetration. Their words were seductive and disarming. On the one hand, they were saying that they really trusted us, but, at the same time, they were taking away from us our ability to confront them later on for their manipulative behaviour.

They were more than willing to give us numerous details about their lives, especially their own history as victims. In group therapy they often expected the therapists and the other women to read their minds and respond accordingly. They expected tremendous amounts of empathy from others, but they very seldom responded to anyone else's needs.

They always asked for the most time in group and always wanted to go first so that they wouldn't get cut short if time ran out.

They also agreed outside of group to support each other against other group members. One of the women persuaded another group member to get involved in some behaviour that was a blatant violation of programme rules. She then confessed the discretions, and, because she came forward first, the other woman was reprimanded.

Overall, I would have to say that these women showed very little interest in really altering their destructive behaviour. They were more interested in going through the motions but really holding on to their pathology. I'm not willing to say that they are untreatable, but they certainly demanded more attention than we could give them.

I want to end with a few suggestions about how the criminal justice and child protection systems can work together for the most effective outcomes for these women and their victims.

We believe that flexibility within the criminal justice system is very helpful and that criminal charges should be filed if there is a viable case. However, these abusers typically do not need long jail sentences. A jail sentence of between 45 days to 6 months usually has a positive effect on these women. The sentence is a tangible statement that their behaviour will not be tolerated and is a crime. The sentence also seems to give the women permission to get on with their lives. They can say that they have paid and now, therefore, have a right to pay attention to themselves and alter their behaviour.

If there is not a viable criminal case, or, if the victim is the perpetrator's child, Child Protective Services should act to remove the child.

If the woman is involved with a coercive male, it is essential to separate them.

We have found that best results occur when treatment is paired with incarceration or interventions, with incarceration being short and treatment being long term.

We also believe it is vital to try to reunify when possible, and the most important factor in that process is the victim. Listen to the victim when allegations of sexual abuse are made and listen to the victims when they say they want to go home. Not all cases are alike, and we must be careful not to interpret the needs of the victim through our own anger or the anger of the foster parents. In spite of all they have suffered, many victims do desire reunification and do love the person who abused them.

6 Barbara's story — a mother who sexually abused

Hilary Eldridge

This is the story of Barbara's journey through therapy: her name and those of her family members have been changed to protect their identities. Barbara is 45 years old. She comes from a middle class background. She and her brother and two sisters were brought up by their parents in the family home. She had few men friends until she met Hugh, whom she married when she was 20. At 28, she had Angie, her only child. When she was 35, she and Hugh separated, and she has lived alone since. Prior to her marriage and after her divorce, she worked as a secretary for a number of different companies. During her 15 year marriage she remained at home, taking in contract typing work.

Barbara sexually abused her daughter Angie. After years of denial she finally admitted the truth of her daughter's allegations, and began to engage in therapy with the aim of learning to accept responsibility, live with herself, and repair her devastated relationship with her daughter.

Barbara has written the story of her own progress through therapy, and I have written a commentary from my point of view as her therapist. Both Angie and Barbara were also abused by Barbara's husband, Hugh, and they have been through trauma and pain. Barbara felt it important to share her story in the hope that it might enable other mothers who have similar experiences to her own, to confide in someone for the sake of both themselves and their children.

Barbara and Angie are still in therapy and it would not be helpful for either to be identified. Hence, we have omitted a lot of the detail, choosing to talk about the process rather than the content of Barbara's therapy. Also, we have taken care to say very little about Angie and her experiences. This is something personal to her, and her story is her own to write at some future stage, should she want to do so.

Angie's social worker, who remains anonymous to protect Angie's identity, and Jenny Still, consultant to myself throughout Barbara's therapy, have given their help and support in the preparation of this chapter.

Barbara's story

I have been having therapy at Gracewell Clinic for just over eighteen months. There have been forty-two sessions with Hilary — some were spent with my daughter Angie and sometimes with her social workers. The period of therapy has been very long and hard and at times very traumatic.

My first encounter at Gracewell was when social services arranged for me to have an assessment done there. I was introduced to Jenny and Hilary and we talked for approximately two hours. Jenny and Hilary took it in turns to ask questions — it was a bit like the Spanish Inquisition but slightly friendlier! I suppose it was the first time that I began to speak about real personal issues. After a while Jenny asked if I believed in rape within marriage. My answer was that I believed it happened within some marriages. I can remember stating emphatically that that was not the case with my marriage, only to be told that I should consider myself a prime case.

Approximately two weeks later I returned to Gracewell with my social worker to listen to the report that Jenny and Hilary had prepared. It was quite a lengthy report and I was amazed that they had remembered so much when they had made no notes during that first interview and no recording was made either. The recommendation was that I undergo a series of therapy sessions, which I agreed to do.

Hilary's story

Barbara was referred to Gracewell for an assessment of the risk she posed to her daughter Angie, then aged fourteen. The background was that when Angie was seven, her parents, Barbara and Hugh, separated. Barbara was homeless and very depressed at that stage and felt unable to provide security for Angie. She left Angie with Hugh and his new partner, Moira, until such time as she had a place to live. Hugh, however, applied successfully for custody of Angie.

When Angie was eight, she said that her mother had sexually abused her prior to the separation. Her father Hugh brought this to the attention of the social worker who had been visiting for some time because Angie had been showing signs of great distress. Barbara was questioned about this, but totally denied the abuse. As so often happens, it was felt that there was insufficient evidence for a prosecution and, although the social worker believed Angie, the matter was never resolved.

Angie didn't see her mother again for some years. However, she became increasingly distressed and disturbed, and eventually when she was ten, she was taken into care. It was clear that she had suffered traumatic experiences even after her mother's departure, but she could not talk about them. After her admission to care, Angie had no further contact with her father and stepmother. Barbara asked if she could start seeing Angie again, and with the social worker's approval, regular access visits were arranged. However, there was a real unease about allowing unsupervised access and overnight stays, because of the mystery surrounding the sexual abuse. Angie didn't want to talk about it any more and Barbara denied it.

When the social worker found out that our clinic did risk assessments on women who commit sexual offences, she referred Barbara in the hope that more light might be shed on the truth, and that the assessment would give a clearer indication of the risk Barbara might present to Angie.

I interviewed Barbara with my colleague Jenny Still who has for many years worked with children and families who have survived sexual abuse. We both have many years' experience in working with male sex offenders and we know the kinds of patterns and attitudes to look for when assessing the risk they present to children. However, it would be wrong to suppose that a knowledge of male sex offending patterns can be used to understand women sex offenders. Women and men behave differently, both in relation to their commission of non-sexual offences, and in relation to sexuality. Hence, women sex offenders may have profoundly different motives, different attitudes, and different behaviour patterns to those commonly found in their male counterparts.

The knowledge professionals have of women sex offenders is relatively poor as only 3 per cent of convicted sex offenders are female. Although some studies have been done, the samples are very small, and it is inappropriate to draw from these anything more than tentative hypotheses.

However, Jenny and I began by making some assumptions. Firstly, children rarely lie about sexual abuse and they know who abused them. Hence we began by believing that Angie was abused by Barbara.

Secondly, most people who do something harmful will seek to justify, minimise, excuse or legitimise their actions. We determined to ascertain what attitudes and beliefs Barbara held which might have helped her to offend without facing the reality that her behaviour was abusive of Angie, or that it was in some way justified. We considered that this might be along the lines that either she or Angie deserved it as a form of punishment, or on the other hand, she may have persuaded herself that it was good appropriate child care, and not abusive at all. Hence some distorted thinking about what is and is not sexual abuse would be noticeable.

Thirdly, women who commit sexual offences often have a coperpetrator. We were particularly interested in the family circumstances, as we were conscious of the fact that Angie had become more, rather than less, distressed after her mother's departure. The limited statistics that are available suggest that half of the women convicted of sexual offences offend with a male coperpetrator. Hence, we wanted to explore the possibility that Angie had been abused by more than one person.

We were particularly interested in finding out about Barbara's own sexual experiences and how these might have affected her sexual boundaries, sexual fantasies, and understanding of what is normal. There were indications that she may have been sexually abused herself and we know that, in some cases, people who have experienced sexual abuse at the hands of those close to them, either as adults or as children, do have difficulty in acknowledging that what happened to them was abusive. This is often for two reasons: one, the offender is telling them to believe that it's love not abuse, and two, it enables the victim to continue believing that the offender loves them really. Where there has been emotional neglect, the victim may also feel that some attention, however painful and compromised, is better than none.

Lastly, we wanted to ascertain the level of risk Barbara presented to Angie now. Hence, we wanted to compare her past and present circumstances, to learn about her current attitudes and behaviour patterns, and her current attitude to Angie. This included entertaining the possibility that Barbara might be primarily aroused to children, and exploring her sexual thoughts fantasies and practices.

During the interview, Barbara stuck to her denial of the offences, but could not explain Angie's allegations. However, she opened the door to further work, by commenting that it was possible she could have accidentally done something to Angie.

There didn't appear to be indications of sexual arousal to children. In fact, Barbara seemed to have blocked off any recognition of sexual feelings or needs. However, she revealed a very high level of repression by her ex-husband, and her life with him seemed to have been typified by her acceptance of physical, sexual and emotional abuse at his hands. Although an articulate and intelligent woman, she talked quite seriously about him allowing her to do some things, and forbidding her to do others. When questioned about their sex life she said it was fine. When asked for detail, she described rape but did not recognise it as such. She believed that her upbringing and her religion dictated that she should do as her husband wished at all times, in order to be a 'good wife'. She also showed herself to be extremely emotionally deprived and needy. Her own emotional needs had been frustrated for most of her life, and it was difficult to see how she could make room for Angie's needs.

In the light of all this, we offered Barbara some therapy sessions to allow further exploration not only of her abuse of Angie, but also to help her survive her own abusive past for herself as a woman as well as in her role as Angie's mother. We agreed that, funding permitting, I would be Barbara's therapist, and Jenny would be my consultant.

Barbara's story

After I was offered the therapy sessions, there began quite a long wait whilst the niceties of funding, etc., were sorted out. It felt rather like having a diagnosis made of a treatable condition without receiving a prescription for the cure! I did begin to wonder whether the therapy would ever take place. Looking back now I can see that the delays were helpful because of events that took place during the waiting time which aided the therapy later on.

Eventually I received notification that the therapy was due to begin. The first session was spent getting re-acquainted with Hilary and Jenny, putting each other in the picture as to what had been happening since we last met and looking again at the report and discussing what would take place over the next few sessions. Jenny and Hilary were good and put me at my ease. They reassured me that these sessions were for me — that this was my time and place and I could feel free to say whatever I wanted.

When I arrived at the clinic for my next session I was informed that only Hilary would be present but that the session would be videoed so that Jenny could see it later and also for future reference. Hilary and I chatted over coffee for a few minutes and then began to talk about my family. It had been alleged by my ex-husband that I had sexually abused my daughter Angie. Angie also remembered me abusing her, but I could not.

I had been repeatedly sexually abused and raped by my ex-

husband during the fifteen years of our marriage and I had locked that
away in the deep recesses of my mind too. It was as if it had never
happened! After a while Hilary asked if I would try to remember and
focus upon one incident in Angie's childhood when she was being
bathed ready for bed. I settled back and closed my eyes.

Hilary began to take me backwards through the sequence of
events — starting with Angie being dressed in her nightclothes,
through the dressing of Angie which took place before that, and
through her bathing.

It was quite a time-consuming process — almost as if Hilary was
dragging the information out of me. I hated it and I wanted to stop but
couldn't. The nightmare that I had lived with all those years was
slowly unfolded in my mind's eye! I hated myself for remembering, I
hated myself for the things I was saying — the events that I was
describing. The remembrance was so painful that I wished in that
moment that I could die!

Because I was so distraught Hilary brought the session to a close
and then over coffee just sort of talked me down and through what I
had said. I was inconsolable! After being together for nearly three
hours, I left Gracewell — but not before Hilary had spoken of the need
to share the contents of the session with Angie's social workers. They
were to be invited to join us the next week.

Hilary's story

I went into the second session with Barbara determined that we would
talk about her abuse of Angie. She had already mentioned the
possibility of accidental abuse whilst bathing Angie. Accidental abuse
is a myth but one which is dear to the hearts of those who abuse. I
knew that Barbara had a very painful secret and I recognised that she
had probably convinced herself that what she did to Angie wasn't
really abusive. We needed to get past her interpretation of events and
talk about what she actually did. Hence, I used a technique I often use
in similar circumstances: I asked her to close her eyes, remember a
specific occasion when she was bathing Angie, and describe the events
in detail. As she talked it became clear that she had washed inside
Angie's vagina whilst her husband, Hugh, acted as both orchestrator
and audience.

I asked her to open her eyes and we sat and talked about the kind
of things that had happened in their household. As she disclosed more
and more information, her voice became quieter and quieter, and the
tears just poured. Her face was blank and she stared into space. At the
end of the session she looked grey and exhausted.

Although in a sense it seemed hard on Barbara, I knew that for Angie's sake, it was vital that Barbara should share what she had told me with Angie's social workers. There were two: one male field worker, and one female residential worker from the community home where Angie was living. It was good that we had videoed our session so that the social workers could watch it and then talk with Barbara. I think Barbara would have found it too difficult to do a complete rerun of everything she'd told me. Barbara was upset at the thought of talking with the social workers, but she immediately recognised that she had to do it. As she left the clinic Barbara told me that she felt worse rather than better after facing her abuse of Angie, but she felt that she'd had to face it. I wondered whether she'd come back next week.

Barbara's story

I think the week after that session must have been one of the hardest and longest weeks that I have ever lived through. If felt as if suddenly everyone knew that I had abused my daughter. I felt like a monster with two heads and that I wore a sign chained around my neck stating that I SEXUALLY ABUSED MY DAUGHTER. I must say it took quite a time for these feelings to leave me and it was only as I came to terms with myself through the therapy that this began to happen.

The next week I didn't want to go back to Gracewell but I couldn't stay away either. I think Hilary was relieved when I arrived! One of the most difficult things was making and sustaining eye contact with Angie's social workers. I felt totally ashamed. I even thought that they wouldn't want to speak to me or associate with me.

We sat through the video recording of that first session and the intensity of pain and shame hit me again. I would rather have been anywhere other than in that room at that precise moment. I know we spent a long time talking about the disclosures afterwards. Both the social workers were very reassuring that the disclosure was nothing less than they had expected all along, and they were relieved that I was now able to start opening up about all the things that had really gone on. The hardest part was that I had to learn to live with what I had done and to learn to live with myself.

Hilary's story

Barbara's sense of shame was very profound. She didn't just feel guilty, she was deeply ashamed of herself as a mother, a woman, a human being. She was very different from most of the male offenders with whom I've worked, in that she didn't at any point try to blame the victim, nor did she try to minimise or legitimise what she'd done. In my experience, most male offenders try to claim that their offence was not very serious and the child wasn't hurt by it. Barbara accepted the essential wrongness of her behaviour, and even though Angie did not recognise some of the abuse as abuse, believing it to be 'normal bathtime', Barbara never used this to claim Angie wasn't hurt. In fact she recognised that the hurt was particularly great because Angie didn't recognise it: her sense of normality had been abused.

Barbara quite quickly began giving more information about her abuse of Angie, than Angie actually remembered. During this time I kept in very close touch with Angie's social workers so they could use what was coming from Barbara to make it easier for Angie to talk. Much of the abuse had taken place when Angie was very young, and like other chidren who have been abused since birth, she had never experienced life without abusive bathtimes, so she did not know what a non-abusive bathtime was like. All she knew was that some aspects of bathtime were unpleasant, but were supposed to be necessary and good for her.

One area in which Barbara's thinking was very distorted was in her belief that, by actually doing to Angie what Hugh asked, she was protecting Angie. She knew from experience, that if she refused to wash inside Angie's vagina, Hugh would do it, and do it roughly. She also knew from experience, that he would punish her for disobedience by the use of physical, sexual and emotional violence. Hence, her belief that she was protecting herself and Angie made sense to her in the context of her distorted belief that she must obey her husband whatever his demands might be.

Although she clearly did have choices as an independent adult, and can in no way escape responsibility for abusing her child, I believe it is important to remember that we do live in a society in which many women are oppressed by their male partners. Barbara felt that she could not choose to disobey Hugh, because if she did she would be choosing to be beaten herself. Towards the end of her life with Hugh, she felt that she could not choose to leave, because Hugh would get custody of Angie. Apparently, he had persuaded Barbara and other people that she was an inadequate, unfit mother who couldn't manage without him. When eventually Barbara left, she felt that she couldn't choose to take Angie because she didn't have the right: she felt she had betrayed both Hugh and Angie.

Although none of this excuses Barbara, it shows something of the work that needed to be done with her if she was to protect either Angie or herself in the future against people such as Hugh.

Barbara's story

The next three sessions were all long ones spent delving further into what life had been like and exploring the truth. Hilary was very good at gently probing to discover the full extent of the abuse. Of course I not only had to come to terms with my abuse of Angie under the cover of bathing her, but also with the abuse I had suffered at the hands of my ex-husband, under the cover of a seemingly happy, loving marriage. It seemed as if at the end of the six weeks we had only just touched the tip of the problem.

One of the hardest things to work through was that supervised access visits with Angie were still continuing on a monthly basis — they were very difficult as I was still learning about myself and coming to terms with my past. The feelings of guilt took a long time to disappear. Even now I still feel a sense of guilt but this fits into the perspective that I now have of all that is past.

Another area that took a lot of working on was that of responsibility. For a long time I had shouldered more than my fair share of responsibility and I was only able to work through this and off-load excess responsibility as Hilary and I worked through a programme of victim survival therapy.

Writing about it now, it seems easy to say that I worked through this area and that area, but some of this work took many, many weeks to get through. There was a period of re-thinking negative, self-defeating thoughts, and learning to think in a more positive way. This helped me recognise where the negative issues were coming from, so that I could change them for myself and not be reliant on others 'talking me up' all the time.

Alongside of this we were still looking at the issues of abuse concerning Angie and how they could be redressed. It was agreed by all the parties, that it would be better to cancel access with Angie until such time as we could work things through with each other. It had been extremely difficult and traumatic for me to continue access with Angie whilst carrying all this guilt around with me, especially as Angie was not aware of all the disclosures I was making. Angie's social worker had regular sessions with her, and I continued seeing Hilary.

Hilary's story

Angie had responded with a combination of relief and rage when she heard from her social worker that Barbara had at last admitted the truth of her allegations. Then with her social worker's help, she wrote a list of questions for her mother to answer. Barbara made a videotape answering the questions, and after it had been seen by myself and Angie's social worker, it was shown to Angie. Angie then wanted to talk to her mother about it and challenge some of her statements. At that stage we arranged meetings between mother and daughter with myself and Angie's social worker present, both in fact supporting Angie.

This was a very difficult phase for them both: Barbara was remembering and talking about a lot of events which Angie still had locked away. Angie's social worker was gently helping her to talk at her own pace. At first we decided that Angie and Barbara should continue seeing each other with supervision as usual. In one sense nothing had changed, Angie and the social workers had always known that Barbara abused Angie. The only aspect that was new, was that Barbara was now admitting it. Angie wanted to see her mother and it seemed wrong to change the arrangements.

However, although access was only once a month, the burden of all that was unsaid but not yet ready to be said, proved too great, and the dialogue between mother and daughter became increasingly stilted. Feelings were on the agenda for the first time in years and this proved very difficult. Barbara had cauterised her feelings during her own abuse at the hands of Hugh and her abuse of Angie. If she allowed herself to feel the pain of being abused, she had also to face how much Angie had suffered, and hence she had to face how much she had been the cause of Angie's suffering. I think she went through times when she wished she could go back to pretending that she'd had a happy marriage and that Angie had never been abused.

Barbara also had to accept the fact that Angie was beginning to show anger towards her, tentatively at first, but increasing in strength and vigour. Angie began at last to feel believed and this had a great empowering effect on her. She began to make choices, and one was to take a break from seeing her mother outside therapy sessions. Access was not resumed for four months until they had had time to talk together about the silent past, in Angie's timescale, in our presence and with our help.

During this period, the field social worker spent a lot of time with Angie and did an excellent job in helping her to ask questions and make challenges and demands. Previously, Angie had been blocked from this by her mother's continuing denial and by the code of silence and fear surrounding the past.

The social worker was a man, and he was very aware of the possibility that this could be difficult for Angie. However, the reality was that he provided what Angie needed at the time: someone who had worked with offenders and knew the manipulative tactics they use; someone who could hear, and showed that he could hear and accept the range of physical, emotional and sexual abuse she had suffered. Essentially, he was prepared to hear the unhearable and imagine the unimaginable. Although the gender of the worker is important, knowledge and experience of offenders and the ability to hear the victim is paramount.

Barbara's story

After several weeks, two sessions were arranged when Angie and I were together with Angie's social worker and Hilary. Prior to this Angie had prepared a series of questions for me to answer. This was recorded on video for Angie to see. After the second session with Angie, I really felt as if I had lost her for good. It seemed to me that it was a total waste of time to continue with any kind of therapy.

At first Angie recalled only some of the abuse. She did not realise that what I had done to her whilst bathing her when she was a young child, was actually sexual abuse. This meant that she had been abused on hundreds of occasions, not a few at all. Her father had been there, directing what was to take place, and at times he had abused her too. Although she knew he had physically abused her, she had not fully understood the sexual nature of his actions. Because her father was no longer around, Angie needed to channel all of her anger, hatred and frustration at me, and that was when I felt that so much damage had been done that it was irreparable.

When it was felt that Angie and I were ready, the social workers began a series of family therapy sessions for Angie and myself. These were separate from Gracewell therapy, but I was able to talk with Hilary over any issues that arose during the sessions with Angie.

Hilary's story

One of the special issues in working with a woman who has offended with a dominant male coperpetrator, who has abused both her and their child, is the apportioning of responsibility. Barbara veered around between blaming Hugh for everything and blaming herself for everything. Although intellectually she began to recognise that Hugh should carry some responsibility, at an emotional level she took responsibility for his behaviour as well as her own. Although she had subjected herself entirely to his will, she kept asking whether he would have been less abusive if she had been even more acquiescent and unquestioning of his wishes and authority! This sat strangely with her self-presentation as an intelligent, articulate woman.

In therapy we used cognitive methods to help Barbara to accept her responsibility for her own abuse of Angie and for not removing

Angie to a safe place away from Hugh. We used the same methods to help her see that she was not responsible for Hugh's behaviour either towards herself or towards Angie. She did not deserve to be raped and beaten by Hugh, nor, given their relationship would she have been able to stop him from abusing Angie whilst they all remained in the same household.

In the early stages of therapy, it became clear that Barbara still thought and behaved as if Hugh was in control of her, even though he had left the area and she hadn't seen him for years. She was still his victim and she was still afraid to even think, let alone say, anything he might consider as questioning, or challenging of his authority. She told me how when she started to feel angry with him, she would hear his voice in her head rebuking her. This was actually visible: her whole affect would change and she would slump in her chair and begin apologising for daring to be critical of him.

Barbara had also suffered sexual abuse as a child and had kept this secret because like so many victims, she felt guilty and responsible. Everyone is a hero in their imagination, and hence Barbara believed she should have screamed, fought and run. At the time of being abused she had frozen, just like most adults and children do when faced with the shock of an actual assault. This combined with her abuse by and fear of Hugh, paralysed her. I think what made this even more difficult was her belief that if she remained afraid of Hugh she could be less responsible for the abuse of Angie; if she stopped being afraid of Hugh she would somehow become more responsible for abusing Angie.

This area proved such a muddle that it blocked her from being able to face Angie's victim experience and recognise how much more painful and confusing Angie's experience as a child in their household must have been than her own. For a time she felt that people could recognise Angie's suffering but not her own, and she felt bitter about this. She had to resolve her past experiences, give up her fear of Hugh, and correctly apportion responsibility between herself and Hugh, before she could begin to face the pain of Angie's experience and recognise her needs. She needed therapy for herself as a survivor, before she could understand and reach out to Angie.

Barbara's story

The hardest area of all to work through was the totally irrational fear that I had of my ex-husband, Hugh. I had been frightened of him for years and our fifteen years of marriage had been a living hell. It was only the fact that he had moved out of the area that made me feel safe enough to make the earlier disclosures. I really was scared of him and wouldn't have been able to open up at all if he was still living locally. I had tried earlier on in therapy to express anger towards Hugh, but I wasn't strong enough in myself to cope with this and soon ended up taking back on board all that I was trying to off-load.

For quite a while Hilary and I worked at changing all the negative, helpless thoughts, and adopting a new assertiveness that had been missing for many, many years. Eventually it began to work and I was also encouraged by entering into a new sexual relationship, which was totally non-abusive, and in which I felt in total control. I began to feel and think like a different person. At the time I was also working on recognising situations so that I didn't get trapped into being a victim again. It was all coming together after months of seemingly getting nowhere.

I must admit that there were times when I felt as if therapy would never come to an end. Hilary was always supportive and encouraging — always saying that there was no right or wrong way to work through therapy, but to adapt it to every single situation.

I was also encouraged that no one would be shocked by anything further that I had to disclose — Hilary believed in keeping an open door for more disclosures to be made. The more that Hilary and I have talked through these areas, the easier it has been to work through them.

Hilary's story

Barbara's long years of experience of abusive sexuality had left her with sexual difficulties. It's natural that when you think of sex and want to feel aroused, you think of your own sexual experiences. This was extremely difficult for Barbara because sexual arousal was fused with being physically hurt, and with shameful unarousing pictures of what she had done to Angie. In a sense she felt it only right to imagine being physically hurt because she needed to be punished for her abuse of Angie. Also, Hugh had persuaded her that she was a person worthy of regular punishment because of her disobedience to his wishes. All this left Barbara vulnerable to making relationships with other abusers.

We spent a lot of time helping Barbara learn to enjoy sex without pain. This started from the basis that sex on your own is better than sex with the wrong person! Barbara learnt by herself to like her body again. Later, she made a non-abusive and enjoyable sexual relationship. However, whilst this was therapeutic, she realised that in overall terms, it wasn't the relationship she wanted long term, either for herself or Angie, and so she ended it. This also was therapeutic: she had enjoyed sex without pain for the first time in years, and she wasn't dependent on the man. She was able to move on out of her own choice, hold on to what she had gained and be her own woman. This term 'being her own woman' was something that Barbara adopted and felt empowered by.

However, there remained the issue of Barbara's fear of Hugh. Although she felt confident in relation to other men, she was still paralysed by the thought of meeting Hugh again. She and I had regular six weekly reviews to evaluate progress and set further goals. I left the goal-setting to Barbara, and in that sense she increasingly directed the therapy herself. When she felt ready, she decided to tackle her fear of Hugh.

Barbara's story

Eventually I reached the point where I could no longer put off having another go at Hugh. This was the last big area to be faced. Hilary provided some large cushions which represented Hugh — the idea being that I could 'have a go' at him — lashing out and hitting the cushions if I so desired. The cushions were on the floor which caused me immense problems for the first few times we tried it. Then I realised that in kneeling down to the cushions, I took on a subservient role to Hugh. After some discussion, I decided to place the cushions on a chair so that when I sat down I was equal to him. It worked really well, and after three further sessions, I felt totally free of him. Looking at a photo of him now, I don't feel frightened or feel the need to curl up and hide from him — *total victory*!

As I became free of Hugh, I felt anger and resentment rise within me towards his wife who had caused many problems for both Angie and myself. I'd trusted her to protect Angie better than I had, and she'd abused her instead. Although it wasn't on the agenda for therapy, Hilary agreed that this area needed addressing as well and so for the next few sessions I worked on her.

Hilary's story

When Barbara began expressing her anger towards Hugh, she tried lashing out at him on behalf of not only herself but Angie too. This didn't work because she could not detach herself from responsibility for Angie's suffering, and the burden of their joint pain proved too great for her to deal with. When instead she began expressing anger for herself alone, she became increasingly strong.

Moira, Hugh's second wife, had physically beaten Angie as well as continuing the previous pattern of sexual abuse in partnership with

Hugh. Later in therapy, Barbara focused her attention on Moira, and began for the first time to rage on behalf of both herself and Angie.

As Barbara began to accept and like herself better, she started to allow herself to care for Angie and feel protective of her. She became less preoccupied with herself and her own feelings and much more concerned with and for Angie. Angie is now seventeen. She doesn't live with Barbara, but says that one day she might want to do so. They are much closer than they've ever been, and for the first time, Angie has a mother who isn't abusive towards her and isn't frightened of anyone. She is 'her own woman'.

Barbara's story

Just a few weeks ago Hilary and I had an interesting session with the social workers, looking over some of the earlier video work that I had done, and comparing early with very recent work to see how far I had come. As we talked through the changes I could really see the difference in me. It was amazing. Looking back over the last eighteen months I can see that at the beginning I was in a long dark tunnel with no light at the end. The therapy has enabled me to travel along the tunnel and to find my way out into the light.

I hope my story will be an encouragement to those who need to go through a period of therapy, or are presently undergoing therapy. It may seem a long process, but take your time to work through it — you will reach the end when you are ready.

To therapists and social workers — be patient with us: we are damaged and hurting and need to go slowly. We will thank you for it in the end.

Afterword on working with female sex offenders – Hilary

My main aim in working with a woman or a man who has committed sexual offences is to reduce the risk of them re-offending. If therapy is to be effective in achieving that end, then the offender's motivation to offend and the way in which she or he has overcome internal and external inhibitors needs to be examined. Therapy needs to address the offender as a thinking, feeling, behaving person and harness thoughts, feelings and behaviour to prevent re-offending. Therapy needs to go at the client's pace, but the overall purpose of therapy, i.e. to prevent re-offending, must never be lost, and there must be a constant eye on the way in which progress can be used to prevent relapse.

When the offender begins to talk openly, she or he may give information which can be used by the child victim's therapist to aid the survival process. It can be used to break the sense of fear and secrecy and free the victim from codes of silence and misplaced feelings of guilt and responsibility. Hence, a positive and open relationship between victim and offender therapists is vital.

Working with women offenders, especially those who have offended in a male-coerced context, is different from working with male offenders. Male offenders have often experienced sexual victim-isation as children. However, as adults they are rarely victims of a man who is also their co-offender. In the case of women, this situation is more common, and it may be necessary to recognise and help them survive their own victim experience before they can begin to fully empathise with the child they have abused.

Women offenders must take responsibility for their own actions, but it is important to remember that some operate in situations of extreme fear of a male offender. Their fears are real: we live in a male dominated society in which women are frequently abused, both sexually and physically, by men. The offending must not be excused, but the context in which it takes place, cannot be dismissed.

7 Female abusers — what children and young people have told ChildLine

Hereward Harrison
Researched By Catherine Cobham

ChildLine is the only free UK helpline for children in trouble or danger. It offers a confidential telephone counselling service for any child with any problem, 24 hours a day. ChildLine listens and provides advice, comfort and protection.

Sexual abuse can be clearly identified as the main problem in 15 per cent of the written records of telephone calls and letters made to ChildLine by children and young people in the year April 1990 to March 1991. Sexual, physical and emotional abuse, however, do not easily separate into discrete categories and it may be, for example, that a child will not immediately talk about sexual abuse but will refer, initially, to general difficulties with parents or other adults or young people. ChildLine's experience, therefore, is that the way children report, and talk about, sexual abuse may very well lead to an underestimate of the number of children who are sexually abused and an over-simplification of statistical information collected by the helpline.

ChildLine's statistics, from children and young people who ring and write, which may not reflect statistics from other sources, show that the biological father is the most common perpetrator of sexual abuse, followed by stepfather, mother's boyfriend, other male relatives and males known to the child. From 1 April 1990–31 March 1991, 8663 children and young people rang ChildLine about sexual abuse. In 91 per cent of these calls, the perpetrators were male and in 9 per cent (780) they were female. This smaller, but significant, proportion of total abusers breaks down as follows:

Sample 780 female abusers	per cent
Mother	34
Other female relative/acquaintance	22
Sister	11
Aunt	11
Stepmother	11
Both parents together	11

ChildLine records indicated that boys were more likely than girls to be abused by females. The perpetrator was reported to be female by 1 per cent of girls who rang about sexual abuse and by 12 per cent of boys who rang about sexual abuse. This may not reflect the true situation but merely be that male abuse is more publicised, and more readily accepted, and that abuse by females is often not recognised by children and young people, or indeed adults, as abuse. In looking at sexual abuse of children and young people by females, we must also refer to an increasing number of children who report sexual abuse at the hands of other children, including female children.

No obvious profile of a 'female abuser' emerges from the ChildLine counselling records, although some characteristics seem to be shared. An absent father was a feature of many reports by children and young people. Parents were often divorced, fathers were working long hours or working away from home.

A teenage boy described how his mother had become increasingly physical with him since her marriage breakup; she was now coming into his room at night and touching him. He was frightened and wanted it to stop before it went any further.

Another caller, whose father was a long distance lorry driver, would not be specific, saying only that 'Mum does things to me and I do things to her'. He felt himself to be at least partly responsible and was very worried that his parents would split up if he told anyone. In a similar example, where an adolescent boy reported having sex with his mother, the caller also reported asking his younger brother to masturbate him, thereby becoming both the subject of sexual abuse and a perpetrator in his own right.

A recurring problem, particularly for adolescent boys, was guilt at the sexual feelings the abuse induced. Female abusers were not usually violent, although there were some exceptions. In one case, a girl was pinned down by her mother's boyfriend while her mother sexually abused her. Other children spoke of being threatened by females with punishment, violence or the withholding of food if they did not comply with adults' demands for sex.

Callers reported enormous conflict between what they saw as inappropriate behaviour on the part of the abuser and the way in which their bodies responded — the 'pleasure' that they experienced. This was particularly true where the abuser was less closely bonded to the caller, such as new stepmothers, schoolteachers, or sisters who were much older. A 14 year old told ChildLine that he enjoyed sex with his stepmother, but that one of his biggest worries was that he would get her pregnant. Several male callers indicated that there was considerable peer pressure to be 'macho'. This tended to increase their confusion about whether or not they should be engaging in sex with their mothers, female relatives and older female acquaintances.

There is evidence from the ChildLine calls that children were unsure about whether it was right to complain or to say no. Many had great difficulty in actually talking about what was happening at all and, when they did tell, they often expressed feelings of guilt and were reluctant to ask for help. A boy spent over half an hour on the phone trying to tell ChildLine he had been abused but revealed little else other than that when his sister came into his room 'things happened'. This is a feature of many calls to ChildLine and indicates that many young people do need time to unravel their 'stories' and that it is essential for counsellors to accept what children say and go at their pace.

Some young people were confused about whether a situation was in fact abusive. A teenager told ChildLine that he and his mother had been having sex for 18 months, but that tonight she had 'sexually abused' him. The caller was not ready to talk more about what was happening to him and the counsellor was left wondering about what had prompted him to phone ChildLine on this occasion.

An adolescent girl told a ChildLine counsellor that her mother embarrassed her in front of her boyfriend, cuddling her and touching her all over. The caller said she 'squirmed all over' every time this happened and had asked her mother to stop but her mother took no notice. The caller was unsure about the nature of the touching; she felt uncomfortable and wondered whether her mother was just jealous and insecure because of her recent divorce from the caller's father. Similarly, a 12 year old girl reported that she felt uneasy about the way her mother was touching her but could not be sure what was reasonable affection and what was not.

During these calls, ChildLine counsellors tried to help children and young people establish the appropriate boundaries which many of them felt were lacking between themselves and their mothers, female relatives and adult female acquaintances. If the young people felt that being touched was unacceptable, or made them uncomfortable, they were encouraged to say so. It did appear in some cases that mothers, or stepmothers, were particularly insensitive to their children's physical and emotional needs in adolescence when they needed more privacy and independence.

There were several examples of callers whose sexual orientation and/or choice of partner had been greatly influenced by their experiences of being sexually abused. A young woman and her sister had been abused as small children by a female friend of the family. The caller reported that at one stage she assumed she must be a lesbian. She believed this because she thought that, if the perpetrator chose her, it must say something about her sexuality.

A boy of 16, whose mother had been forcing him to do 'what his father wouldn't do', now lived with a much older man which made him feel less threatened. Another caller of the same age whose concerns probably reflected those of many others, said that the sex initiated by his stepmother made him feel very unsure about what was right and wrong, what this meant about his relationship with his biological mother and whether he would be able to form 'proper' relationships as he grew up.

The experience ChildLine has gained from the many thousands of children and young people who have phoned or written to the helpline about being sexually abused by adults or other children and young people has helped place the issue of female abusers in context. The overwhelming majority of abuse of children and young people reported to ChildLine is perpetrated by males. The publicity that has been given to these male abusers, however, has meant that many children and young people, as well as adults, have not been able to think of women, or other children and young people, as abusers. The calls to ChildLine are clear evidence that children and young people do suffer abuse from men, but *also* from women and other children and young people. It is essential that we keep our minds open to these possibilities and understand what they mean for the young people who are being abused.

8 The paradox of women who sexually abuse children

Olive Wolfers

If we take the stance that women do not sexually abuse children and that it is purely a male activity, or if we assume women only abuse in conjunction with men, we ignore the effects of prevailing male ideology on women; we set limitations on women's ability to change; we rule out women's ability to understand the structural faults in our society and to draw their own conclusions about themselves. We ignore women's potential.

Although a minority of people, excluding victims/survivors, have been aware of child sexual abuse perpetrated by women, the subject has only recently emerged as an issue. Caring agencies, generally speaking, are not geared to detecting women's involvement in child sexual abuse and, consequently, frequently leave children unprotected.

This chapter is a tentative attempt to present a theorisation of women sexual abusers of children as emerging from a situation of powerlessness. The central contention is that powerlessness results in a far greater resort to violence and intimidation practices than is currently acknowledged and represented in the literature. In order to clarify this broad hypothesis, a number of issues will be examined: substance abuse; pornography; intergenerational abuse; networks; and denial. These will be related to a theory of power.

The objective is an attempt to generate a broad macro-theory of women's place within a power structure, the consequent dangers for children, and some of the practical implications for professionals.

Violence and its relationship to powerlessness

Violence is defined as any act which involves the use of physical or emotional pain, fear of physical pain or injury in order to either degrade the victim or force them to comply with the behaviour of the assailant. Johnson and Shier (1987) maintain that the vast majority of female molesters use persuasion rather than physical force or threats. It is proposed here, however, that there is a strong likelihood of violence in situations where women are involved in sexually abusing children.

Investigation of ten cases of women offenders (Wolfers 1990) revealed that seven out of ten women subjected their victims to a very high level of physical and emotional abuse. Children were kicked, beaten, burnt, locked in cupboards and threatened with witchcraft, the nature of which appeared sado-masochistic in one instance. Perpetrators went to tremendous lengths to set the scene, culminating in bizarre acting out of religious fanaticism, bondage and imprisonment. Despite the small sample and recognising the involvement of male co-offenders in each case, nevertheless the level of violence is high. Clearly, it would be useful to examine co-offending situations more closely to determine if women are less violent in the absence of men.

It is well documented that male perpetrators objectify their victims and it is currently understood that this acts as a disinhibitor, enabling them to both sexually and physically abuse children. It is possible to speculate that women offenders may behave in the same way. Violence may be a way of instilling fear and preventing disclosure allowing the perpetrator to obtain maximum power.

Money (1980) suggests that, whilst a given type of sexual behaviour may be shared by males and females alike, the threshold for its arousal and expression will be different. Nevertheless violence in conjunction with or as part of sexually abusive behaviour by women appears significant. Similar sentiments are expressed by Faller (1987) and Finkelhor and Russell (1984).

How much is violence linked to women's feelings of powerlessness? Ong (1985) states that, although women may feel powerless outside the home, the structural powerlessness of women as mothers in the public sphere, turns into one of total power as a mother in the private sphere. Alternatively, co-offending may leave women feeling powerless outside the home as well as in it when partnered by what seems to them to be a very powerful male perpetrator.

Although child sexual abuse is a misuse of power, people who abuse power may not necessarily feel powerless. Powerlessness may be a conscious state of trying to achieve control and the use of violence, indeed the involvement in child sexual abuse, may be an attempt to achieve control by some women in powerless situations. This, of course, is likely to be only a part of the equation. Women who themselves have been abused as children, either physically or sexually, may suffer cognitive impairment resulting in distorted thinking patterns and identification with their aggressor. A study by Fowler et al. (1983) maintained that 80 per cent of incest offenders had been sexually or physically abused as children. Groth et al. (1982) believe that former incest victims become offenders in an effort to resolve unresolved sexual trauma.

It is important to look at situations in which women child sexual abusers are violent and to identify what makes some women 'act out', given societal expectation that women internalise abusive experiences, whilst men are said to externalise them. Many women face extreme internal conflict: the internalised dominant ideology of women as nurturers and carers, as moral arbiters within the family and the external social reality of their existence, creates feelings of self-blame and lack of worth, which in turn reinforces feelings of powerlessness. Leonard (1984) states the intricate relationship between these external and internal means of constructing the activities and feelings of women is such that the internal experiences are already spoken for externally. It is perhaps this conflict which results in violent behaviour for some women, producing a heady addictive mixture of clandestine activity, eroticism and power when linked with sexual abuse.

Practitioners have been attempting to deal with the effects on children of physical and emotional abuse by men and women for many years. What we have failed to be aware of is its link in some instances with sexual abuse and, in particular, women's involvement. If feelings of powerlessness are the result of internal conflict arising from the experiences of women and societal expectations upon them, and if violence is an attempt to resolve this conflict, then it would seem reasonable to speculate that there may be a higher incidence of violence perpetrated by women abusers than is presently recognised.

Substance abuse and pornography

Substance abuse and pornography could be considered a broadening of the spectrum of violence and an important additional factor in child sexual abuse. There is general recognition that drugs and alcohol act as disinhibitors. Although some women perpetrators are involved in substance abuse, there is no proven link in the general population between substance abuse and child sexual abuse, except in situations where sexual abuse appears to be used for monetary gain in order to fund the use of drugs and alcohol. Wolfers (1990) found in a sample of ten women offenders there were three cases of alcohol abuse and one of severe drug, alcohol and solvent abuse. The latter case involved a network of male and female abusers, drugs were administered to children as well as being used by abusers. In addition, children were used for pornographic purposes.

It is possible to speculate that in these instances children are more likely to be drawn into abusive networks and pornography, resulting in serious implications for women and children, who may be at the mercy of a large number of abusers, crossing cultural and gender boundaries. Consequently their access to control is likely to diminish and feelings of powerlessness increase.

Wolf (1984) is of the opinion that male offenders are prone to acting on their impulses, which are frequently manifested in the area of alcohol or drug abuse, sexual promiscuity or physical aggression and indeed this is borne out by approximately four years' experience of group work with this client group by the writer.

However, there are important differences in the way men and women are socialised which, in the writer's view, radically affects the way women respond. Bringing up a family is still seen as predominantly women's responsibility, a task which may be isolating and both physically and emotionally demanding, particularly in the case of women who lack supportive partners. Succeeding as a mother is seen as crucial within our society and yet little value is placed upon it in reality. Drugs and alcohol may be one way of attempting to cope with the conflict and possible powerlessness this engenders. Unfortunately problems then tend to be internalised. The imbibing of chemicals effectively blocks reality, at least for the time being, and alleviates the need for the individual to examine the real difficulties. As a consequence they tend to be exacerbated and dependency and powerlessness are reinforced, control is abdicated to substances and ultimately to other people.

McCarty (1986) revealed that 46 per cent of independent offenders had a serious drug problem, whilst 22 per cent of co-offenders and 20 per cent of accomplices were involved in substance abuse. Whilst feelings of isolation might be the initial reason for drug dependency, rather than sexual abuse, it nevertheless points to the possibility of independent women abusers being vulnerable to involvement in networks and, of course, in some instances this will also apply to people who co-offend.

The writer's early study (Wolfers 1990) revealed four out of ten women were addicted to substances. Three abused alcohol and the other used drugs, alcohol and solvents. Children in the latter case were subjected to multi-perpetrator male and female abusers co-offending with their mother, who sometimes acted together, though on occasions offenders were all female. These children were also abused by their mother in isolation. Drugs were administered to the children from an early age and victims used for pornographic purposes.

If women who sexually abuse children are involved in substance abuse and if, because of the addictive nature of these substances, they then become involved in networks in order to fund them, then children are at greater risk of abuse by multi-perpetrators, resulting in increased emotional and physical trauma. In addition, the danger to health in terms of exposure to HIV and drug/alcohol addiction are phenomenal and the pressures not to disclose intense and sustained.

Children in these situations learn a powerful lesson; they learn that, generally speaking, they are powerless to stop the abuse. They know how it feels to be powerless and without hope. Small wonder that some of these children grow up to view sexual abuse not only as a normative experience but also to see it as a way of achieving control and overcoming powerlessness. If current research is correct and more female children are abused than male children, then it is logical to assume that not only will some of these children become adult offenders but that there may be a larger number of women perpetrators than we imagine. Clearly this awaits further research.

Denial

If we consider the intense pressures and conflict already outlined, then it is not unreasonable to suppose that there is very little initially to persuade women to admit their sexual involvement with a child and that they are as likely to deny offending as male perpetrators. The writer's earlier study revealed six out of ten women denied sexual involvement with a child and, although this is a small number of offenders, the high level of denial has been confirmed by practice experience.

Women who co-offended with male partners will be subjected to the same pressure to deny as that to which they have already succumbed in order to become involved in the first place.

The inability of many women to see themselves functioning in the absence of men, in situations of powerlessness, may mean they are prepared to go to any length to preserve their relationship with their partner, even if this means sacrificing their children. This is described by Justice and Justice (1976) as the symbiotic characteristic of abuse family system.

Intergenerational abuse may be an added dimension in these circumstances. Mothers may never have experienced being parented and consequently make unrealistic demands of their children, expecting a parental response from them. There tends to be a lack of psychological investment in their children, which may be due to early emotional deprivation or lack of social skills (Zuelzer and Reposa 1983). Additionally, a process of normalisation will probably have taken place, making it extremely difficult for children and perpetrators to extradite themselves.

Given this social reality, how realistic is it to expect such women to admit abusing their children? Particularly as there is very little likelihood of their receiving help at the moment if they were to do so. Whether women abuse in co-offending situations or independently, they may be as isolated as the children they abuse.

If we are to move women beyond denial then we must look at the underlying issues. We must address their individual needs, whilst crucially not losing sight of child protection issues. The ultimate aim must be to confront the offending behaviour.

Conclusion

Set in the context of powerlessness, this chapter is intended as a contribution to the debate on the current topic of women child sexual abusers. However, the subject is intensely complex and individuals are subject to a wide variety of variables, requiring ideas and theory to be constantly adjusted. Clearly there are considerable practical implications if we are to attempt to address some of the issues previously outlined.

It may not be possible to elicit information from women offenders unless there is sufficient evidence to either prosecute them or enable removal of the children. Therefore there is every likelihood that, like male perpetrators, they will be an unwilling group.

Cases of child sexual abuse involving women tend to be particularly difficult, partly because of the very nature of the relationship between women and children, but also because of frequent links with networks and multi-perpetrator involvement. The use of violence, as previously contended, can create tremendous fear and anxiety for victims, accentuated where children may have to testify against both parents, making retraction a strong possibility and reducing the chance of prosecution. Prosecution is crucial if we are to acknowledge victim harm and allow women the opportunity to admit their offences and obtain treatment, that is assuming treatment is available. Unfortunately there is a tendency within the Crown Prosecution

Service to decriminalise sexual offences committed by women (Wolfers 1992).

We need to set women's offending in its historical as well as its current context within systems. If we are to obtain a clear overview, information on women must be separated from that on male offenders, though cross-referenced where it is appropriate. The context and nature of the offending needs to be carefully logged, together with a record of victims. Perpetrators who have offended sexually should be separated on index cards from women who have physically abused children, unless there is knowledge of both types of offending. It is a matter for conjecture whether most agencies do this.

Recent research (NCH 1992), together with practice experience, indicates that male perpetrators commence offending at an earlier age than previously thought. Further research is required to establish if this also applies to women offenders, together with investigation into the linking of violence and eroticism. Without this information, the implications for placing children together will remain speculative.

The same society which creates powerlessness in women, also ensures that children are without power and it is the powerlessness which is primarily the reason children become first of all victims and are then unable to disclose their victimisation. The harmful effects of victimisation are both symptomatic and a reinforcement of that powerlessness. Hopefully, in the light of on-going debate, future research and pressure on government to commit resources, we will move towards a solution of this issue.

References

Faller, K. C. (1987) 'Women who sexually abuse children' *Violence and Victims* 12 (4) pp. 236–76 Springer Publishing Company.

Finkelhor, D. and Russell, D. (1984) 'Women as perpetrators' in Finkelhor, D. et al. (eds) *Child Sexual Abuse, New Theory and Research* The Free Press.

Fowler, S. et al. (1983) 'Against sexual assault, Phoenix AZ counselling the incest offender' *International Journal of Female Therapy* 5 pp. 92–7.

Groth, A., Nicholas, Hobson, L. and Gory, T. (1982) 'The child molester: clinical observations' *Social Work and Child Sexual Abuse* pp. 129–44, The Howarth Press.

Johnson, R. L. and Shrier, D. (1987) 'Past victimsation by females of male patients in an adolescent medicine clinic population' *American Journal of Psychiatry* 144 p. 4.

Justice, R. and Justice, B. (1976) *The Missing Family* Human Science Press, pp. 60–80.

Leonard, P. (1984) *Personality and Ideology* Macmillan Education Ltd.

McCarty, L. M. (1986) *Mother Child Incest Characteristics of the Offender* Child Welfare League of America, pp. 447–58.

Money, J. (1980) *Love and Love Sickness: The Science of Sex, Gender Difference and Pair Bonding* Johns Hopkins University Press.

National Children's Home Committee of Enquiry (1992) *Report of the Committee of Enquiry into Children and Young People who Sexually Abuse Other Children* National Children's Home.

Ong, Bie Nio (1985) 'Understanding child abuse, ideologies of motherhood' *Womens Studies Inc Forum* 8 (6) Pergamon Press.

Wolf, S. C. (1984) Paper presented at the 3rd International Conference on Victimology, Lisbon, Portugal, November 1984.

Wolfers, O. (1990) Women Child Sexual Abusers: An Exploratory Study, Unpublished Dissertation, Bradford University.

Wolfers, O. (1992) 'Same abuse, different parent' *Social Work Today* 23 26.

Zuelzer, M. B. and Reposa, R. E. (1983) 'Mothers in incestuous families' *International Journal of Family Therapy* 5 (2) Harron SciencePpress.

9 Women abusers — a feminist view

Val Young

Female sexual abuse is a difficult subject for a feminist to discuss objectively. Any purposeful writing needs to acknowledge the points of view of survivors, therapists and, most importantly, the children being abused, and to propose ways of moving forward.

While there are reasons why feminists limit discussions on women abusers, these reasons are valid only to feminism. It seems we are willing to go only so far in acknowledging women's negativity, and always put this into the context of patriarchal oppression. Merely stating what is, and why, offers no hope of any positive solutions.

It is disillusioning, to a lifelong feminist, to observe what seems to be a clear avoidance of the contemporary holistic principles of self-actualisation, which include the awareness that negative behaviour is one expression of a natural quality, and therefore readily transformable. Any exploration of women's negativity can be balanced by the evidence that women are more likely than men to stop abusing and seek help once they are aware of the harm they are doing to a child.

Perhaps there is also some reluctance among feminists in being the providers of yet more bad news about human beings, because of the sense of powerlessness that accompanies each series of revelations. Yet secrecy and denial perpetuate abuse, and as it is the powerless who become the abused, it will require a collective effort to develop enough strength to challenge a deeply embedded myth that even twenty-five years of feminism has failed to dispel: the purity of the mothering instinct.

Such a huge task can only be made manageable by the awareness that the ultimate (if idealistic) purpose of any discussions is to put pressure on society to take responsibility for the prevention of all forms of child abuse, rather than to reinforce the burden on victims or their representatives to report, prove and stop abuse.

Female sexual abuse is the least understood and the least believed, and carries perhaps the greatest emotive shock. Revelations in this book and elsewhere may force those still in denial to face the reality of what many children in our supposedly civilised society have to bear. Britain is a nation in which known child abusers work in children's homes and other areas of social work (only minimal police checks are carried out on potential staff) and which then affect horror at the news that yet another home is at the centre of an abuse investigation — with some relief, however, as it takes the focus off what is happening in suburban streets a mile or two away.

The real horror is the fact that child abuse, like murder, is largely a domestic crime. Since we are living, now, with the consequences of generations of child abuse (including, as we now know, female abuse) it is hard to understand what fears or fantasies about the results of acknowledging this have prevented successive governments from taking action on prevention, as they have done for the past ten years in, for instance, Australia.

Examining the reasons for the feminist resistance to acknowledging female abuse realistically provides us with clues to society's denial of the wider problem. The reasons, as those working in the field know, are to do with maintaining a status quo that is recognisably fragile. The short-sighted view is that there is no profit in prevention, and, while child abuse remains a domestic crime carried out in secrecy, it is treated as not worthy of concern, and it is left to charities and survivors' writing to counteract this. The statutory child protection workers' remit is to carry out a form of damage limitation, and previous archaic laws which decided a child was an unreliable witness resulted in a derisory small number of prosecutions. 'No one believes children' is the message. However, some members of society do believe survivors.

In the context of this book, it can be seen that the effects of female abuse on adult behaviour, political alignment or sexuality follows no clear pattern apart from one: the conviction that society as a whole has a responsibility for the reporting and prevention of all forms of child abuse.

Now that the lid has been lifted off 'the last taboo' (though there are no doubt more and worse revelations to come) it is time to forget about politicising and concentrate on the essential task. Since it is undoubtedly feminist pressure which has caused such advances in child protection as we now have, it will fall to feminists to take on an educative and advisory role in terms of female abusers. This article is one contribution to this task.

Female abuse as a threat to feminism

Until late in 1990, it was taken as fact that all child sexual abusers were male. This was the child protection agencies' experience, and was matched by survivors' stories. Women's experiences of rape, pornography, male violence, sexual assault and sexual harrassment contributed to the understanding that all abuse victims were female.

Political feminists, supported by this information, were able to prove a central theory: that sexual abuse is about power, and is one of the ways in which females are oppressed by patriarchy — the form of society in which males have all the power, and in which the male way of doing things is held in the highest esteem. (Just as an illustration, more than 90 per cent of judges are male.)

More recently, it became clear that boys were also sexually abused, and gradually a horrific and alarming picture emerged of one in four girls and one in eight boys experiencing some form of sexual abuse during childhood. Reports of multiple abuse in historically incestuous families appeared, along with cases of cult and ritual abuse and child pornography rings in which women were involved.

Inevitably, it emerged that women, too, abuse: not in itself surprising, since this possibility has been recognised in law since 1933. Information, though sparse, came not so much from survivors but from child protection workers and women's crisis centres or helplines; one or two reports came from the probation service. The first national press article appeared on 8 April 1990. Feminist contributions to such debates which followed were notably minimal, and appeared only in radical quarterlies. The most courageous attempt to tackle the subject was at a small London conference held by a lesbian group, though the organisers requested that no reports appeared.

Just as individual survivors of female abuse believed, until recently, that they were the only ones, women's project workers thought that the cases they heard about were rarities, and that abusing was one part of a pattern of 'dysfunctional' behaviour and was invariably male coerced. Along with wider political campaigning, the feminist priority was, and remains, increasing public awareness of the far greater problem of male abusers: it is accepted that over 90 per cent of abusers are male.

While there is no typical feminist, there is also no typical female abuser, and deciding that all fall into the category feminism has allotted them is in itself a form of denial which is both offensive to survivors and demeaning to feminism. While the basic tenet of feminism is correct, we as feminists are the first to be aware that all theories can be challenged, and all systems, however fair and just, can be exploited to the point of absurdity. It must also be acknowledged that many survivors are feminists (some also abused by males) and readily accept the need for women to protect each other, to the extent of holding onto their secret, effectively sitting on what felt like a time bomb.

Survivors attending the KIDSCAPE conference in London in March 1992, relieved that a responsible children's organisation had finally opened up the subject, were shocked when, a week before the conference, a press report made it clear that many feminists had known for some time that some women sexually abuse children. This report (in the women's page of the *Guardian*) questioned the wisdom of holding the conference in the light of the far greater problem of male abusers, stating that in a political context, feminists — and many social workers and other professionals — identified such women as victims of patriarchy, that is, of previous male abuse or of male or cult coercion. Whether the writer meant it or not, one implication was that women abusers were not responsible for their behaviour. The other was that a women abused as a child is likely to become an abusing adult. Survivors at the conference — including one of the women speakers, who withdrew from the platform — were deeply offended at this implication.

They also felt betrayed. Feminism, the great and powerful substitute mother, who could be relied upon to right all wrongs, had known all about female abusers and yet had kept this information out of the public arena. This was almost as painful as the child of an abusing mother realising that her favourite aunty knew and said nothing.

In the two years prior to the conference, despite wide media coverage of the subject, KIDSCAPE say they received no offers of support from feminists or formal feminist input. On the contrary, they received angry letters and phone calls from feminists berating them for bringing the subject to the attention of 'the public', though the conference was, in fact, for professionals. An opportunity was sadly lost for an important contribution to our understanding, as it was clear on the day that information is scant. The content of what local conferences there may have been — one in Scotland, the small private one in London the previous year, and results of a college research project — were not made available to KIDSCAPE.

What is now clear, from this book and from the various children's charities' files (including KIDSCAPE's own, it must be said, in which the cases had previously been considered as rarities) is that feminists in the field may have made mistakes in their analysis of women abusers, and, particularly, in not communicating their information more widely. Survivors of female abuse frequently point out that they were not believed by therapists, and ask whether child care workers allow for this possibility, or even believe children who are able to disclose this experience. Some survivors who are therapists or child protection workers did not disclose, for fear of being disbelieved, until faced with a client whose experience was similar. They, too, speak of feeling isolated even among colleagues and are now those most committed to child-focused discussions and open forums for survivors.

Child abuse is everyone's issue. However ardent and radical one's commitment to feminism, however painful the realisation that some of the women whose battles we fight are sexually abusing their children, however small the incidences are, however caring and compassionate we may be, the fact that women are capable of sexual abuse is not going to go away, and we as women, whether feminist or not, can no longer deny it.

Each survivor may have privately wondered why the subject was never mentioned in training manuals or books about survivors' experiences (if they had access to them) and each drew the conclusion that they were the only one. Or they believed that if it was never mentioned, it was impossible, and that they must have imagined it. Kathy Evert, a survivor of female sexual abuse and the writer of the first widely available book on the subject said, in 1987, that she had yet to talk to another human being who was abused by their mother or any other female.

Though it is important to respect theories, and to maintain privacy, it is more important, in any discussions about the extent and nature of child abuse, that the focus is on finding way of stopping abusive behaviour, and of putting the responsibility firmly onto the perpetrators. We hold men responsible for regulating negative male behaviour, so, in the spirit of feminism, women need to take responsibility for acknowledging negative female behaviour. Indeed, this is the only way that women can exercise some control over discussions of the subject.

One of the concerns is of a backlash from feminism's opponents, primarily men. Since male survivors are increasingly saying women do abuse it seems worthwhile to pre-empt any such backlash by preparing responses for what challenges may be made. A productive initial response would be to agree with the criticisms while pointing out that arguments distract from the main task.

Challenging the theories

There is no question that any outreach, or official attempts to stop
abuse or confront abusers, cannot be effective without a realistic
recognition of who abusers are, how they think about themselves, and
an acceptance of the true nature and extent of child abuse. There is no
typical abuser, though there are commonalities. There is no single
way of communicating with them.

No one denies that more than 90 per cent of sexual abusers are
male, and that this is a reflection of, and a product of, the power of an
abusive patriarchy which allows it to continue. Yet the academic
feminist belief that all sexual abuse is always about the abuse of power
(that is, the wish to control) is questionable. This theory requires us to
accept that women are not 'powerful' enough to initiate abuse, and
that they are most likely to be former abuse victims perpetuating their
own experiences. This does not give a complete picture.

The greatest challenge to this theory is the existence of women
sexual abusers who are nothing like victims, and, more significantly,
of the greater majority of survivors of female (and male) abuse who
have never resorted to abusive behaviour. Those survivors free to
speak also talk of women being sole abusers, which contradicts the
male-coercion theory.

How have the accepted theories arisen? Could feminist academics
have made assumptions, or, more likely, found the exposure of
patriarchal forms of abuse more urgent?

For instance, it is true that sexual abuse can be about unconsciously re-creating childhood experiences, and about the misuse of
power. It can also be about any of the following: anger, self-
gratification, objectifying children, comfort, possessiveness, a distorted type of love, transference of the abuser's suppressed sexuality,
immaturity, sadism, making money out of pornography, aggression,
a form of sexual addiction, and, frequently, the misinterpretation of a
child's natural sensuality as sexuality. Some abusers claim they are
'educating' their children about their own sexuality. Psychologists
observe that abusers have low (or zero) self-worth and are out of touch
with themselves, either because of substance dependency or personality disorders, including psychotic episodes. 'Male' behaviour? Primarily, yes.

But how can we classify this when it is women who are doing it? Is
it still 'male' behaviour? As it is, obviously, the children who are the
victims, it is hard for even the most compassionate survivor to define
exactly what such women are victims of. Those who try to do this
grow up feeling pity for their abusers, and find it impossible to
recognise the extent of their own damage, and therefore to heal.

Abusers also know about the victim theory. Part of abuse is that children are led to believe that they are responsible for their abusers' behaviour, and this (along with threats) ensures their silence. Children accept their abusers' adoption of victim or martyr status. When your life depends on pleasing the person who cares for you, you have no choice but to believe what they say about themselves. Abusers exploit this too. That is why what they do is called 'abuse'. Abusers — consciously or unconsciously — have a considerable investment in their own survival, and therefore their priority is self-protection. This includes controlling a child so that the family secrets are not revealed.

Adopting the role of victim is therefore a classic abusers' stance, so giving any abuser such reasons or explanations is very dangerous — it may encourage them to think of themselves as not responsible for their behaviour, and thus to continue abusing. Reputable therapists who work with such abusers set as a target that the abuse should stop before dealing with the client's own experiences of childhood abuse.

Any theory or belief can be misused. Perhaps if they were all abandoned, sexual abusers would stop justifying themselves. It is in any case irrelevant what the abuser thought he or she was doing. Child abuse is always measured by the effect on the child, never the intentions of the abuser.

Through feminism, we have arrived at a set of values for women who are destructive towards adults, and have, perhaps unwisely, applied these to those abusing children. We see them as desperate mimics, acting out male aggression, often to protect a child from worse abuse. We understand that battered women kill men in self-defence, and have actively campaigned (not always successfully) for lenient sentences.

What risks are there in widening discussions of female abuse? A lessening of responsibility by men to see males as the main perpetrators? Providing vindication for feminism's opponents? Perhaps. The information could be used against women in general, and there is a risk that rapists (for example) may plead for clemency on the grounds their mothers abused them — the 'eroticisation of anger' theory, and a new twist to an old argument. Stating that exposure of women as abusers could affect the credibility of feminism is reasonable; however, to survivors this comes across as having to carry the responsibility for protecting an abusive status quo, just as they were made to do as children. Exposing mother is not attacking feminism. That said, for women to be constantly perceived as 'victims' is in itself disempowering as it helps to maintain women's internalised patriarchal attitudes. As we know, these inevitably lead to abusive and self-abusive behaviour.

There is no denying that our society remains abusive to women, who are constantly exposed to mild and extreme forms of sexism.

Every step forward in terms of legislation is accompanied by a
wearying sexist and homophobic backlash, such as reports on
women's violence, films about women murderers, or the increased
expectations for actresses to appear nude in explicit sex scenes on
stage, on TV and even in opera. Women are continually portrayed
either as sex objects or as vacant creatures whose lives are concerned
only with a choice of washing powder or chips or boys without
dandruff. Every time there is a successful sexual harassment case, you
can be sure men pop up and claim that they, too, have been harassed
by voracious women. The 'wicked stepmother' makes her annual
appearance. A young actress who becomes the mistress of a powerful
married politician finds herself exposed as the 'scarlet woman'.
Women who are strong, independent, resourceful and self-
responsible are considered (negatively) as 'masculine'.

Men continue to claim that women have the real power, and that
everything which goes wrong in society is women's fault (particularly
mother's) ever since Eve ate the forbidden fruit. Every so often, a
'whither feminism?' book appears, followed by a highly publicised
debate. We may have better laws, but it takes more than a generation
for an ideology to be accepted. We remain surprised at how small the
feminist movement is, yet men continue to attack it.

The credibility gap in society — including among many women —
about the validity of feminism has a great deal to do with an unrealistic
view of women, as well as an inaccurate view of feminism. The whole
point of feminism is individual women's self-definition, and the
respecting of differences. Politically, feminism is primarily about
empowering women (and other oppressed minorities) and gaining
them rights equal to, not greater than, men's. Feminism is basically
humanism, though it is as impossible to make blanket statements
about feminists as it is to make them about women.

All the feminist claims about the position of women in society are
true. What is also true, and rarely addressed objectively by academic
feminists, is that some women, within the limited power that they
have, can be abusive, vicious, cruel, possessive, domineering, violent,
manipulative, aggressive, dishonest, self-deceptive, and criminal.
While behaviour may be a reaction against patriarchal oppression, no
one can make another adult human being feel in a particular way. We
need to establish when female abuse is reactive, absent-minded, or
opportunist, and when it is deliberate, premeditated and continuous.

The reality of female abusers

Why is it so hard to believe that some women initiate sexual abuse? As
it is still women who have the greater care of children, it is they who

are the closest and most likely victims of women's sexual aggression. It is true that many such women are out of touch with themselves, possibly addictive, disturbed, perhaps mentally ill, exhausted, depressed, trapped, despairing and frustrated. It is also true that some women who remember in later life that they were abused as children may suddenly recognise that their behaviour to their own children is abusive.

However, it beggars belief to claim that all abusing women are victims of patriarchal oppression and are merely mimicking male behaviour.

You might as well believe that abusive men are also all victims, or are mimicking women, an idea totally unacceptable to feminists and, for that matter, to most men. (Feminist men, though they may perceive themselves as humanists, however, recognise that we are to an extent all oppressed by the peculiarly British form of heirarchical society which values power and wealth above love and human decency.)

Part of sexism is the belief that women are innocent and somehow sexually dormant until claimed and sexualised by a man. So it is actually sexist, rather than feminist, to disbelieve initiatory female sexual abuse.

Feminism recognises that it is feminine to be strong, powerful, assertive, self-directing, decisive, creative, and responsible for our own sexuality. This appears to mean that one cannot be both feminist and a victim. Or perhaps that women abusers (being victims) do not 'qualify' as feminists. Just as all theories can be rendered absurd, all systems, however positive and just, are open to exploitation. For the sake of the innocent, we allow the same rights to the guilty and think the risk that they will exploit this is 'acceptable', despite knowing that abusers are experts at such exploitation. Sooner or later, someone will ask if any feminists are abusing their children, and whether this is why they don't like the subject discussed.

It is hardly surprising that abusive women are the first to exploit feminism, picking out the parts they like (self-empowerment, assertion, the right to be heard and validated) and ignoring the concepts of co-operation, individual boundaries, equality and respect for others. Mothers who do this are considered in some branches of psychiatry to be narcissistic and grandiose. They grant themselves automatic rights over the lives of their children, and assume that a natural biological function brings with it sudden wisdom and total power. Many a young girl, sexually abused or not, is expected by her mother (or other female carer) to minimise her own needs and to be attentive, caring, supportive, tolerant, reliable, entertaining, self-sacrificing, yielding, affectionate, respectful, even reverent, forgiving and — of course — motherly.

This has long been understood by feminists and therapists alike, who see such mothers as immature, politically unaware, ignorant, or copying their own female carers, or (because they are victims) demanding of their children what they never had themselves or what they cannot get from partners. We feel sorry for them; seeing them as wartime or ghettoised mothers, damaged, needy people, and we feel guilty naming their behaviour as abusive while observing that this mental and emotional abuse is no different from the way many men treat their wives. The sexual aspect of this insidious and damaging behaviour in women has been side-stepped by feminist academics, who tend to state that it is patriarchy which causes girls to be raised to be all things to all people, and sacrifice their own needs. In feminist therapy, problems in young women which are self-destructive are seen either as direct results of this type of upbringing or the effects of sexual abuse by a male.

In one of the most important books of the decade, which dealt with women's sexually addictive behaviour, there was not one case mentioned of a girl sexually abused by a woman. It seems the issue was side-stepped in an otherwise compassionate book which traced all forms of destructive and self-destructive women's behaviour to childhood experiences of abuse.

While we can understand that women who may be abusive in non-sexual ways do not recognise their behaviour as such, are we asked to believe that they do not know that sex is where to draw the line? If we accept that sexual abuse is compulsive behaviour, we would then need to understand that they merely see children as objects for their private use, and do not care or think about the consequences. We could then rationalise this by believing that these women unwittingly reflect patriarchy's attitude to powerless children, valuing themselves no less than they value their children because they are oppressed women. However, this does not hold, as they apparently value themselves enough to expect sexual and other forms of gratification.

If such women are mimicking their male partners' behaviour, men ask where men learned it, and we are back to the Eve principle. How far can we go in allotting ancestral blame? At what point can we expect adults to take responsibility for their abusive behaviour?

We cannot assume that all women who have experienced self-denying mothering perpetuate it. It is more likely that today's mother works hard on herself to prevent behaving in this way to her own children. Many women abused by women distance themselves from their children, afraid of harming them, and many, of course, avoid any contact with children at all.

There is another aspect to consider in asking how patriarchy influences women to abuse. Women who cannot cope with their own sexuality, and who may have sexual feelings towards children, decide that it is the children who are seductive — one legacy of the Freudian 'Oedipal' theory, later withdrawn. Patriarchy, religion and Victorian values have meant that many girls are (as their mothers were) punished for their natural sexuality. Often this is also because their mothers are jealous of their naturalness or embarrassed by their sexuality, setting up a lifelong association between sex and shame. This is considered a 'female' reaction, while abusing is a 'male' reaction to children's natural sexuality.

Other girls, as we now know, are exploited and used for the sexual gratification of older women — mothers, stepmothers, grandmothers and aunts; older girls have been known to use sex games as forms of punishment for younger ones. This contradicts those theorists who see female abusers as trapped in historically incestuous families, or controlled by cults, or coerced by male partners, or who collude to prevent the child from worse abuse.

Various aspects of motherhood and parenting have headed the agenda at almost every post-war feminist conference and the achievements have been considerable in terms of mothers' rights: pregnancy leave, support for abortion, amniocentesis and other tests, more choice over birthing methods, single mothers' housing and allowances, child benefits paid to mothers, legal protection from abusive male partners, separate taxation, nursery and creche provision (where funding permits), and much more — not the least, widespread information.

Our new approach to motherhood surely did not need to include the message that planned and deliberate sex with your son or daughter is a blatant reversal of the carer–child relationship, and an obscene distortion of a natural bond? If it did, then it seems we must endeavour to state this message.

Who are the real victims? Can there be any argument, feminist or otherwise, about this? Squabbles about who the greater victim is are in any case ridiculous, and surely now beside the point.

A positive role for feminists

When dealing with child sexual abuse, there is little value in theories, academic studies, or statistics. As has been shown, it is easy to demolish theories. All these traditionally 'masculine' approaches were once important, as it was male beliefs which had to be challenged, and feminists needed to speak to them in their own language. We need to take another approach, and to use women's language. Just as 'victim' and 'survivor' communicate the severity of abuse, we have a graphic and unmistakable vocabulary which allows universal recognition of rapists as hunters and perpetrators of brutal crimes, paedophiles as predators, and sexual abusers as men who methodically violate their children. These are active, male, aggressive words, and full of menace. It is understandable why female sexual abuse is, to many, inexpressible.

Perhaps a first step is to create a child-focused language, as we need, in any case, to stop analysing abusers and trying to explain their actions. Victims and survivors spend much of their lives trying to do this. It would also be valuable to stop thinking about 'treatment' plans, as if abusing was an illness that could be cured. We may also have to forget about debating female abuse in a politically correct context, as it will require a considerable stretch of the imagination to continue providing what seem to be excuses, and a waste of energy and effort that can be better used.

Apologist theories are out of date, and self-responsibility is the issue of the 1990s in every area of life, whether it is saving the planet, personal growth, recovery from addiction, or buying a pension plan.

At present the resources aimed at children are for letting them know that it's OK to tell, rescuing them, attempting to identify abusive families and working with them, attempting to prosecute perpetrators, providing survivors with supportive counselling and therapy. Though these are enormous steps forward, they also still place the responsibility on children to report abuse.

What is needed is a clear message to abusers. What we, as feminists, could be doing is accepting that equal rights means equal responsibility and using whatever means possible to put pressure on society to inform abusers that they should stop, and of the harmful effects of abuse on their victims' lives.

The Home Office surely has a duty to issue frequent and widespread warnings about the nature of the crimes of child abuse and the likely sentences. Money is spent on advising us of the dangers (and consequences) of drinking and driving, of not paying our TV licence or Poll Tax, or of jumping a red traffic light, or of unprotected sex. We know that theft, fraud and insider trading are illegal and carry stiff prison sentences. What the Government appears to be saying is that sexual abuse, since it happens mostly in the home and is kept secret, does not cost society any money, so is not worthy of concern.

Bodies such as the Press Council need to be asked to produce guidelines for responsible reporting about sexual abuse, bearing in mind the tendency of some newspapers to give the parents' side of the story and to castigate social workers — including giving prominence to cases where social workers abuse children in their care or hold them responsible for the abuse, and in some cases murder, of a child known to be at risk.

No steps will be taken to care for children currently being abused by women, or of adult survivors, until realistic information is available and healthcare services alerted. Since therapists and child care workers are bound by rules of confidentiality, the most reliable source of information (as with the first conferences and books about male sexual abusers) will come from survivors, though no one would ask them to assume responsibility for this educative role, nor to give up their anonymity.

We could spend the next 50 years researching and exposing the reasons for and the nature and extent of child abuse. It seems, however, more urgent to create a new approach for preventing it, as it is becoming impossible to define.

We now know that sexual abuse never exists alone, and that in adult survivors it affects a great deal more than sexuality. If we accept the feminist view and cannot separate women abusers from cults or incestuous families, we cannot therefore consider abuse as gender-specific, nor is it only 'sexual' abuse.

Reaching women through the few feminist outlets we have is unrealistic. Not all women are feminists. Most women, trying to get on with their lives, do not read radical publications, academic books or MA dissertations, and nor do they have access to professional magazines, such as those read by doctors, social workers or counsellors. Even in Central London, there are thousands of women who have never heard of Wesley House and do not know that there are seven women's centres in the Borough of Camden alone. Many who do know feel unsure about using them. Perhaps they are afraid of powerful women? If they have a history of abuse by females, this would not be surprising.

If it is true that 'only' five per cent of abusers are women, reaching them is not going to be a mammoth task. If they are male-coerced, they need to be told that it is safe to report this. What is the best way to reach them, accepting that the male-dominated media is unlikely to co-operate? Police stations which have domestic violence units often display posters about incest helplines. As it is mostly women who tramp to post offices to collect child benefits, perhaps posters could be displayed here too.

Another possibility is the health services. Women see a variety of professionals around the time of pregnancy; these professionals have a unique opportunity for sensitive assessment of the woman's domestic life and her ability to nurture a child. If the woman is being forced by a male to abuse a child, provision of information on domestic violence services could be given routinely with ante-natal care.

A better understanding of post-natal depression and a less sentimental approach to motherhood could allow women safe expression of their negative feelings towards small children. At present health visitors tend to be the first to hear about new mothers' doubts. Again, the popular media could approach the subject less unrealistically. As an example, the usually responsible and widely read magazine *Practical Parenting* headlined a recent issue: 'Bonding with baby — a love affair that begins at birth'. The feature itself opened with: 'As you hold your baby in your arms for the very first time, so begins *the most powerful and passionate love affair you'll ever know*' (my italics). Both these statements were in fact misleading as the feature itself was realistic and fair, if a little coy. One can only assume that such headlines increase the readership, and that some mothers hope to feel 'passionate love' for their babies as much as they want to bask in possibly their first experience of unconditional love.

It is just as likely that some women experience the overwhelming sensuality of childbirth, breast-feeding and daily intimate care as sexual, and are unable to share this with anyone. It is certainly some abuse survivors' experience that their mother (or carer) expressed a lustful, passionate and possessive attitude towards them. It has been noted elsewhere, and particularly in the more honest US publications, that a child can experience this attitude as sexually abusive, even if actual sexual contact never took place.

Such frank information, usually only available between therapists working with survivors, could be of great benefit to new mothers, and more importantly to their children, should any general publication be courageous enough to risk making it available. Here, feminists, always willing to tackle difficult issues, could take the lead, remembering to be non-judgemental, uncompromising, and respecting and validating different needs — that is, being active and receptive rather than analytical and producing yet more labels, which is merely a controlling device.

Another valuable initiative could also provide information about mothers' real experiences, and information about women abusers, to the services sector, and find ways of monitoring it to be certain it is not being misused. Care should be taken that survivors' input is included. There is also an urgent need for recognising which women — feminist or not — are most likely to suffer from publicity about female abusers: lesbian mothers seeking custody, and those applying to adopt. These women are likely to be the primary targets of self-righteous heterosexist attacks. It is assumed in much of society, thanks to irresponsible reporting, that all paedophiles are homosexual, so it will inevitably be assumed, wrongly, that all female child abusers are lesbians. This belief can hopefully be counteracted with the information that child abusers objectify their victims to the extent that their gender becomes irrelevant.

It would be naïve to underestimate the enormity of the task of communicating with abusers, male or female. It would be an even greater task to change society's attitude to the nature of abuse. What the public, the media, our legislators and judiciary, and many branches of the health service still fail to understand is that sexual abusers are not necessarily psychotic 'monsters' or even a sick minority: some are just as likely to be apparently healthy, well-educated and financially successful adults. Mainly interested in self-gratification, they see children as freely available to meet their needs. Perhaps a first step would be to make this clear.

Part 2

Survivors

Introduction to part 2

This section has been written by men and women who have been sexually abused during childhood by women. Although many of the survivors wanted to be known by their real names, for legal reasons this was not possible. Therefore, all the names and biographical details have been changed.

The vast majority of the survivors said that the abuse caused them life-long distress, though a few said that it had not adversely affected them. Many commented on how lonely and isolated they felt, and how difficult it has been for them to come to terms with what happened. One of the most common themes for the survivors of sexual abuse by mothers is the life-long quest they have been on to find mother love and bonding. Despite the emotional, physical and psychological damage inflicted on them, many of these survivors have managed to cope with taking care of their elderly mothers. Some have, through therapy, self-help and the support of friends and family, found a way to cope with their own pain and go on to lead productive lives.

For most of the survivors who have contributed to this book, taking life one day at a time and finding personal and professional help has allowed them to go forward. In sharing their experiences, they are helping others to be comforted that they are not alone and that there is hope for healing. For their help in compiling this book and for having the courage to speak out, these men and women have my deepest admiration and gratitude.

MOTHERS' DAY

How do I celebrate Mothers' Day
With a Mother I wish was dead
Or that I had never been born
Or that she was not my mother

Do I send a bunch of flowers
Or a card
To a woman who gave birth to me
And then hated me

Who needed to kill
What life and joy I possessed
My spontaneity and self-worth
To leave me an empty shell
Like herself

An horrific and
Pathetic vampire
Who could only exist
Through sucking
The emotional life-blood
of her child

A woman whose
Only sexual fulfilment
Was, to arouse
Her daughter
And then punish her
For having the orgasmic release
She could not experience herself

A sadistic mutilation
Of my sexuality
Leaving me
With painful
And humiliating
Images and fantasies

A sexuality labelled perverted
With shame and self-loathing
Which has driven me
Many times
To the brink of despair
And the desire
To kill myself

A self-hate
Which has made me
Unable
To touch my daughter
Without the fear
Of contaminating her

So how do I celebrate Mothers' Day
Do I send a card
Or a bunch of flowers
To an old, shrivelled woman
Who has always existed
In the shadows
Of the semi-dead

So afraid
Of the pain within herself
That all feelings must be killed
In herself
And her children
And joy and love never experienced

Do I add to her pain?
Or to my own?

Pat Bell

Pat Bell works as a gardener, is divorced and lives with her teenage daughter and a house full of dogs and cats. She has undergone much psychotherapy of the last ten years and has done some training as a humanistic psychotherapist. She only recently recognised that she was sexually abused as a young child by her mother. She is still struggling to believe it and deal with its effects through therapy. Pat cares deeply about her mother, although at the moment chooses not to have any direct contact with her.

10 Women survivors' stories

Eleanor Stevens

Eleanor Stevens is from the Home Counties, is divorced and lives alone. She has 3 children aged between 25 and 35. Eleanor is 53 years old.

Eleanor's story

It was a Sunday morning in summer. The kids were playing in the garden, my husband was working in his studio, my parents were on the motorway coming for their fortnightly visit, and I was in the kitchen preparing lunch. What appears to be a normal domestic scene was not, for I was drunk, at 10 am on a Sunday morning. I could still operate, I could do the cooking, etc. but I was numbing a fear that lay deep within me. A fear that I could not put a face or name to but it was ruining my life. After several more of these sham Sundays that got worse and worse as time went on, plus a few attempts at slashing my wrists and a spell in a mental hospital I knew I had to seek help and then confront that fear head on. Confront it, look at it full in the face and then leave it behind. So began my journey to truth.

I was born in 1939 just a month before war was declared. My parents were a young couple, recently married, and living in the suburbs of Birmingham. My mother didn't want to get married and she certainly didn't want to become pregnant and give birth but it was the done thing in those days and pressure had been put upon her to conform. When I was born and was a girl it was like the end of the world for her. At first she wouldn't pick me up, let alone care for me, but yet again pressure was put on her and she did as she was told. For a while things were OK but as the midwives and other carers left, things deteriorated. My father, because of ill health, didn't join the armed forces as such but was a member of 'Dad's Army' so together with his job he was away from home for large chunks of each day. This left my mother and me alone in the house. At first the abuse was mild. She used to lie me on the bed, take off my nappy and gently stroke between my legs. She never said anything but her eyes never left my face. Neither did she make any attempt to penetrate me, just the rhythmic stroking, up and down, up and down. Somehow I soon learnt that by wetting myself I broke her trance and she would stop. After gently scolding me, she would put me in a clean nappy and put me back in my cot, so ending the nightmare for that day. This went on for two or three years, past the time when I was out of nappies. She would suddenly come, squat down beside me whilst I stood up. She would put her left arm around my shoulders and hold up my dress with her left hand. Pulling down my knickers with her right hand she would then once again begin that awful stroking. I learnt to wet myself as soon as possible. The rest never varied, a gentle scolding and then a complete change of clothing and it was as if it never happened. She then became my 'normal mummy'. The end came when she sent me to ballet school. One day I wet myself there and told the concerned teachers 'Oh it is what I always do, it is what my mummy wants'. When she came to fetch me that day there was a lot of whispered worried consultation. My mother called me a wicked naughty girl for telling such awful lies. Needless to say I never went to ballet again.

After that life was reasonably normal for a time. My mother looked after me in as much as she fed and clothed me but there was no sign of normal love, she never played with me or read to me. I was just given toys and left to amuse myself. She took me with her from room to room in the house but never did she talk directly to me.

One fateful day she took me into the bathroom with her. I was to play on the floor with my toys whilst she had a bath. When she got out she put the lid of the toilet down and sat on it. Bracing one leg on the bath and the other on the side of the airing cupboard she drew me to her. She took my hands and guided them towards her genitals. Looking me full in the face once again she told me that inside that hole was a warm cosy nest where I had first been until I was big enough and then I had just popped out. She encouraged me to find that cosy nest. I was terrified, with my child's logic, I thought that if I had just popped out what was to stop me from popping back in. Then I would be lost forever and nobody but my mother would know where I was.

However, she persisted and slowly with my tiny child's hands I tried to do as she wanted. Her breathing grew heavy and faster and eventually she threw back her head and let out a large scream. A climax of course, but I could not understand what was happening. Then she let me go, came back to the mummy I could cope with and life went on.

When this happened again I didn't want to do as she asked and I tried to keep my hands away from her. However much she persisted so did I and eventually she roughly took me by the arm and pulled me into my bedroom, shutting the door behind me. She didn't lock it but she didn't need to. Houses in the 1930s had their handles two-thirds of the way up and it was a round knob that had to be rotated. No way could I reach it let alone turn it. I was to all intents and purposes locked in. There I remained until the next day. In the morning she came in, my normal mummy, and without making any comment she cleared up the mess I had made, washed and dressed me and took me down to breakfast. Life went on.

This went on for some time and the fear within me grew. If I did as she asked she became the mummy I didn't like but if I didn't she shut me in my room. I was trapped and full of fear. I became a very unhappy child indeed. This of course caused comments from other people, relatives, neighbours, etc., but when I tried to tell them why I was so unhappy all I ever got in reply was 'But she is your mummy dear, of course she wants a cuddle'. They could not, or would not, understand, so there I was alone with my fear.

Eventually because of my now obvious distress and the resulting questions from people the abuse did stop and I pushed the memories away, but the fear stayed with me.

As I grew older I learnt that as long as I was busy I could cope with life. I married early, had three children and ran a bed and breakfast house for PE students. I also had a part-time job in a shop, ran a guide unit, went to night school, joined the local consumer association; the list was endless. But I couldn't run for ever and as the fear grew my life began to crumble and that was when I realised that I had to get myself some help. Eventually I found a counsellor with whom I could work and slowly the memories began to surface. It has taken eight long years for the memories to fully surface and for me to learn how to deal with them. My life has changed completely during those years. I have lost my marriage, my beautiful home and my job but I have gained so much more. Now I have control over my life, I am happy and at peace. The journey has been long and hard but worth it.

During these years I have learnt a lot and perhaps it may be of some help to others on the same journey to share some of my experiences. The very first thing to do is to find a counsellor who you feel you can truly trust and with whom you are at ease. This may not be the most obvious person or indeed the first one you approach. For me there were many false starts but when I met Robert I knew at once I could work with him. I learnt to trust what he said and at least to try the things he suggested I should do. One of the first things he did was to send me away to a convent at very regular intervals. He said I needed a place where I could find peace away from the turmoil of my life. 'Help!' was my first reaction, 'what am I doing here?' But once again I learnt to trust this small community of Anglican nuns. The love they have shown me has been endless. Many, many times they have taken me in, 'patched me up' with regular meals, rest, and love, and then sent me off on my journey again. To them I offer my heartfelt thanks — I will be back!! Next I needed to build up a small circle of friends that knew what I was doing and were willing to help me. Through group sessions at Robert's I met these people. There is Jane who has a small farm not far away. Once I had learnt to trust her, and that was not easy for my natural inclination is to mistrust all women, I learnt to 'role-play' with her and she would become my mummy whilst I hurled the anger and abuse at her that I have never done with my real mother. There is a monk who is at an abbey not far away; I can always ring him up and he will sit with me for an hour, perhaps while I just cry; and there are other abused people on the same journey. All have been vitally necessary for me and to all I say 'Thank you'.

Once I had a little peace in my life, a safe place to go to and friends to help me the memories began to surface. I shall never forget the first time I faced Robert and said 'I have been sexually abused by my mother'. I couldn't believe my own ears — what was I saying? This couldn't be true, it was a pack of wicked lies, I really must be crazy. It seemed as if my voice was saying one thing whilst my mind was rejecting it at the same time. But that is what I had been doing for over forty years. It was perhaps the biggest hurdle I had to get over. I had to believe myself. It wasn't easy and it took a long time. I had to say it over and over again and my supporters had to keep reflecting it back to me before, in the end, even I had to believe it. Once I did that I began to make progress. I read what little I could find on the subject, talked about it a lot and now at long last I have come to terms with it.

That then has been my journey to truth. It has taken a long time, the best part of eight years and is perhaps the hardest thing I have ever done in my life, but it has been the most worthwhile. Now I am at peace.

Lynne Marie

Lynne Marie is 40 years old, she is married and has one child. She is from the midwest in the United States.

Lynne's story

I grew up in small towns in the Midwest, USA. I was sexually, verbally, physically and emotionally abused by my mother, whom I know was at least physically abused by her father. The effects of abuse continue to wreak havoc with every aspect of my life.

My parents married when they were in their thirties. It was the first marriage for both of them. I think they finally married to get away from the obligations and bad situations they were experiencing at home. My father was hearing impaired and relied heavily on my mother. She was more than willing to dominate him as she later would me. I was born a little less than a year after they were wed. Mother said she had me so she would have someone to love her. No other children followed.

I was a disappointment from the very beginning. Mother had a difficult delivery with several serious complications. Both my parents hoped for a healthy baby boy. I was a sickly female. If Mother had to have a girl, she wanted a very petite young lady. Instead, I was an average-sized tomboy.

My father was absent most of the time due to his work. Mother slept with me nearly every night as far back as I can remember. The initial memories of abuse were that of being fondled, which probably began in infancy. By the time I was three years old, Mother was having me touch her as well. Later I was introduced to oral sex. This sort of behaviour occurred almost nightly until I was twelve years of age. This in itself was horrible enough; but by the time I entered school, Mother started torturing me in sexual ways.

The first time I remember being sexually tortured was when Mother took me into a wooded area fondled me, had oral sex with me, and inserted her fingers into my vagina. I cried and screamed because of the severe pain. This only made Mother angry; so to shut me up and to threatened me, she picked up a large stick and shoved it inside my vagina. This incident taught me the lesson of silence and to turn off feelings of pain.

At age five, I wanted some attention from Mother; but she was too busy ironing. I accidentally knocked off the old sprinkling bottle and broke it. Mother was furious. She dragged me off to the bedroom and chained me, spread eagled, to the bed. Then she took a piece of the broken glass and lacerated the inside of my vagina with it.

Another time Mother got angry with me for some sort of infraction. My punishment on this occasion was an ice pick in my anus. I suffered from a perforated rectum.

One December Mother and I were going to sleep on a hide-a-bed in the living room, because it was too cold to sleep in the unheated upstairs bedroom. Mother began stroking my genitals. Then she put her fingers inside me. I knew if I fought back or made any noises, It would only make matters worse for me. It was Christmas time, and our tree stood near by. I just concentrated on it and its twinkling lights. I shut everything else out including my emotions. It's been so many years since then, but I still demolish our Christmas tree at least once during the holiday season.

There was one time when Mother put a candle in my vagina. I must have done something to provoke her, but I have no idea what it was. Anything would set her off, from my presence to the weather conditions.

Once I picked a bouquet of flowers for my Mother from our neighbour's garden without permission. Mother fumed. She forced me onto the dirt floor of our shed. She sat on top of me to hold me down while she pried my legs apart and shoved the thorny rose stems into my body. Since that time, I've never been able to pick flowers. Even accepting them as a gift is hard for me.

I recall being in bed against the wall one night. Mother had an infection in her fingers. The doctor had given her some medicine to put on her wounds. It turned her hands purple. Mother came into my room and molested me. I remember feeling so trapped by that wall and those purple hands coming after me, touching me. I'm still frightened by the colour purple, and I will not sleep next to a wall.

Mother was knitting one afternoon. I showed up from school. It was poor timing on my part, apparently my presence distracted Mother, and she got very angry with me. Mother tied me down to the coffee table and poked a knitting needle into my rectum.

Scissors were another instrument of torture. I was cutting paper dolls on my bed and accidentally cut a tiny hole in the bedspread. As punishment, Mother once again tied me to the bed and clipped the edges of my vaginal opening. A wave of nausea sweeps over me every time I have to use a pair of scissors.

There was a time when Mother forced the handle of a wooden spoon into my vagina. She'd also prod inside of me with a coat hanger. Mother would use pencils to pry at my inner parts. Lit cigarettes were put inside of me, too.

Abuse also took place when Mother would take a bath with me. At eight years old, I was still made to bathe with her. Mother would fondle me and coerce me into touching her breasts and genitals. I recall a time when I objected to this. Consequently Mother took a bath brush and put it inside of me. When I attempted to resist, Mother held me under the water to get me to co-operate. I choked on the water and couldn't breathe. To this day, I can only take showers, not baths.

Mother never hit me or left any outward signs of abuse. She always preached that I would have to learn to control my temper the way she had. This message was a contradiction; but Mother thought that as long as she wasn't hitting me, she wasn't abusing me. If she lacked the energy that torture required, Mother would simply lock me up in a closet, attic or basement until she calmed down or needed me for something. There were times when I'd be locked up for a couple of days with no place to go to the bathroom, nothing to eat, and nothing to drink. Mother told me that the confinement was for my own good. Mother used locking me up as a way to control any beatings she might have the urge to inflict upon me. When I was locked up, Mother knew she wouldn't be tempted to hit me. I would have preferred beatings to the sexual abuse and torture, but sometimes even the torture felt better than receiving no attention at all or being totally neglected.

Once when I was locked in the basement, there was a live turkey down there. My parents had won it for Thanksgiving. I didn't know it was to be killed and eaten. I made friends with the turkey while we were locked up together. Then Dad took the turkey to be killed. At Thanksgiving dinner, I couldn't eat it. Later Mother fed me tabasco sauce and anchovy paste. When I threw up, Mother tied me to the kitchen table and inserted an old-fashioned potato masher inside me. Still today I can't eat turkey; I get extremely ill. I even break out in a rash on my hands if I handle turkey meat. One Thanksgiving had been destroyed; and years upon years, there has been no traditional turkey at Thanksgiving.

At the only birthday party I can recall, Mother commented on how pretty I looked. Then she summoned me into the house away from my guests. I knew what she wanted, and I refused to go inside. Mother sent my playmates home. After they left, she smeared dog faeces all over me and told me I was shit. I've felt like that ever since, and I have no desire to look appealing again.

As I got older, I started to develop. Hair grew in places where I'd never had any before. At age twelve, I was too young to have it, according to Mother. Then she sat me on the toilet and shaved all the hair off. I felt that I couldn't even mature properly. I was embarrassed, humiliated and ashamed. It was the last physical and sexual abuse I remember, but Mother never quit sleeping with me until I went away to college at age eighteen. I haven't a clue as to why those abuses and torture stopped so suddenly then. I just thank God that they did, but Mother still continues to abuse me emotionally and verbally. Manipulation through guilt is her favourite ploy.

I was threatened not to tell anything that went on in our house; but age ten, I attempted to tell the nun who was my catechism teacher. She slapped me across the face telling me never to lie and to honour my parents. I never found the courage to tell anyone again until just recently when I began therapy with a very special, caring, and understanding woman.

I was once in a support group for incest survivors. Since the incidence of women abusers isn't often heard of, I felt extremely out of place in this group where all the abusers had been men. I then found and joined a different support group in which the abusers were both male and female. I felt more like I belonged, but my fear of people prevented me from continuing with the group.

I have been diagnosed as having multiple personality disorder. With the help of my therapist, I am working toward integration. It will probably take a lot more time before that happens though.

I am also afraid to go out of the house alone. I find it necessary to have someone accompany me most places, and then I still can't go away for very long periods of time — I can only cope comfortably with a few hours, I'm usually very shy and withdrawn.

There is an eating disorder, too. At first I overate to avoid attracting anyone's sexual attention. I used the excess weight to keep people at a distance and to feel somehow protected. Now I don't eat much of anything. I lost approximately 200 pounds in fifteen months. I just want to disappear, so everyone will leave me alone. If they can't see me, they can't find me to hurt me. The not eating could subconsciously be some sort of death wish, too.

I suffer from periods of severe depression, as well. There have been times when I have seriously attempted suicide. I have been hospitalised on four occasions for emotional problems. I've been on several types of medication, none of which helped to any great extent.

I have a problem with self-mutilation. This is not a suicide attempt! The cutting works as a release. I don't feel the physical pain until the cutting is done and over with. I am suffering and miserable, but no one can see it. The cuts make it visible. They make it real and justified to me. I often feel so unreal. When I see the blood, I know that I am real. By letting some of the blood out of my body, I feel that I am also letting out some of the suffering and pain.

I have been married for almost twenty years. I have one child, a girl. She is my special miracle, since doctors said I'd probably never have any children because of the internal damage. My abuse has caused additional problems in my family life. Intimacy with my husband is difficult. I feel no desire or arousal. I've learned to shut that part of me off completely. I do not have orgasms except on rare occasions, after which I always cry. I suppose I feel guilty for experiencing pleasure in a sexual way. I am tender and loving toward my husband, but sex makes me feel used. I just want to get it over with.

I don't mind non-sexual touching from those few I can trust, but I can't stand to touch other people. Mother taught me to be sensual in my touching, and I'm afraid I'll touch someone in the wrong way. This, of course, has created difficulties touching and bonding with my daughter. I know adults who were abused as children can sometimes continue the abuse with their own children. I've always had the fear of hurting my daughter.

These memories are very new to me, and I'm being troubled by flashbacks. I know there are even more memories to come. I have no feelings as far as these memories are concerned. I have learned to shut down my feelings. I'm not even appalled that these things could happen to any child anywhere. I have to relearn how to feel. I'm not angry with my Mother either. I think that is part of the multiple personality disorder. The abuse did not happen to me; it happened to one of the other personalities. Emotionally, I can't relate to the abuse even though my life has been so adversely effected by it.

My father died a short time ago. That's when I really went over the edge. My Dad always fell short of my expectations. I guess I always hoped he'd rescue me from Mother. Then when he died, I knew I'd be alone to cope with my Mother until one of us died too.

I believe Dad didn't know at first what was going on, but I can't believe that he didn't know as time passed. He must have wondered about the hospitalisations and numerous trips to doctors. It was always a different doctor or a different hospital. What excuses did Mother give everyone for my many injuries?

We were constantly on the move. We didn't stay in one place very long. I think Mother was afraid of being found out; she must have known what she was doing was wrong. Because of the numerous moves, I had no consistency or stability in my life and not many chances to make friends, now I refuse to move anywhere even within the same town to a newer house. Mother kept me extremely isolated. I was her possession and only hers. She allowed no one to get close to me. If I developed a relationship with anyone, Mother quickly put an end to it. I felt so alone, but I learned to amuse myself and to enjoy my own company.

Anxiety attacks and worrying about what could happen prevent me from having any pleasure or experiencing joy. Trying to anticipate what lies ahead makes me feel a bit more prepared for the unexpected. I try to predict what's going to happen, because nothing in my life was ever predictable. Rules, regulations, and punishment varied according to Mother's moods and whims. In the morning, I'd do one thing; and it would be acceptable. By afternoon, I'd be punished for having done the same thing. This makes it difficult to set rules and discipline my own child. I don't trust my instincts. I can't be spontaneous. I feel forewarned is forearmed.

I am a perfectionist. It gives me a sense of control over my life after not having had any while I was growing up. No matter how perfectly I do something, though, it's still not good enough to suit me. My self-esteem is so low that it's practically non-existent. I can never measure up to the standards of perfection I have set for myself. Yet, I keep trying, because that sense of control makes me feel like I have some strengths and power in my life. I also think that some of my perfectionism comes from wanting to please Mother and the expectations she had of me.

I used to blame myself for most of what happened, but I'm getting beyond that stage. I've never blamed Mother. Consequently, I have no reason to forgive her. My entire life has been spent being hypervigilant of Mother's moods and needs. That has expanded to include anyone with whom I'm in contact. I've spent a great deal of energy trying to please, care for, and protect my Mother. Now that she's older and alone, I continue to feel it is my responsibility to do that, especially since I am her only child. There is no other family close by. I will not confront her; I have no need for that. It would only upset the delicate balance my Mother and I have in our relationship. I have a difficult time being with her, but I want to do the responsible thing for an ageing parent. She'll always be my Mother no matter what she did. I guess I'm still looking for the Mother I never had. It is a strange relationship to say the least. Mother has changed some since my father's death; but I suppose, deep down, I know I'll never get the nurturing I've always wanted from her. I have to learn to get what I need from other sources. I also have to learn to nurture myself.

I don't have much hope at this point. My therapist has that for me. Right now, I'm keeping my therapy appointments three times a week and gently pushing myself along the way. I do as much as I can while taking one moment at a time.

The prism

It hits the prism as white light,
But the prism refracts and bends it
Into fragments of coloured light — the spectrum.

As a tiny child, I was the white light.
My prism life bent and twisted me
Into a fragmented adult.

The Queen of Spades

If you've ever played
The card game of hearts,
You know that the Queen of Spades
Counts thirteen points against you.
I really wouldn't say
That I've had all the cards
Stacked against me from the start
In the card game of life.
I was just unlucky enough
To be dealt the Black Lady.

Sexuality

Through the process of growing up,
We all receive an education.
At a young age, I found that
The body is something that
Shouldn't be seen or touched.
Later as my chest blossomed,
I realised that certain people
Don't always abide by the rule:
'Thou shall not touch.'
As I further matured,
I was taught that this process
Wasn't considered natural by everyone.
My new growth of hair was shaved off.
After becoming a woman,
Despite the forces which
Were against that,
I discovered that sexual relationships
Aren't always by consent.
I learned my lessons well.
I received my education.

The mask

The mask is a false smile
That hides the sorrowful tears
Behind a pair of laughing eyes.
The mask conceals all the years
Of anguish, pain, and lies.
Why the continual charade
With this deceiving mask?
I can't let others see
Living's such a difficult task for me.
If they learn what hurts me,
They'll then use that knowledge
To hurt me over and over again.
The mask is my only salvation
From others who commit this sin.
My jovial mask is my protection.

Jill Myers

Jill is a 36 year old professional woman, living in a long-term lesbian
relationship.

Jill's story

I am very angry about what happened to me when I was small. I was abused by my father, I can't remember when it started — I was very little. When my brother was growing up, he wanted to touch me as well and I let him because it was, after all, only the things my father did and I really did think it was my job. My mother also touched me, and she sometimes beat me on the head, but I have only just realised that what she did wasn't normal care of little girls, but was for herself.

The abuse by my father was part of my normal life. It was something I grew up with, a weekly event. The abuse from my mother is something I am still trying to come to terms with. My father forced me to have oral sex and asked me if I liked it. I didn't know it was alright to say no, so I said yes. My mother began abusing me when I was about five. She would take me into the bedroom and rub cream into my genitals. I dreaded her doing it. It went on when I was old enough to know it wasn't right. It always went on in private, when no one else was home. It was a secret in exactly the same way as the abuse by my father was a secret.

It's odd that the abuse by my father was not as awful as the abuse by my mother. There's something about a mother. When you're small, she should be the first person you go to if you're hurt; the first person to cuddle you. She should clothe you, feed you and give you physical love and care, as well as emotional support. So when she's the one who abuses you, it leads to an even greater sense of despair than when your father abuses you.

As a result of all the abuse, I felt as though I must have had a label around my neck because I was also assaulted by two men outside the home, at the local swimming baths. Again, I didn't know then that I had a right to say no — I thought my role in life was as a convenience for all the men around. I also thought that there was something really stupid about me because I didn't like what was happening and I thought I was supposed to like this big special secret. So I started pretending, acting, and became a different person on the outside. The real me was only alive deep inside me — the other was all an act. It still is to a certain extent. It is something I am trying to come to terms with now.

I am 36 years old and really feel that I shouldn't be so distressed about my childhood. I have never talked about the abuse before, but not for want of trying. I have been fairly depressed and one of my colleagues at work found me a counsellor. The counsellor has helped me enormously, although my mood swings are frightening and depressing.

When I was small, there was no one I could turn to and as I grew up I became aware that people did not want to know. They couldn't cope with hearing about it. So I buried it down further away, where it has been festering inside me. I fear losing control more than anything in the world. Recently I lost control and it felt as though an unexploded bomb went off inside me. It made me afraid that I would not be able to put on my mask sufficiently to manage in life. I like to portray myself as someone who can cope, be in control and I feel so far removed from that at times. I hate admitting that I need help, but I know that my outwardly strong, capable character is really a weakness, not a strength. They are the strong ones who face up to it and get help and that's what I want.

When I think about it, I realise that so much of my mental energies went into training to lock away things as they happened when I was small, that I found the ability to do so remained with me. Counselling has helped me to begin to adjust to new patterns of behaviour, but I was totally unprepared for the emotional impact of all the things I had so successfully buried in my other selves and they frighten me. I sometimes wonder what else will appear — nothing worse, surely. I forgive myself little in my rational, organised, able thinking self; how much less I forgive in my other less rational self is left to the imagination. I am sometimes very afraid that, while functioning in one of these other selves, during times of stress, I will kill myself. I felt this way particularly when I unlocked another memory — one that has caused me more suffering than anything else in my life. I became an abuser. I have repeated on innocent children the same abuse that I experienced. I started when I 'initiated' my playmates. As I got older, friends my own age objected, so I turned to younger children. Much to my shame and regret, I also abused children in my care when I was a teenager and young adult. I undressed them and touched their genitals and made them touch me in ways that were inappropriate between a child and an adult.

Intellectually I know *why* I did it. That is no excuse. Knowing the pain and hurt it caused me as a child, particularly when my mother, a woman, did it, I feel complete despair. I also know that I could at any time repeat that to another child in my care which makes me feel untrustworthy. I now ensure that I am never left with any children. I have no children of my own and my partner (a woman) and I do not want any. I think that, as long as I have help and support, I will not abuse again.

I am haunted by what I have done and by my fantasies of what I might do. When the fantasies come, I want to kill myself. I have tried many times, but not recently. My father disappeared from my life years ago, but I still see my mother. I am torn between love and hate — unable to do either. I have forgiven my mother for what she did, but I cannot forgive myself. I blame myself for abusing my friend's children and for the abuse from my mother. In my dreams I castrate my father and suffocate him. But I don't attack my mother. I attack a little girl and the little girl is me. She shouldn't have let it happen, and I suffocate her.

Jane Swann

Jane is in her early forties and lives in South East England. She is an artist and the mother of one child.

Jane's story

I have two points I would like to raise both related to my own experiences of abuse. The question is often raised by new mothers, doctors, psychologists, etc. as to what constitutes 'good mothering' (or parenting). As I am referring here to women as carers I will continue to use the term 'mothering'. Often the kind of sexual abuse alluded to is 'overtly sexual' in nature, either as isolated incidents or as part of a child's upbringing. Intercourse, masturbation, the insertion of implements, etc. are mentioned. There appears to be a problem on how to identify sexual abuse, particularly when it is endemic to the child's upbringing. Professionals have claimed the child is fantasising, or the mother is 'too protective' of the child. They might misinterpret the child's (or adult's) 'ramblings' and searching for words as indicative of some other problem. The description of the mother's behaviour might be construed as 'immature' but not 'abusive' because the meaning of her actions (described by the survivor) is misunderstood. What I shall go on to describe is 'perverse mothering', where the activities of mothering itself are used as a means of sexual gratification. However, in this context, the ultimate gratification is complete power over the victim (as in the case of rape), a desire to take over and destroy as opposed to nurture.

From the age of four, when my father remarried and my stepmother took primary care of me, until the age of eighteen when I left home, I was subjected to abuse that was so endemic to my upbringing that for many years it was impossible for me to pick out certain areas and describe them in such a way that a professional, such as a psychiatrist, could identify the cause of my emotional distress and attribute it to sexual abuse by a female (mother or stepmother). Also, I was incapable of expressing myself clearly because 'the words would simply not come out'. I existed, emotionally, behind a wall of silence. The 'perverse mothering' I endured included many of the activities performed at some point during a child's upbringing, but done in such a way that could only on reflection be considered a cruel distortion of nurturing.

I was bathed weekly until I was sixteen. I slammed the bathroom door in my stepmother's face at that point and she never attempted to enter the bathroom when I was there, again. When I was bathed I was 'treated like a baby'. In my teens I can remember her staring at me fixedly whilst I was in the bath which made me feel extremely uncomfortable and 'dirty'. Other aspects of my upbringing included never being able to choose my own clothes, they were always given to me, so I never made a decision about what to wear. I was never allowed to wash my own hair when I wanted, my stepmother insisted on doing it 'because I would never do it properly'. If we went out and had to use a public toilet I never used a separate cubicle until way past the age of ten. This was not to save money. We were not hard-up.

I remember being on holiday with relatives and I had to get changed to go swimming. My aunt took me to the changing cubicles and I automatically went in with her, although I must have been ten or eleven. She showed surprise at my behaviour. When I went out with my stepmother I was made to hold her hand at all times, again until way past the age when such hand-holding is necessary to keep children from running into the road. I was subjected to a lot of verbal abuse directed at my anatomy. The first outburst I remember occurred when my stepmother first came to live with us. I had put on a pair of dungarees and had forgotten to put my knickers. I was subjected to a tirade of abuse for being 'so disgusting' for not covering myself properly. She, on the other hand, habitually put on her knickers in front of my father and me and laughingly said how she had forgotten to put them on.

I was asked constantly if I had washed 'down there'. I was physically abused over trivial misdemeanours and hit around the head and body so vehemently I had to crouch in a corner with my arms over my head to protect myself. The way she hit me did not leave any obvious signs of bruising. I bruised myself a lot anyway because I was so clumsy. She never apologised for any of her behaviour and never once showed any signs of remorse. However, to the outside world I would not have appeared uncared-for. I did not come from an apparently deprived background. My parents were lower middle-class, my father worked in a bank. At school I was considered shy, intelligent though apt to daydream and well behaved apart from a particularly difficult time when I was about ten or eleven. I suddenly started behaving totally 'out of character'. I became rude and abusive to other children, I became depressed, I developed a terrible self-loathing for my own body. I wrote a story at school about the life-story of a cat. She worked very hard having kittens and looking after them; when they grew up she could think of nothing else to do and only wanted to die.

When the family visited relatives, I was dressed up and must have looked like a little doll in a pretty print dress, white nylon gloves with frills round the wrists, white socks, buckled shoes and curled beribboned hair. To my stepmother I *was* a doll. Everyone commented on how pretty I looked, how well behaved, how quiet and how I was so willing to make myself useful. I remember other women telling my stepmother how they envied her for having such a good child who 'never got up to mischief' and who always found ways to amuse herself. To the neighbours I was a model child. They never heard the screaming. My stepmother regarded all other children as 'brats'. She constantly enthused about how I 'must not behave like them', though instilling me with the sense that I was like them, despite my efforts to be otherwise in order to please her.

Female abuse is damaging because it is so subversive. In day-to-day caring a mother, or mother figure, will physically handle the child a great deal as part of the child's upbringing. When a child's life is so dependent on being fed, clothed and loved by the mother, who is usually the most predominant figure, and subsequently that person takes advantage of their unique position of power and authority, then the devastating effects of sexual abuse can be recognised as deeply wounding to the point of being likely to destroy the ability of that abused child to ever be able to form safe, happy relationships with anyone else, possibly for the rest of his or her life, unless it is discovered and treated with understanding and compassion. If the mother is emotionally disturbed or very immature she will be unable to perceive the child as a child but simply as another person, like herself, or not even as a person but as an object like a toy or plaything. Children have an awareness of their developing sexuality and will often 'flirt' unwittingly with an adult, particularly with a close relative with whom they have a lot of physical contact. An immature or disturbed adult will respond instinctively to these signals in the same way as two consenting adults. The result of this for the child is a crippled personality and a distorted view of their own sexuality.

Throughout my childhood I lived in a state of continual fear. I believed my stepmother spied on me when I was out of her sight, even to the extent of believing she might possibly have hidden microphones and cameras. I had nightmares about her. I dreamt of fires in my parents' bedroom, me trying to run out of the house but unable to. I imagined the whole house to be 'evil' but I couldn't run away, neither in my dreams nor in real life. (I was frightened of the dark, indoors not outside, until I was in my thirties.) When I reached puberty I was humiliated in front of my father when I was menstruating. If I complained of stomach pains I was thrown out of the house. I suffered from teasing by my peers at school. I found it difficult to make friends and in my teens, any kind of social life or boyfriends was totally out of the question. However, despite everything I did manage to create areas of my life to compensate for all the unhappiness. I loved drawing, music (singing, playing musical instruments) and made efforts to teach myself, dancing to records or the radio, or no music at all, play-acting on my own or sometimes with another child. I had a vivid imagination which enabled me to escape into my own world. I needed to find places to be on my own, such as the garden, although at the same time I often felt terribly lonely. I had no need of other people most of the time. This was far from true. When I reached adulthood I was totally unable to cope on my own away from home. I did not know how to make fully independent decisions, or organise my life properly without the risk of a 'breakdown'. In the following I shall describe my early adulthood to show how my childhood experiences affected me. This account should be particularly useful to those working with offenders, battered women and drug–alcohol abusers. I shall leave the reader to draw their own conclusions.

I left home for the first time when I was eighteen. I lived on my own for a few weeks, then shared a room with a friend for a few months. I was unable to confide in her about anything. Not long after I left home I began to get feelings of 'being in a car that had gone out of control'. I could not form a proper social life. I had a job which I disliked (I had been unable to stay on at school past the school leaving age of sixteen). I found myself being drawn towards violent situations. I 'unintentionally' got drunk until I passed out. It was as if I wasn't able to control what I was doing any more. After a few months I started to become literally 'sick with fear'. I suffered bouts of vomiting, diarrhoea, giddiness, palpitations, agoraphobia, weight loss caused by an inability to swallow food easily, and insomnia. I felt emotionally 'blocked up'. I couldn't cry even though I desperately wanted to. I had tried to talk to people about my parents both before and after I left home. People laughed. I was an adolescent, all adolescents fall out with their parents, it was normal. It was worse when I mentioned my stepmother. 'Wicked stepmothers are a figment of the imagination, fairy stories and the Brothers Grimm.' I took an overdose because I was ill, confused and desperately unhappy. I was asked in casualty if I wanted to go home to my parents or go into a mental hospital as a voluntary patient. I was admitted to hospital. In a locked admission ward of a psychiatric hospital (this was 1972) I rapidly regained 'normality' for me, though I was given anti-depressants which made me fall asleep a lot. I soon regained my appetite, put on weight, cried a lot and for the first time ever, began talking to people freely, something I had never been able to do before. I did not talk much about myself, not what was deep inside me because I never seemed to be able to find the right words.

The psychiatrist who saw me could find no signs of mental illness, apart from the fact that I was 'a bit neurotic', he said. He exclaimed I was a 'creative genius' (whatever *that* means) but how could I create anything if I couldn't express my feelings? A social worker told me I was a delinquent and a nuisance to my 'nice' parents, who had been interviewed by the psychiatrist. No professional diagnosed abuse in childhood, let alone sexual abuse from a woman. No one attempted to ask the right questions or gave me time to talk. I was constantly told I was 'normal' and given a bottle of pills 'to make me better'. I became addicted to tranquillisers because professionals at that time were unaware of tranquilliser addiction. I was admitted to hospital, at my request, eighteen months after the first admission because I had tried to do without tranquillisers. Again I was diagnosed as a 'genius' and sent off with another prescription. The sister on the ward was astounded by my 'remarkable recovery' a few days after admission. My anxiety prior to admission had been so severe I had lost the power of speech and had to write everything down on a piece of paper. I then realised I had a choice. I could stay 'locked up' or take more tranquillisers. Inevitably I formed an abusive relationship with a partner to mirror the horrors of my childhood. This was not what I wanted, it was what I knew. The familiarity with a situation alone gave me the stability I needed to function.

I got out of that situation many years later when I had a child. When my son was three it was my own anger and inner turmoil that caused the 'sick with fear' feelings to return. I left my husband and began a new life. This time I had to find out what was wrong with me in order to protect my son from the possibility of enduring the same terrible childhood I had suffered. Luckily I found the help I needed. It took me a long while to find the courage and confidence to talk. Abuse in childhood was diagnosed and also sexual abuse from a female (my stepmother). Much of my rehabilitation has been 'self-healing'. I have written a great deal, for myself. I had therapy for a period of five years, although even talking to a therapist is difficult when there is an ingrown inability to trust anyone. I have had to realise (painfully) how I could be as much a perpetrator of violence, as a victim of it. I had to recognise how much I had actively sought out violent relationships to mirror my childhood environment. If I wanted to change I had to accept responsibility for my own part in these relationships and not see myself always as a victim of someone else's violence. I had to learn to love myself, discover self-esteem, learn to live independently.

Looking back, I consider myself now to be very lucky because I am a *survivor*. I am still undergoing a 'healing process' and no doubt I will remain so for the rest of my life. I cannot ever see a time when I will be 'over it' completely. I consider myself as 'much better than I was' and 'continuing to make progress'.

Karen Green

Karen is a 48 year old and has a degree in physics and mathematics. She is married and has three sons aged 24, 22, 17 and a daughter aged 11. She moved from London to Shropshire in 1978 and has been running a book and record shop in a small town ever since. She comes from a Jewish middle-class professional family, and did not leave home until she married when she was 21.

Karen's story

I was sexually abused by my mother from the age of one until I was ten years old. When I was 13, she forcibly broke my hymen so that my father and brother could rape me. When I was 19, my parents injected me with a tranquilliser so that my father could again rape me. I remembered nothing of this until my mother died eleven years ago. I am now 48 years old and have been flooded with terrible memories, having suppressed what happened for all those years. I wonder how many other people have had this experience.

The events leading up to the discovery were as follows. I had been taking Valium daily from age 22 and when my mother died in 1980 and my daughter was born I decided to stop taking it.

From then on I followed a journey back into my past, contacting relatives whom I had not seen for 25 years. Ours had been a very enclosed family and we were not allowed contact with the wider extended family. I did not know what I was searching for, but just that there was something very wrong inside of me which I had to discover. I gradually picked up small pieces of information about my parents' past, and then, out of the blue, I went headlong into a breakdown which I now know was the struggle between the two parts of me — the one part that had been totally unaware of what had happened and presented a cheerful front to the world — and the child in me who knew all that had happened.

It took another two years before I had a dream that I was sexually abusing my daughter — to my horror. I woke up and it came to the fore of my conscious mind that my mother had sexually abused me.

The irony is that I come from a highly respectable family. My father was a doctor, so trying to get help was out of the question. No one would believe me. My mother made me perform oral sex and she always whispered that she loved me. I coped by splitting her image into two and carried that of a loving mother in my head, completely denying the reality. I then decided that the outside world was dangerous, rather than my mother and consequently suffered from agoraphobia until I became aware of what had happened. I also had continual panic attacks and depression, all of which seem to be fading as I live though more of the abuse.

The only people I felt safe to tell were my husband and my older children. I am afraid to tell friends as I am worried that they might be shocked or even deny it. Sexual abuse is somehow acceptable by fathers and men, but not by mothers. It bothers me that, when the subject of childhood comes up in a social situation, I have to pretend that mine was normal. It seems a betrayal of the child I was.

It is still hard for me to believe that I knew nothing about my childhood and, in fact, made up a happy family in my mind. However, the reality was that normal communication in our family was impossible. Everyone's relationships were so distorted, yet everyone knew that the abuse was going on. It was an open, unspoken secret.

I have spent the past three years remembering and living through emotions from the past. Suddenly the rest of my life made sense in a way it has never done before. There must be thousands of women (and men), perhaps suffering from agoraphobia, who are unaware that they have been sexually abused. I think that sexual abuse by females is buried in the mind very deeply as the loss of trust in one's mother is actually life threatening at a very early age.

I told my sister, who I found out was also a victim of the abuse from my mother, father and brother. I think, looking back, that my mother was also abused by her mother. She occasionally made comments about it, although she said it was done in the name of love. My mother told me that this is what her mother did to her and then when I had a daughter I would understand. When I talked to my sister, I suspected that she went on to sexually abuse her own children, now grown up.

I don't know why some people abuse their children, while others don't, but those that don't have a good chance of one day becoming free of it all. Those who go on to abuse turn all of their rage onto their own children. Those who don't turn it inwards on themselves. I have had two breakdowns in adult life and never knew the cause. My family and friends were amazed that I suffered a breakdown, which illustrates that you can carry on leading a fairly normal life, hiding problems from everyone. The only trouble is that this is at the expense of being unable to experience any real positive feelings.

The hopeful aspect is that you can come through this, as long as you can find someone to trust and who believes you. My husband and children have been wonderful. It has also helped to write this as I know that this time I will be believed. No matter what you have to go through to deal with the abuse, it is all worth it in order to be free.

Gillian Balas

Gillian was a teacher, head of department and workaholic with a drink problem. She discovered the root of her problems in analysis and, to her horror, realised that she had sexually abused her own daughters. They have all had therapy and Gillian has since become a therapist herself.

Gillian's story

Most of the abuse I experienced was from my father and uncles, but the events in which my mother was involved, though few, were, I think, some of the most damaging. I know from some of the things she has told me and my sister that she herself was probably abused as a child, and I am certain that the events I have recalled, with the help of a therapist, are completely buried in her mind. She even told me once that she has a place right down at the back of her memory where she pushes the unhappy times.

I was about five. I remember being in my parents' bedroom staring down at my baby sister in her cot and thinking, 'They love *her*'. I began to wallop her on her well-padded bottom, but when she started crying, I became scared, and stuffed the blanket into her mouth. I was caught. My mother took my sister away downstairs while my father made me get on the bed face down, took down my knickers and hit me six times with his belt.

He paused after six and grunted, 'Six of the best'. I knew I had a choice. Either he would go on hitting me or I had to suck his penis, which I could see was erect. I crawled over and put my mouth on it — he pushed my head down and eventually came. He gave me a handkerchief and left the room; I lay breathless and exhausted on the bed.

My mother came back with the baby. She put her in the cot and then turned to me as I lay limp and without knickers on the bed.

She took the hairbrush from the dressing table and rammed its handle into my vagina — I have a lasting memory of the fury on her face. The pain was enormous. Then she stopped that and instead began to fondle me, using her finger to bring me to a climax. I had an orgasm which overwhelmed me and then she seemed angry again, slamming the hairbrush handle back into me and saying, ' Don't you ever do that again'.

I realise now that she meant hitting my sister, and since recovering that experience from my memory, have also at last recovered the ability to have an orgasm. I realise, too, that she was beside herself with anger and fear for the baby, and this must have caused her to repeat a forgotten pattern of her own childhood.

A later episode was also important: I must have been about six when something similar happened again. As she fondled me, my whole body stiffened, knowing that I must not let go, mustn't let it happen. She laughed and said, 'when you're a big girl, when you're bigger'.

At last, and ironically, I had arrived at the cause of my weight problem. Every failure has been met by my unconscious drive to be bigger. I have been helped, though, to understand and to forgive, and because of that I feel that I am healed.

Rachal Robinson

Rachal Robinson was born in England in 1947 and spent her first few months in a private nursery awaiting adoption. Her mother, a member of a large family of emigrant entertainers, decided to keep her and broke off relations with the disapproving family. She worked as a dressmaker and later started a small theatrical hire firm. Rachal met some of her cousins when she was five or six, and was often taken to shows and concerts in which they were appearing. The freedom and excitement of their lives compared to her own drab and claustrophobic childhood, along with her mother's wish for her to become a star, led her to take dance lessons at school and go on to study drama. She has worked in provincial rep, musicals, commercials, and radical feminist theatre in Britain and the USA. She occasionally wrote poetry and scripts for comedy sketches. Her generation of performers joined the CND and supported gay liberation and the PLO. Rachal was also a feminist activist.

Long periods of depression and drink and drug problems affected her ability to work and she spent time in a therapeutic community. She decided to concentrate on writing plays — so far unsuccessful — and is now studying to be a drama therapist, partly for her own healing. She is single, has never wanted children, and for most of her adult life has lived as a lesbian.

Rachal's story

Being sexually abused by my mother has for meant a lifelong search for identity, particularly sexual identity. I wish I'd known at 20 what I know now, at 45. I can explain it now, understand myself, though not completely. I can do what I was never able to do — name my feelings, find reasons for them, express them, discover my needs and ask for them to be met, recognise the boundaries between me and other people, see where being a lesbian is an asset rather than a source of deep shame. Say I was sexually abused by my mother, rather than saying my mother was a mad old bitch. But it's far from over. This is the first time I have written about it.

It's not just the abuse that I denied, it was all the feelings that went with it. Oh, yes, gradually through therapy, groups and reading I accepted (as other people do) feelings like pain and fear. Even anger was OK, self-hatred, low self-esteem — all those disempowering feelings were OK, what I call the 'victim' feelings. What was never OK were all the other feelings: shame, rage, resentment, bitterness, jealousy, humiliation, craving for love, being mad sometimes, feeling violent, being domineering, sarcastic, cold, superior, cunning, man-ipulative, vengeful, having a short fuse in terms of friends' behaviour — called 'being intolerant'. Many of these are what I call the 'fighter's' feelings. That's the bit the books miss out — you go from victim to survivor. But where do you get the courage to do the exhausting and painful work to become a survivor? I think I got it from being a fighter. Though people have always thought me easy-going, friendly, responsible, amenable, even strong, they eventually picked up some un-named hostility from me, a 'back off' message if they got too close, or pushed me too far. I'd switch off. No one ever saw the terrified wild animal underneath, claws ready, snarling, adrenalin pumping through me, hissing and spitting, craving for someone to recognise this paralysing defensiveness and to reach out and soothe me, calm me, still me. Instead, I took tranquillisers.

I was fit and strong, a gymnast, good at most sports. I never sought confrontation with anyone — anger always meant violence to me and I would soothe, negotiate, discuss, batter with logic, and defuse potentially violent situations. Another part of me would actively seek danger. The Universe, in its funny, obliging way, would send me muggers, groping drunks, mad dogs, even once a war — situations in which I could legitimately scream, punch and kick, run away, seethe and curse and, later, collapse, sobbing, and be comforted and congratulated on my narrow escape or my self-defence tactics.

As a young adult I found plenty of people to hate, to rage and storm against. Ours was the generation of demonstrations, sit-ins, protest marches, slogan-chanting, wrestling with police or soldiers guarding nuclear bases. Perhaps most of us were abused children, raging and storming against our parents and other supposedly trustworthy adults who had messed up our world, taken away our childhoods, beaten any self-esteem out of us, and controlled us with their so much greater, even omnipotent, power.

It was always men, of course. No one then ever said that women were abusive. Although I hated being a lesbian, in the early days of the women's movement I was admired as a genuine separatist, a real feminist, a women who owned her sexuality with pride. All these labels were welcomed by me, though underneath I thought these women were nutty sentimentalists. What did they know? It hadn't been a political decision. I knew I was a lesbian from the age of 14. So did my mother. She hated me for it and told me I was abnormal, disgusting, shameful. At the same time she was intensely curious and read books about lesbians, and ask me if I'd read them. I read one which explained how I felt about myself — a 'sane schizophrenic': part of me denied it to her, another part flaunted it, determined that she would find out.

It was all very mixed up. I knew I didn't want children, though I didn't know why. I didn't really want sex, though I did have relationships with men in my twenties, so I opted for women, which seemed less like sex than love and companionship. It was, of course, not quite like that — it was a desperate searching for myself and sometimes a strange sort of voyeurism. When the sex was good, which wasn't often, I would switch off because of a deeply uncomfortable feeling that my mother was watching: I called this feeling 'guilt', and later 'internalised homophobia'. There were a lot of labels in those days, plenty of pop psychology books available to those of us trying to define ourselves. I stuck each new label onto myself.

My mother told me once, when she got into spiritualism in a big way, that she went astral travelling at night and watched what I was doing. She never said what she saw. However, because of this sense of her being there somehow, I believed her. It was inhibiting to my sex life, and it became easier, for a while, to keep sex in my fantasies.

I was the ideal feminist — strong, powerful, independent, assertive, an individual, a fighter for just causes, champion of the oppressed. How I managed to keep this up I do not know, because the early feminists, frankly, terrified the wits out of me. Some were big, loud-voiced, harsh, angry, and deliberately wore shapeless 'working' clothes. Some sneered at me because I wasn't working class. They didn't trust me because I was an actress. I thought they were right, that sooner or later I would be 'found out' (as what, I did not know). They made rules about what was and what wasn't a right-on feminist. In camps or overnight hostels I would feel repulsed by their big hips and their flab, and felt guilty for my repulsion. Later I understood this. I would join groups, get involved, then leave without explanation. I kept moving house, changing jobs, joining new groups, becoming involved in political projects, then dropping out. Nor did I feel comfortable with other lesbians, unless I had the upper hand somehow — running a project, organising a club night, editing a newsletter, being on the end of a helpline telephone, being a rescuer of women in distress. I only had relationships with younger women.

During this time women became more assertive, laws changed,

rights were achieved, and we didn't have to fight and battle quite so much. We were allowed to be ourselves and enjoy life. Single women could get mortgages. It was OK to be a feminist. There was feminist theatre. It was OK to be a lesbian. There was lesbian comedy. At the end of the 1970s it was even in vogue. We began to be a community with a culture rather than a protest group of oppressed victims of patriarchy.

I went into a deep, panic-stricken depression. Happiness terrified me more than anything else. I was still taking tranquillisers and drinking too much. I had no outlet for my resentment and rage and envy, or my fear of being 'found out'. I didn't know why I felt like this — I had so much. Plenty of work, friends, a nice place to live, a little car, enjoyable activities. What could possibly be wrong with me? I went to therapy, even managed to find a lesbian therapist. She wouldn't let me talk about my sexual problems. Turned out that she had them too.

This was before the term 'sexual abuse' came into common use. We'd heard about 'incest', that one-in-a-million phenomenon in which a father fell in love with his daughter, or a brother and sister lived together in Byronic exclusivity. Someone was making a film about it. We knew about battered children and battered wives, because we'd helped to set up women's refuges. We knew about rape too. We didn't know anything about sexual abuse until the mid-1980s, from painful books written by US feminists. We never met anyone who had been sexually abused. Gradually, a few brave souls crept out of their private hell-holes and began to talk about it, just a little, and only in very safe and long-established therapy groups.

One or two incest survivor groups were formed. More books appeared. I read them. I used to think, 'If only I had been sexually abused I could join these groups, I could get some help'. Then I'd feel terribly guilty about those thoughts — those women were so much worse off than I was.

I knew my mother was physically violent, verbally abusive, emotionally manipulative. I recognised that what I had experienced was also mental cruelty. All my childhood I felt sorry for her. Since I was tiny, she had told me heart-breaking stories about poverty in the 1930s, deprivations of the war, not having enough to eat, men who had deserted her, how she'd had to skivvy and scrub floors to feed me, how shameful it was to have an illegitimate child. (My father had 'raped' her, she said.) And how lucky I was to have her, she who would never leave me, who would always love me as only a mother could, however horrible I was. Oh, she was clever. She knew which of her stories would make me cry and comfort her. She programmed me so well that she had only to say a word or two and I would crumble and give in to her. The desperate feeling I always had — a mixture of intense pity for her and a terrified longing to get away from her — was what she called 'love'. She would also tell me how much I loved her. Sometimes I would sob from exhaustion and weakness and frustration and she would tell me it was because I loved her so much that I was feeling bad because I'd 'hurt her feelings'. Whatever I felt was something to do with her. She had lots of labels ready to stick on to me too. I believed her, of course.

I only had to allow a tiny tentative thought of myself to creep into my consciousness — perhaps 'I want to read a book by myself' — for a great dollop of guilt to come crashing down inside me. I wouldn't allow myself to want anything. I wouldn't even allow myself to think. I waited to see what sort of mood she was in, what she wanted me to do, which meant what she wanted me to do for her. Much of the time she expected me to know. I would look blankly at her as she got more and more furious, racking my brains to think of what dropped hint I may have missed (as it must have been my fault) and then she would snap and hit me, sometimes punish me more, for being insensitive or selfish, or unloving. 'No one will ever love you', she would scream.

One thing my first therapist did was to make me sit in a chair and pretend to be my mother, seeing her point of view. This I could do very easily — there was never any other point of view in our home except hers. Friends and relatives told me that I should forgive my mother as she was obviously 'a bit unhinged because of her terrible childhood' and 'not responsible' for her behaviour.

There were more books. I kept recognising myself in them. I had most of the problems survivors talked about, though not as severe as some. There were never any women abusers, though. So I decided that my mother was right, there was something wrong with me — I was mad and unloveable, sexually abnormal, insensitive and selfish, hard as nails, a liar and much more. However, I kept my distance, visited her as little as possible, talked endlessly about her to friends who also had domineering, damaged mothers. On one level I began to understand it wasn't really me; on the other level — where all that shame and resentment still dogged me — I knew it was me. I was, after all, a lesbian, wasn't I? There must be something wrong with me. I never wanted children. That, to her, was abnormal too, since she prized motherhood above everything else. This was how she had given herself permission to abuse me in every way she found possible. She was my mother; she owned me, she had absolute rights over my body, my thoughts, my feelings, even my soul. For this I also had to be grateful.

More therapy, a group. I began the painful separation process from the mother I'd never had. The needy child in me searched for gentle, motherly people, for happy families, and particularly for unhappy children who I could play with and communicate with and offer some love to. I did some clowning. I wasn't too good at finding the gentle people though — what I found was a lot of rescuers. I found that, once again, I was in relationships with 'victims' who controlled me.

Weekend workshops, another group. Many more women were now talking about sexual abuse. Though deeply ashamed of doing this, I made up some stories about having been sexually abused by an uncle. I had been sexually assaulted when I was nine years old by a man in a park, though I had managed to get away in time. I built that up too, since I'd never told anyone. At least I had sympathy and attention, and reasons for all the problems I'd experienced — drink, soft drugs, tranquillisers, self-sabotage, low self-esteem, self-hate, hopeless relationships, dependency, strange fantasies and night-mares, eating problems, sexual problems, repressed anger and pain and fear. But the collective pain of the women in the group wore me down: I began to be supportive of them, understanding, and compassionate. I suddenly realised I was doing what I had always done, and left the group.

I was very lost and alone. I felt alienated from the whole human race. Labels like 'feminist' allowed me to have little to do with men. (I had, actually, been sexually abused by two teenage male cousins who were playing doctors and nurses, though I didn't remember this until much later.) Labels like 'lesbian' allowed me to have reasons for feeling alienated and oppressed and a little bit crazy. It was even right-on to be celibate. Yet I felt that none of them really described me. I had a great big hole inside me. Sometimes it ached for ordinary human companionship. Acting came easily to me.

Then I met a woman who looked so like my mother that all my friends commented on it, though I couldn't see it myself. I fell on her like an addict. We had the most passionate sexual relationship I had ever known, the sort of relationship you only read about in books — no taboos, no inhibitions, pure lust. It was wonderfully freeing for me to be with someone who enjoyed sex so much, yet who was unpossessive and independent. It took some weeks before I had, finally, deep orgasms during one long, passionate night. I couldn't stop crying afterwards. She was kind at first, then impatient and bored. I wouldn't let her touch me for weeks. It happened again — we were crazy about each other — and I reacted in the same way. She suggested that I get some help, and left me.

People have died, friends have emigrated, I have experienced other losses, but the grief of the ending of this short relationship was unbearable. It was my fault, I was a failure. I couldn't work, I couldn't see anyone, I cried and stopped eating and felt suicidal. I read thrillers and horror stories, erotica and pornography. I didn't know why. I wrote, too — strange abstract pieces which, the next morning, looked like the scribblings of someone demented. I threw them away. I decided I was possessed by a devil of some sort. I was. It my mother.

I was exhausted and high from lack of sleep and I went to stay at a friend's place in the country, near some woods. Though I'd managed to give up alcohol, I wanted to get off the tranquillisers, I was running out of money and needed to work again. I knew I needed rest and healing. Alone in that little cottage, I felt that menace lurked in the woods and that there were ghosts all around. I couldn't sleep at all. Just before dawn, I had a sense of being pushed and pushed from behind, and then an 'out of body' experience. I floated around in hell. It was like the DTs the alcoholics in one of my groups described, feeling weightless and powerless, and totally alone, vivid colour and patchworks and terror, pure terror. There were monsters, writhing snakes, mud and steam and disembodied screams, people with harsh voices calling my name. I heard myself begging and pleading for it to stop, for the monsters to go away. I knew I was mad. I felt my body again, hung on to the bed, breathing hard and staring at the dawn light through the curtains. I think I even prayed. Then I sank into a dreamlike state. When I awoke, I thought it had been a dream. I made some tea, and realised that it was a memory.

I had been sexually abused by mother, in various ways, from the age of two until the age of nine. I blessed the friend that had lent me her cottage, my years of reading, all the women in my groups, and the therapists, for all the knowledge and understanding that I had which helped me through the remainder of that week. I would walk about, feeling the rage and tension and tell myself it was OK, it was only a panic attack, because I'd stopped taking the tranquillisers. I recognised my reactions from books I'd read. I wrote some things down, though I burned them all. It seemed cleaner to do that. It was intensely difficult to feel positive about being a lesbian. I sat, shocked, thinking that I was a lesbian because my mother was. I understood, later, that this wasn't the case at all. I looked back on the relationships I'd had with wild, addictive, passionate women and saw elements of my mother in all of them. I'd always felt these women to be normal. I saw them as trapped souls, full of remorse for their wrongdoings (they always apologised) innocent because of their ignorance (I'd lend them books) or still suffering because of their childhood experiences (I felt sorry for them). I cast around for that sympathy, tolerance, understanding and forgiveness and tried to give myself some of it.

As the memories returned, so did the feelings. All of them together. Claustrophobia, jealousy and powerlessness; rage, shame and rejection; love, desire and excitement; eroticism, self-punishment and fear; self-hatred, contempt and humiliation. And guilt, guilt, guilt. Guilt for the times I had loved her and sought her love. Guilt for being too weak to say *no*.

From the age of two, she had held me responsible for all her feelings, including her sexual feelings, and for her headaches, tiredness, backaches, food poisoning, accidents, lack of money, lack of freedom: everything was my fault. Even my illegitimacy was my fault.

She often shamed me in public. She would tell people — strangers, shopkeepers — that I wet the bed, or that I had odd little obsessive habits, that I made up strange stories, or that I bit my nails or was 'always snivelling'. In my teens she would say I was neurotic and highly strung. She often hit me. She was an expert at mental cruelty. Yet I was so well programmed that I rushed to do her bidding, even when I was older, when the sexual part of the abuse stopped.

Nothing I ever did was enough. I'd feel guilty about that. It was not enough that I was attentive and compliant, willing to massage her and smooth lotions onto her face, her breasts, her stomach and thighs. It was not enough that I remained quiet when she sat me across her naked thighs, and gripped my small leg against her genitals and bounced me up and down while clinging onto me so hotly and tightly that I thought I would choke. It was not enough that, in bed, I lay across her while she rocked me against her body. She wanted more — she wanted me to enjoy it, even to ask for it. She wanted to be kissed on the lips, courted and admired. She wanted me to be the perfect lover. She taught me to sit astride her, froglike, and bounce up and down. She wanted me to tell her every detail of my day, every thought. Later, in bed, she'd use nauseating pet-names, depending on what had caught my attention that day — tadpole or hamster or plum. She wanted a house servant, too. If I didn't wash up properly, or bring her coffee in bed in the morning, she would spank me, then, that night, kiss my bottom better, then she would turn me over and stroke my budding genitals, saying what a naughty girl I was, and how lucky she loved me. No wonder I was constipated, though I stopped telling her about that because she said I'd have to have an enema. She'd told me once about giving enemas to wounded soldiers when she was a VAD.

Her moods would change in moments. She would be funny, affectionate, hurt, furious, insulted, critical, sneering, violent, crying, grimly silent, punishing, interested and curious, seductive, disapproving, secretive or exhaustingly talkative, all in a single evening. So frightening were these moods that I would do anything she asked. In my anxiety I would, of course, do it wrong. My hands were too small, I was stupid and insensitive, I didn't like exploring her vagina, and it hurt when she put her fingers inside mine. She said I would like it when I was bigger, and to my undying remorse, I did once or twice get some pleasure from it.

Yet she pushed me to achieve at school and win at games, and she complained to the teachers if I wasn't given special attention. Other girls said I was lucky to have my mother on my side. If I failed — I was an average pupil and exams made me too nervous to do well — she would beat me for shaming her, and the usual 'How could you do this to me?' tears would follow. She only wanted my achievements so that she could boast about them. She sent me to have elocution lessons. She wanted me to be a model, then a film star, though she kept saying I wasn't pretty any more. She wanted me to have my nose fixed, my teeth capped, my hair blonded and permed.

As I got older, and withdrew, the sexual abuse stopped — perhaps because she'd started the menopause. She became more violent and venomous and sarcastic. She told the doctor, teachers, my school friends' parents, that she was worried about my moods, or my lack of concentration, or my rudeness or lack of respect. She asked if I was on drugs. She asked if I had been messing around with boys. She would say she thought I was 'a bit mental'. She would check my physical development, scream at me to unlock the door when I was in the bathroom. I was continually being sent for tests to psychologists, neurologists and gynaecologists to find why I wouldn't eat and why my periods hadn't started and why I took so many laxatives. If 'I answered back' she said I was schizophrenic. If I failed to tell her every detail of what the specialists said, she told me I was 'hiding something'. I had no friends any more. She interfered with every relationship I had, and continued to do this until I was almost 30 years old. She still called me her 'little girl'. She said I had got my 'sickness' from my father.

In that cottage in the woods, I could feel her breathing down my neck. 'Don't you dare criticise me', she used to say. I felt guilty and scared even remembering all the things she'd done to me. She'd often told me how 'in tune' we were — that she knew my every thought, my every move. I was convinced she could see me now and hear me ranting and raving around the woods (which, luckily, were deserted, though I startled a few deer). She haunted me. She haunts me still. Then, I thought I was the only girl in the world who had been sexually abused by my mother. I could never tell anyone; no one would believe me. It was impossible, since only men did that. I still felt it was partly my fault. I still thought I must have imagined it. I wondered if Freud's theory was true, that children have sexual fantasies about the opposite-sex parent, and since I only had one, my fantasies involved her. I couldn't connect with it or make it real.

I didn't know who to tell. I'd be betraying her, she might find out. I couldn't tell my feminist friends — I'd be betraying feminism. I couldn't tell my lesbian friends — it would open up too many questions about lesbians and mothers of lesbians. I wasn't ready to take on all that responsibility. I went home and found some work, and as soon as I could afford it, I found a therapist. It took me 18 months to blurt it out. She believed me, and she helped me work out what to say when I next saw my mother. I had to see her, for family reasons.

She asked me why I 'neglected' her, and I told her, stumblingly, that it was because of what she'd done to me as a child. I was still very frightened of her. There were too many knives around, and I remembered, then, that she used to shake knives at me and tell me she'd kill me. She stared at me, that familiar menacing glare. I trembled, but held my ground, watchful. She must have realised that I remembered everything. Eventually, with a struggle, she relaxed her expression. 'Surely you don't blame me for that?' she said. 'I loved you so much. I couldn't refuse you anything.' Mentally, I flipped. Up rose a deep, deep shame. For a moment, I believed her — it was my fault, after all. I hadn't the courage to contradict her. I left as soon as I could, and I haven't spoken to her since.

I'm grateful to KIDSCAPE for setting up the conference on female abusers. The different parts of me fell together when one of the speakers was describing a patient she had found impossible to treat: she sounded exactly like my mother. Someone understood. I hadn't imagined it. I wasn't alone any more. But I wish I could get rid of the feelings of contempt for her, and the resentment for my lost childhood, my problematic sexuality, my own lost chance at motherhood; the waste. I think the grief I felt at the loss of my lover was the grief and pain about all that; the tears were also about experiencing the happiness I'd never known — it was too much for me to handle while all those memories were so close to surfacing.

And still, deep down, I am unable to expose my mother, or to punish her any more than I already have done by ignoring her. I realise she was, and still is, deeply disturbed. Someone told me that she was always on some kind of medication. This may be a reason, though I don't see it as an excuse. Maybe I am still afraid that she'll find a way of punishing me for finally talking about it.

Sue Rogers

Sue Rogers is a 40 year old professional woman working in the publishing field.

Sue's story

When I was about nine years of age, I became involved with a teenage neighbour, she was roughly seventeen at the time. I considered our relationship to be a kind of extension of 'play', but she was also a babysitter/minder for me, and as the daughter of the caretaker of our block of flats, my mother trusted her. What began as a friendship, rapidly became a sexual abuse situation. Although I enjoyed our first 'sexual' experiences, I began to realise that the issue was taboo, and found that friends my own age were shocked. I learnt the word 'lesbian' as something incredibly negative (this was 1965–67), and tried to distance myself from the woman and her 'games' with me. My abuser was actually involved in a kind of prostitution and tried to involve me in sex with men. Her whole pretext for abusing me was in the guise of 'training for heterosexuality'.

She began to verbally abuse me, calling me a 'dirty lesbian' and also 'dirty Jew'. I was blamed for her abusive behaviour, and I believed I was guilty. I had no one to talk to about it, and eventually she began waiting for me to come back from school, and beat me up 'for being a lesbian and a Jew'.

I believe I was a lesbian then, and would possibly have found a real relationship during adolescence, but in the circumstances, I just threw myself into 'escaping' the memories which made me feel so guilty. At twelve I was actively trying to 'make myself heterosexual', and trying to lose my virginity at any price. I believed I could escape my experience, by having as many relationships with boys as possible. I was consequently a 'slag' but relieved not to be branded 'lesbian'.

I came out as a lesbian when I was 21 or so, and it was only during a relationship with an incest survivor, when I was 28 or 29, that I remembered I had been abused.

For me the consequences still follow me. It has taken me years to regain a sense of a caring relationship. If a lesbian advice worker I met at a party hadn't told me that my experience was sexual abuse, I would have continued to bury it with ignorance. Abuse was the first experience I had of sex, and I believed I wasn't a lesbian because I wasn't an abuser. If I had been born a few years later, and if information had been available, I might have been able to come to terms with it, and live my life better, at a younger age. Instead, I was a suicidal, and ashamed teenager, desperate to cover up my feelings which I felt were 'criminal'.

I hope your work can bring some of this horror to a sane conclusion.

Helen Smith

Helen is a middle-aged professional woman, who grew up in a desirable English village. She has degrees in psychology and science and is considered to be extremely competent. Her parents are still alive and she maintains contact with them, though she has not yet confronted them with her memories. She continues in her profession-al role and in counselling. Her husband has been supportive, but there has been great strain on the marriage because of the problems resulting from the abuse she suffered as a child.

Helen's story

Around forty years ago, a mother took her three year old daughter to visit a friend who worked for an important man. I do not know what the man was. The friend seemed to work in the kitchen. During the visit, the child was 'examined' intimately by two male employees in the presence of the mother and her friend to establish how 'big she was down there'. Subsequently, and after a period of instruction and training in the child's house, the child provided services for gentle-men, who would visit her at her home. These services were paid for, the mother being the recipient. This went on for about two years.

Concurrent with visiting gentlemen, the child was introduced to the 'important' man. She became very attached to him, liked him and tried her best to please him. He benefited from the child's rather special talents. The situation came to an end because of the injuries caused to the child by another of the visiting gentlemen. The child was able to classify men into two distinct groups: those wishing to have a good girl and those wishing to have a bad girl. If the child was good, then she did what was asked of her. If the child was naughty, then she had to resist, to fight. The child dreaded being naughty because she was always hurt on those occasions, but there was no way out for her. If she tried to be good, the man or men would make her naughty by hurting her until she actually was naughty.

The child was dangerously hurt and eventually a family confer-ence resulted in a doctor being summoned. She recovered, but officials came and took her away when she was better. While she was away from home, in a hospital-type place with people in uniforms, she was repeatedly interviewed by a woman who maintained that she was the child's friend. The child knew she must not talk about what took place in her home or about her 'important' man. However, she did a drawing and was aware that she had drawn a man in addition to her family. Although no one else recognised it, she became very upset because she had done the wrong thing. The interviewer lied to the child and said that her mother had said it was alright to talk to the interviewer. The child did not yet understand what a lie was and told about the 'important' man. She had no feelings about the visiting gentlemen, but did love the 'important' man.

The child went to court, but the man did not. He went away and she was told that people like him do not go to court. The court had to decide whether she would go back with her parents. This confused her terribly. Her mother and father were there. Her mother was very upset. The child was questioned about whether her mother knew what the men had done to her. The child was sure her mother knew because mothers know everything. However, the questioner then told her that her mother did not know, which completely confused her. The child decided that perhaps little girls lie, but mothers do not. The child was allowed to go home and was thrilled. She thought everything would be alright now.

The next day, the mother told the child that she had known. This devastated the child, who felt as if parts of her body were being ripped away. Other things were said and the child thought that everything she had worked at learning was being snatched from her. She forgot how to walk and talk. She had to relearn these things all over again.

The mother subsequently told the child that she would never love her ever again. She still maintains that and has expressed to third parties that she regrets the daughter survived repeated suicide attempts as an adult. When the child was about seven, she accidently walked in on her mother satisfying herself. The mother was furious and taught the child how to satisfy her. This went on for about 18 months, the child hating every minute of it. At one point, as a punishment, the child was forced to perform her services on her unconscious grandmother, who subsequently died of cancer after an extended illness. This grandmother was a much-loved figure to the child and this episode caused her enormous distress.

The child's story has never been told before. She grew up to become a most distinguished adult who established herself professionally as a teacher and a social worker, receiving acclaim in both fields.

The abuse affected her in many ways, however. She developed strong phobias about travelling by any means of public transport — trains, planes, buses. Between the ages of 17 and 24, she was in and out of psychiatric hospitals and remembered nothing of her past. It was as if she had appeared from nowhere at the age of twelve. She self-mutilated and attempted suicide. Then she started seeing a counsellor, who helped her not to suppress some thoughts. What she started to think was horrendous. She denied it. Such things happen to others, not to her. She was frightened that she was remembering, not imagining. She spent much of the 18 months feeling sick before every counselling session. She knew she had to go on and now feels that she has sought and found the help she needed.

As an adult, she feels that the most harm was done to her by the interviewer pretending to be a friend, while encouraging her to betray someone she loved. She says that the damage caused by making children innocently betray their parents is worse than the damage caused by the abuse. 'It can never be acceptable to use the child to reinforce society's current norms. People interviewing children should state clearly what they are doing and stay with what the abused child says, not with what the interviewer needs the child to say'.

Sarah Miller

Sarah is an American living in England. She is currently in therapy. She is married and has two teenage children.

To Mother

Mother, I want you to know how I felt, what you did to me, how I remember you and your abuse. I want you to feel for my pain. I want you to know what you have done to a small innocent child, a child who was eager to be good, eager to learn and to love you. I want you to know what you did to a little girl who all her life wanted to be good enough for you: how cruel you were to her, and how evil.

My earliest memory of you is of being afraid that you would leave me. I was alone in my crib so much! Morning times and nap times were always starting and ending in tears because you would be so angry that I was awake and asking to get out of the crib: angry at *me* for wanting to get out, and I learned quite early just to wait and not to make any noise. But time would seem to go on and on and sometimes I would be sure that you had abandoned me and I would climb out of the crib to go find you. Your anger was terrible then, the spankings not just a certainty but accompanied by such rage against me that I soon had to be absolutely terrified of being left to dare to do it. I would hold Lamby-Baa-Baa and tell him over and over that you would be coming soon, aching for you to come and rescue me. And when I heard you coming, I couldn't greet you with joy; I had to pretend to be asleep, because you would be angry if I was awake. What kind of cruelty made you do that to me, mother? I was just a normal child, wanting to get on with life, but you caged me in for hours and hours in that crib, with terror and fear and despair because I couldn't be the obedient doll you wanted. That was abuse, mother.

When you were toilet training me, mother, how did you do it? I don't remember. But I know that I was terrified and ashamed whenever I wet my pants, and got spanked when I dirtied them. I was always so scared of being wet and dirty. After Dada abused me and I had to wear nappies again, I remember you telling me I was a bad, bad girl; that I was making extra work for everyone. It must have been obvious that I was torn down there; I remember bleeding a lot and both weeing and pooing hurting terribly; not just stinging, but really hurting me inside, but you treated me as though I had done it on purpose, just to be naughty, just so I wouldn't be able to control myself. I remember crying with the pain of weeing, mother; crying as it ran down my leg because I had tried not to go for so long and had to, and it hurt so much. And there was too much for the nappy, and you spanked me for it; *spanked* me on my bottom which had been torn and hurt so much I couldn't move, couldn't sit or walk without pain. You spanked a hurt and defenceless little girl for being so abused that she was in constant pain and fear. That was abuse, mother. You showed me no compassion, no understanding, no decency. That was abuse.

When you put your fingers up in my tiny vagina and rubbed my clitoris, and my body responded either with pleasure or with discomfort or with pain; when night after night you gave me attentions like that, talking constantly about how dirty I was, how filthy, how difficult to get clean, and I was too young to know what you were doing, too little to know that you were sexually exciting yourself with my body, too desperate for your love to realise that those attentions were not even care or affection, let alone love: that was abuse, mother; that was abuse. Rocking on the tub like you were in pain caused by my mythological dirt, that was abuse, mother. Making me squirm, telling me not to wriggle when you knew that what you were doing was meant to make me wriggle, hooking me up with your cruel fingers; rubbing me raw and sore, that was abuse, mother. That was abuse. No child should ever have endured that, mother.

Catching my terrified body like an evil doll and swinging it round by the legs, trying to batter my body by bashing it against the door, the towel rails, the walls, the floor; trying to smash my head in against the walls and the towel rails, making me rocket through the air like a toy on a string, like a thing; trying to smash my body and my spirit for daring to protest your cruelty; trying to kill me for daring to be human; that was abuse, mother. Holding my head under the bath water where you had thrown me like a broken doll, trying to kill me, that was abuse. Putting me on the floor with my face almost in my own vomit while you cleaned it up with one of my nappies, saying what an evil, awful, dirty child I was, ignoring my agony, my hurt face, my hurt head, my hurt hands and arms, my hurt back; that was abuse. Washing my hair and then rubbing my crack raw and hooking me high with your fingers and saying 'Never say that again . . .' That was abuse, mother; that was abuse. No person should ever have endured that, mother.

Making that little girl's experiences into a laughing matter and pretending that you were her saviour rather than the perpetrator; that was abuse. Never allowing her to own her own body; that was abuse; never listening to her ideas or thoughts or desires or feelings; that was abuse. Forcing her to say over and over in public how much she loved you; what a wonderful mother you were; that was abuse. Always criticising, never allowing her to make a mistake; blaming her for *your* inability to ask clearly for what you wanted; blaming her for being a child, just an ordinary little girl, who couldn't understand everything, who couldn't mother you; that was abuse, Mother. That was abuse.

I am crying, Mother, but not for you. I am crying for the little girl who survived your evil against all odds. I am crying for her pain and confusion and terror, all caused by your evil. I am crying for her misplaced hopes for love from her mother. I am crying for her loneliness and the unfairness of having to live through all your abuses again just to be able to get rid of them. I am crying for her mistrust of kindness, mistrust of appreciation, mistrust of self.

I am crying with compassion for that little girl, crying because I love her. I am crying for myself.

My dream

The little girl stood naked in the bathroom, disgruntled. She didn't want a bath; she didn't want the soap and the wash cloth touching her; she didn't want her mother's hands rubbing her, cleaning her, invading her. Her mother reached towards her to lift her in, but she shook her head. 'No, mummy,' she said, 'no'. And as her mother's face blackened, she whirled around and ran out the door as fast as she could go, running away from the anger she knew was there, running away from her mother's hatred, running away from the punishment she knew she deserved, running, running terrified into the dark hallway. Her mother was coming closer, furiously reaching for her shoulders, trying to grab her, trying to carry her back. She whimpered in terror. 'No . . .' Then 'no, no, no,' she screamed, 'please no, please no, please . . .' She felt her body lifted up roughly . . .

'Put her down,' a voice said quietly; 'Put her down right now.' The little girl looked round, astonished. She thought she was alone, and suddenly there was a strange woman as well as her mother. She started to cry, but the woman knelt down as her mother slowly released her grip. 'It's all right,' said the woman, I won't hurt you ever. I've fought battles to get to you, to be with you, to be here for you. It's all right little one, it's all right.' And she stood up and unfolded the softest, whitest towel the little girl had ever seen. She walked over to the little girl and asked, 'Would you like it round you? Would you like a cuddle in my lap? It's all right to say no if you don't; I'm here to give you what you need. I'm here for *you*.'

Slowly the little girl nodded, and found herself gently wrapped up, her nakedness covered. 'I'll get it dirty,' her small voice worried.

'No you won't,' said the woman firmly. 'The dirt in this house is your mother's not yours. *You* are perfect, just the way you are, and always have been. The dirt is in her, *in her* . . .' She patted her lap as she settled herself on the floor. 'Would you like a cuddle?' And the little girl found herself warm and safe on the woman's broad lap, with her head resting on her chest, and she heard the soft sweet words of The Mockingbird lullabye being sung gently to her, and her little hand curled itself loosely around a fold in the woman's blouse, and she slept.

When the child was asleep, the woman's face changed, becoming hard; implacable. She glanced up at the mother. 'Well, what do you have to say for yourself?' The mother's words gushed out; torrents of lies, rivers of denial, streams of hurt, waterfalls of confusion, boulders of abuse and hate and perversion, all mixed up with pebbles of love, muddy care and occasional ripples of kindness. The woman waited patiently until the words slowed to self-serving pleas, and then she spoke, deliberately. Her words were honed like razors.

'The child is no longer yours. She should never have been yours. You have forfeited any right to her. You abused her physically, sexually, and emotionally. You used her like an object for your own pleasure. You tried to kill her. You treated her like a thing, when she was a beautiful delicate child. You dressed her like a doll and treated her like one. You purposely hurt her body and her spirit. I could tell the world what you have done . . . would you like that?' The mother turned white.

'Give her back. I'm her mother! She is mine, *mine*, my child!'

'When were you a real mother to her? When did you love, protect and cherish this child? When did you listen to her? When did you care what she thought or felt? You are only a birth mother; only a mother in name. You have no rights to her at all. You will be lucky if she can remain civil to you, lucky if she doesn't eventually denounce you to the world.'

'And since when does a woman as fat and ugly and stupid as you have any rights? What makes you think *you* can do any better? Who gave you the rights to my child? Who would believe *you*?'

'The child believes me. The child has chosen me. The child will tell me what she needs to heal from your evil. And if I chose to tell the world what you have done, who will believe anything *you* say? You will be shamed. You will be locked up. What you have done is *criminal*.'

'Give her to me!' screamed the mother lunging for the child, her red nails clawing at the woman's throat and face. The woman bent her body over the child protectively, and the nails raked her. Still protecting the child she carried her to the door at the end of the hallway, and laid her gently on the floor, still sleeping. She turned to face the mother. 'If you even try to touch this child again, I will kill you,' she said softly.

'I won't give her up!' As the mother reached for the child in the doorway, the woman grabbed her bony feet out from under her and drew out a carving knife. She cut the mother's head off with one swift slice. Blood spurted into her face; she spat disgustedly, and shook her head. 'Filth,' she said, as she cut off the mother's hands. 'Filth.'

The woman went calmly to the bathroom and washed. She returned to the sleeping child, kicking the mother's body aside as though it were a piece of rubbish. She gathered the child gently in her arms and carried her down the stairs and out of the house. She kissed the top of the child's head softly as the child stirred and nestled into her shoulder. 'Go back to sleep, little one. I am here. I am here now; I am here.'

Amanda Mitchell

Amanda is 41 years old, unmarried and not in any long-term relationship. She trained as a teacher and then as a counsellor.

Amanda's story

It has taken me 7 months to be able to write to you from the time I decided I was going to write to you. I met you and heard you speak at the KIDSCAPE Conference on Female Sexual Abuse on 31 March 1992. Today is the 31st October and at last I've got the courage to write. I only hope I'll have the courage to post it.

I found that day in March devastating. I had come along, telling myself that I needed to hear this because of the work I'm doing with victims of sexual abuse. More and more I had been hearing about mothers, aunts, grandmothers and babysitters who were abusing children and I felt I needed to hear more about it . . . that's what I told myself but another voice in my head as I travelled said 'This is your own agenda, Amanda, this is for yourself you're going' and of course, it was true because I had been abused as a child by both my uncle and my aunt and the female abuse was by far the worst and most destructive for me.

I've been so depressed over the past few months that I feel I need to talk to someone. Like many people, I am in the kind of job where my needs must never come to the fore — I work with people who have been abused — of course, it will be immediately obvious to you why I would be doing this kind of work — in many ways I just bury myself in it and try and work out my own problems through the people I meet every day — the trouble is that deep inside I've started screaming for help — no one on the outside knows this, of course, so it's a big step for me to be writing this. I don't expect anything from you in response, it just may help to write to someone who will believe me and understand and someone who is far enough removed from my situation not to judge me incompetent or unable to do my job because of what's happened to me. That's one of my biggest fears, that people will find out about my background and realise that I am not the strong, efficient person they all rely on. I earn a very good salary for my job, yet I alone know that inside I am just a wreck!

First of all let me tell you why the Conference devastated me — it was the anger in the audience — the people who were getting up and shouting trying to say that females didn't abuse and that female abuse was not as cruel as that of men; I wanted to scream at them and tell them that it was worse, much much worse. I was touched by the fact that you had organised support groups for the end of the day. I thought it was extremely sensitive of you. However, I was unable to attend because I just wanted to hide away and cry. I cried all the way home on the train and have rarely stopped crying since. My doctor has given me anti-depressant drugs but I know they cannot be the permanent answer.

Let me tell you as briefly as I can about my story. For some reason, I think because my mother had post-natal depression, I did not bond with her. From a very early age I had the impression of being a deep disappointment to her. When I was four I was left alone with my baby sister, 3 weeks old, and she drowned — for years and years I had assumed that I killed her — I saw myself lifting her and putting her into the bath of water but just over a year ago I had a clear 'flashback' to the incident and saw that I was helping my mother to bath the baby. My mother left us to answer the doorbell saying the words 'hold on' but the baby was wriggling and I couldn't hold on and when my mother returned the baby had drowned. All hell was let loose and I was banished up to my room where my older brother told me I'd 'killed' the baby. Something in my head exploded and I remember nothing more of that day. The baby was never spoken of again by anyone and my mother never smiled now or laughed or sang and I knew for certain that she hated me.

When I was about 10 years old my mother asked me to help her bring my uncle home from the pub — she could see him staggering across the field to our house and knew he was the worse for drink. I went upstairs with him and my mother began to undress him for bed and then she left me and told me to 'finish off'. My uncle began making sexual advances asking me to touch his penis and saying he would give me money if I did it properly. This became a regular occurrence that I would go to my uncle's room and he would give me money for satisfying him sexually. He told me it was our secret and that I was special to him and he even said I was beautiful — no one had ever said that before. I knew that what I was doing was wrong but I also had a sense that it would make my mother angry if she knew and I was glad about that. By the time I was twelve he was having full intercourse with me and, although he was a huge man (23 stone), I cannot say that I hated it — I didn't. I loved the attention, I loved the secrecy and I loved the money.

At the same time as this was going on I had become very close to my cousin James, who was the same age as me. We used to play for hours on our bikes together but our favourite game was 'wrestling' on my parents' big bed. My mother used to go mad if she caught us, saying it wasn't decent for a boy and girl of our age to behave like this. Late one night I heard her and my father talking about sending James to boarding school but they couldn't afford it and then they said they'd send him to another aunt and uncle in the city so that he could go to the big public school near them and just pay day-fees. I told James this and we decided we would run away together that night. I had plenty of my uncle's money stored away and he said he knew where his real mother lived (his mother had had a breakdown when her husband committed suicide and that's why my cousins lived with us). Eventually we found my aunt's house but she just phoned my mother and said we were there. Next morning she sent James back saying he must go to school as his father would have wanted it. I was violently sick that morning so she told my mother I could stay for a day or two till I got better. But I was sick next morning too and the next so she took me to a doctor. The doctor told her I was pregnant. She went mad — she thought it must have been her son. When she calmed down I managed to tell her what my uncle had been doing. She arranged a termination and said I needn't go home again if I didn't want to. I felt she was my saviour — I could see the sun shining through her — to me she was everything that was wonderful because she had rescued me from hell.

At first it was great, she was so warm and loving and caring and sleeping beside her was sheer joy and even when she first began to touch me sexually I never thought it was bad or wrong, in fact I liked it and would do all I could to seduce her into these situations. However, as the years went by she began to make more and more weird demands on me almost all of which involved terrible physical pain. If I ever talked about leaving she would remind me about having been pregnant and 'killing my baby'. I believed that's what abortion was and, of course, what I didn't realise, this also had echoes in it for me of the baby I'd drowned when I was four — I felt I was a double murderer and terrible as it was to stay with this aunt it felt like just punishment.

I have had psychiatric help over the years notably when I myself had a breakdown but even though I've told doctors about being abused — it was only ever my uncle I could tell them about —

somehow being sexually abused by a man seems acceptable while the other is just a big dark secret hemmed in by other dark secrets. I would never be able to tell anyone the details of what my aunt did to me and yet the memory of it is eating away at me like a cancer, she totally degraded me and blamed me for it, totally; at 16 I walked out of her house and did not see her again until I heard she was dying five years later and that she was asking for me. Stupidly I thought there would be a reconciliation, some kind of forgiveness which might lead to forgetting, I had this silly notion of it all coming right on her death bed so I went to see her. It was awful, she showed me her cancerous wounds and said I had caused them — she taunted me to kiss her breasts full of puss — 'You once were quick to kiss them and bite them,' she said. I fled the room in tears knowing she was going to the grave cursing me.

I feel exhausted having written all this and to someone I don't even know but maybe my story will help others. I have survived but I'm a very short way along the road to recovery. I know, and the 31st March made me realise it, that I need to get some therapeutic help for me, that I cannot keep hiding behind the pain of others.

Thanks for all you're doing for those who've been abused. I need a good therapist but where do you find them? That's a rhetorical question — I'll keep looking — don't feel you need to respond to this letter in any way, I needed just to write it.

11   Men survivors' stories

Richard Carter

Richard is a 41 year old psychotherapist who works with other abuse survivors. He is married with four children.

Richard's story

I was born in 1951. At the age of seven I had to go and live with my aunt, mainly because the family were under a lot of pressure, and I know now that my parents were on the edge of divorce. My eldest brother had just been sent to prison, but I did not know why, this was used to great effect against me later.

My aunt would have been around 28–30, she lived in a large house in the country and had always been known for being strict. When I arrived, I was told the rules about keeping my room tidy and reminded that I had been told to do what she said. Things went alright for the first week or so, then she started to smack me for the slightest reason. She always took my trousers or jeans off first, saying she wouldn't waste her energy hitting clothes. Soon after this started, she said I was always so naughty, she had to spend most of her day hitting me. Because of this she bought a note book (out of my pocket money) so she could mark down all the times I had been naughty during the day, then after my bath at night, she would give me what I had coming. After my bath, I had to put on my pyjama jacket, then go and wait for her in her bedroom, no matter how good I had been, there were normally between 10 and 20 wrong doings, each one meant a smack.

My uncle was away from home a lot because of his job, when he wasn't there she would walk around the house in her underwear or nightdress, she would laugh at me because I was embarrassed. One night I was in bed and she called me into the bathroom, she was in the bath and told me to get her a towel, when I passed it to her, she stood up. I gave her the towel and went to leave, but I was called back. She started to shout at me, asking what was wrong with her body, then she made me stand and watch her dry herself. When she had finished, she wrapped the towel around her and got out and told me to undress and get into the bath. When she saw I had an erection she again started shouting and hitting me while she called me names. When I got in the bath, she showed me how to wash it until it tingled. After that, she bathed with me whenever my uncle was away, sometimes I had to stand in the bath and wash it, while she washed her vagina. Other times we would wash each other's.

I can't remember how long it took her to move onto the 'dry and powder' but I remember one day there was only one towel in the bathroom (another black mark in my book), she took the towel and dried me off, I was then told to dry her. After we had finished, she laid the towel on the floor and told me to lie face down. She then rubbed baby powder on me top to toe, front and back. I then had to do the same to her. (I still hate the smell or feel of talcum powder.)

As a child, I wet the bed a lot, one night, after I had received my punishment, I was told I had to sleep in her bed because mine was still wet. During the night, I woke up because she was shaking and moaning, one of her hands was inside my pyjamas. I remember feeling very afraid as I tried to wake her. When I told her what had happened, she said she must have been having a nightmare. She said that if it happened again, I was not to wake her, what I had to do was hold her as tight as I could, and gently rub her tummy or back. I now know she was masturbating, although at the time I felt sorry for her and wanted to help her. Needless to say, it happened quite a lot. Most nights when I slept in her bed, in the morning we would end up with no clothes, although we had night clothes on when we went to bed.

The next step was for her to show me how much she loved me. The first time this happened was after a bath, she had powdered my back and told me to turn over. She said she wished I wasn't such a naughty boy as she loved me so much. As she said this, she started to fondle me. When I was hard, she said she would show me how much she loved me. When she bent her head down. I thought she was going to bite me. She stopped after a short while and asked if I liked it. Even if I didn't I wouldn't have told her — she was someone you never said no to. I said it felt nice and she said I should put my hand on top of her head, when I wanted her to stop, I just had to take my hand away. When it was over, she said she knew how much I had enjoyed it, because she felt me push her head down when I started to tingle. I don't think I did, but again I didn't argue. I had learnt from her that, if anyone does anything nice to you or for you, they expected something in return, this time was no exception. She said that now she had proved how much she loved me, I had to show her how much I loved her. She explained that women have a penis, but that it is only small, if I loved her, I would suck it for her. She laid down and made me look at her, with the finger, she pointed to her 'penis' and gave me instructions how to suck it, she put her hand on top of my head saying she would move it when she wanted me to stop. Of course it never moved, and I knew she pushed me down harder. I felt sure I was going to suffocate and tried to get up. I now know she had an orgasm, but when it happened, I thought she had wee'd in my mouth. That was too much and I threw up all over her thighs. Of course I received a beating, and had to do it again after she had had another bath. After this, she would often get me to show her how much I loved her. Sometimes it would be when we were downstairs alone, but most times it would be just before my punishment. If it happened downstairs, she would pat the settee for me to sit next to her saying, 'Come and show aunty how much you love her.' Sometimes I had to do it before she hit me, I had to say, 'If I show you how much I love you, will you rub out some of the marks in my book?' She always said yes, but I feel she smacked me just as many times. We nearly got caught a number of times, once my uncle came home early, I was powdering her when he knocked on the bathroom door. She put her dressing gown on and told me to get back into the bath. When she opened the door, he looked at me and asked her what was going on, but she managed to convince him, she said the bathroom door wasn't locked (it never was) and he could have walked in if he had wanted to.

The other time, we were downstairs on the settee, I was showing her I loved her when my mum came in the back door. As she shouted out my aunt's name, I was kicked across the other side of the room. She managed to pull her skirt down, but her knickers were still on the floor. When we were alone, Mum asked me loads of questions but I lied to her, I think she knew I was lying but nothing was done. I still get pangs of guilt when I think about those two times. If only I had said something, it would have stopped, but I was so afraid of her. When my Mum left I received the biggest beating ever. Aunty was sure I had told Mum what we were doing, no matter how much I claimed otherwise, she kept hitting. That night I was in the kitchen making a cup of tea and I remembered seeing a box in one of the kitchen drawers. I can still remember it was a yellow box with big black letters, the one word I was interested in was gun. When I found it, I took it out and opened it, praying she would not come in and catch me before I was able to shoot myself. I was so disappointed when I found it was only a flash gun for a camera.

It was around this time that I started to have problems at school. I had always found learning easy, and was usually in the top form. Nobody questioned me as to why my grades were slowly going down, or why I no longer played with any of my friends. I was always fighting or getting into trouble. When I was around 10, I stayed after school had finished and drew rude pictures of myself and my aunt on the pages of the class register. They soon found out it was me and I was expelled for three months. Nobody asked how I knew about such things, they just called my aunt to the school, told her what had happened, and she took me home. Of course she wasn't very pleased, and left me in no doubt what my fate would be when she got me home. It was the first time she used a cane on me, telling me as she hit me that, for the next three months, I would always get the cane as she didn't have to worry about leaving marks on me.

One day a friend's daughter stayed with us, she was about a year older than me. While we were upstairs playing, she asked me if I would show her my willy, I am almost certain my aunt was waiting outside the bedroom door, because the instant I took my trousers down, she came in the door with the cane. She made Amanda sit on the bed while I was punished, she told her that she would get the same if she ever did anything like that again. I saw Amanda a few years ago, and she told me she was 23 before she had the courage to do more than kiss her boyfriends, she still often has guilt feelings when she makes love to her husband.

During my three months away from school, I was introduced to full sex. Again it was in the bathroom, as she was drying me, I was told she had a special treat for me. Whenever she said this, it always meant some new form of abuse. Once she explained what I was to do, I tried, but without success. She got very angry, saying I was messing it up on purpose. She tried several ways to get me to do it properly, but ended up with her on top of me. She seemed to be enjoying herself, but I didn't feel part of it, I knew that she didn't care about how I felt. She was ignoring me completely. I wanted to speak to her, to remind her I was there. I remember I started to cry but she didn't even notice that. Then I had to stop myself from laughing as I watched her breasts bounding up and down, looking at them made the whole situation seem so comical for a while. When she had finished, I was told to get dressed and go and sit on my bed to wait for her. When she came in, she was holding a book and a newspaper. She sat next to me and asked me if I had enjoyed what had just happened. I said 'yes' because if you said 'no' to her, you were punished. She said did I know what I had just done. I said 'had sex'. She said 'yes, but do you know what incest means?' She passed me the book and told me to look it up. I couldn't spell it so she told me, but I still couldn't find it. She snatched the book back and found it and told me to read what it meant. I read some of it but I couldn't read it all so she read it out for me. I still didn't understand, so she said it meant having sex with a relative could send you to jail.

She then asked if I knew what rape was. Without waiting for an answer, she looked it up and read it out. It sounded like what I had done with her. She then opened the newspaper and showed me a story about a man who had been jailed for ten years for rape. I thought I was going to jail and started to cry. She put her arms around me and told me not to worry as she would never tell anyone. But she said I had to promise that every time my willy got hard, I had to tell her by saying, 'I need to rape you again Aunty'. She said that way, I wouldn't rape anyone else and go to prison. Every time I got hard, I was so scared I told her and we would have sex. The reason I was so afraid, is because my brother had been sent to jail, and I thought he had done the same thing to her. She knew I was unaware of his crime, and often said, 'Do this or do that, or I shall send you to join your brother'. Sometimes when I told her I was hard, she would say 'I was being too naughty and to teach me a lesson, I had to go and rape somebody else.' She would then make me go outside. I always sneaked around into the garden shed and sat and cried, terrified of my own erection. I soon found that masturbating made it go away, on one occasion when she sent me out, she found me in the shed. Without giving me a chance to pull my trousers up, she dragged me up the garden to the house. Her neighbour was in her garden, and she shouted to her, telling her what she had just caught me doing and pointed to my erection. As well as the beating I received, I also had to tell my uncle what I was caught doing. He gave me a long lecture about how wrong it was and that at my age I shouldn't even know about such things. Boy was I confused after that.

Not long after that incident, when I was having sex with her, I had a searing pain in my penis, it was so bad I started to cry. When I told her what was wrong, she called me a liar and made me carry on. This went on for about two weeks, until she believed me and took me to the doctors. All that morning, and on the way to the surgery, she made me go over my story. If I was asked if I had ever had sex, I was to say I once did it to a girl at school. To me, this was telling the doctor I had raped someone and I felt certain this time I was going to join my brother. She insisted on staying with me during the examination, obviously making sure I didn't say anything. Luckily enough, it was a routine problem, but it meant I had to go to hospital to be circumcised. Then she told the doctor she had caught me in the shed, and asked if that could be the cause, even though he had already told her it often happened to boys my age. An appointment was made at the hospital in two days' time. By now, even an erection caused me great pain, and true to form, she made sure I got an erection as often as she could. She also told me I was going into hospital to have it cut off, because I couldn't control it, and that when I came home again, she would have some pretty dresses for me as I would be a girl.

When I got to the hospital, she left straight away and I was left to get into my pyjamas. Soon a nurse came through the curtain, and asked me questions. I couldn't believe what happened next. She undid my pyjama bottoms, pulled them down and started to touch me. I can still remember thinking, 'All women are the same, even nurses'. All that day I cowered whenever a nurse came close. The next morning I was to have the operation done, another nurse came to my bed, drew the curtains and told me to undress. I started to cry and said I wanted to go home. She told me not to be silly. If I didn't get undressed, she would undress me. This made me become hysterical, and another nurse was called to hold me down, I was then given an injection. I was still crying as they undressed me, I don't remember much after that.

When I opened my eyes again, there was another nurse touching me. When she saw I was awake, she smiled, just the same way as my aunt did when she touched me. As soon as she had gone, I checked to see what they had done to me. Was I ever relieved to see my penis!

The next two days, I was examined by the nurses. Again, my feelings seemed to be pushed to one side. If I objected, I was forced. During my stay in hospital, I had no visitors. One nurse even asked me if I was an orphan. I have never felt so alone and unwanted. Those few days did nothing to build my faith in women. When my aunt came to get me, the nurses had already told her how I had behaved. The first thing I was told by her was what was going to happen to me when she got me home, and she kept her word.

It wasn't too long before the abuse started again, but each time she complained saying 'It's not as good now, they cut the best part of it off'. Often halfway through, she would tell me to stop, I would then have to give her oral sex, or we would masturbate together. On one such occasion, she said I would have to start to use her 'little boy's hole'. She put some vasoline on me and told me what to do. As soon as I entered her, it felt so different, I felt I was part of it and actually felt pleasure. Then when she said I had to be gentle as I was hurting her, I felt great and lost control of my actions. Then I had my first real orgasm, she must have felt it because she acted like she had never done before. She acted like she was crazy. After she had calmed down she made such a fuss, saying that I was now a real man, and that I had to do that each time from now on. Of course it wasn't long before she used it against me. She told me that is what two men do together, and for me to have done that inside her, I must be a queer. Sometimes she would hit me until I admitted I wanted to do it to a man, or she would threaten to get another boy and make me do it to him. For years afterwards, I was uncertain about my sexuality, so much so that when I reached my teens, I had sex with as many girls as I could, trying to convince myself I was not gay.

I was about 12 or 13 when I went back home and I no longer seemed to fit in. I was always the odd one out, or the one who was always in trouble. Even when I was home, she didn't stop. About three weeks after, she came to visit and looked at me when she told the family she was expecting. I really thought she was going to say I was the father. I don't know if she was expecting or just enjoying herself at my expense, either way she never had the child. I joined a group of Hells Angels when I was 14 and ran away from home several times. At 16, I moved into my own flat. Each week I had a different girlfriend, unable to understand why, when they got too close to the real me, I would reject them. I started to drink heavily and smoked pot. At 17 I married. When I was 19, I decided I had to do something with my life, so I joined the army. I had always been a violent person, and this was the ideal way to let out my anger, I put an end to the drinking, and started to do well. On the surface, everything seemed OK. I had two children and a good marriage. I didn't realise the abuse was still affecting and controlling me. Problems started to surface, mainly to do with sex, I couldn't stand being touched. Even walking through the town, if my wife held my hand, I would start to panic. In every situation, no matter where, I had a ready excuse to move away from her. If I found myself getting aroused, I would feel so guilty I would have to leave the room, or get out of the bed. I often remember saying to my aunt, 'I don't want to'. But she would point to my erection and say something like 'That tells me what a dirty boy you are and that you do want to'.

It wasn't long before I started drinking again, when this happened, my first wife left me because of the demands I was putting on her.

It was around this time that child abuse 'went public', although at the time I didn't connect my problems to my abuse. It was only when my second marriage started to go the same way as the first, that I told my second wife. Instead of the rejection I was expecting, she listened and stood by me. We found Penny Parks through the Samaritans, I went through therapy and out the other side. Now I understand that it wasn't just the sex, it was the hurt and the humiliation I was put through. It cost me one marriage and cost my children years of missed love and affection. I never had any thoughts about abusing them. In fact, it was just the opposite. If I gave them a cuddle, I was afraid it would go further. If I sat them on my knee, or even if I was alone with them, if someone came in, I felt they were thinking that I had abused them. I became afraid to be with my own children. I have managed to make up for a lot, both with my children and my wife, and now I have managed to separate sex from abuse. I can accept love and affection for what it is, without feeling threatened.

Tony Schreiber

Tony is married with two grown sons, and lives on the West Coast of the US. He is a member of Parents United, a support group for those who have abused and for their families. He has not confronted his aunt, who abused him, because 'she is in her seventies and not even aware that I remember anything. I don't relate to her any more. I feel very sad and used when I think of her, but I don't want to hurt her either. She hasn't long to live and I can't see me destroying her peace.'

Tony's story

As near as I can tell, my aunt started to molest me at about the age of three. At about that time, I had to sleep with her since we did not have enough beds. The abuse continued until about the age of six and a half, when my mother found out and stopped it, as well as making different sleeping arrangements for me. I was molested virtually every night during that time. She made me perform oral sex on her, held me on top of her and caused my small penis to penetrate her as much as it could. She taught me how to 'hump'. During the day, since we had only one bathroom and she was in charge of me, she would go into the bathroom with me most of the time. She would sit on the toilet and open her legs to allow me to urinate into the toilet between them. When I finished, she would rub my penis in her vagina and attempt to get it erect. She would periodically purchase new underpants and I was forced to watch while she tried on each pair in front of me, turning at the last instant so that I never really saw her sex organs for any length of time.

I have to explain that I was born a bastard and was an object of shame to my family, and particularly to my mother. Our family had lived in the same area since 1732 so that everyone knew us and everyone knew of my birth and the shame that attended it. The only person who touched me in a caring way was my aunt and she molested me until I thought it was normal. The only thing which made it strange was her insistence that I 'not tell anyone' and that 'it was our secret'. I never told.

One day I was in the bathroom when my mother sat on the commode. I had to go and so I asked her if I could go between her legs like my aunt had made me do. She questioned me and beat the hell out of me when I told her what had gone on, although I never really told her just what had happened and how extensive the abuse had been. From now on, I had to sleep with my grandfather. At about the same time, I was caught indulging my normal sexual curiosity by looking at my girl cousins and playing with them. Again I was beaten. By now my mother was convinced that I was a full-blown sex fiend. I was not yet seven, a budding pervert and I had lost the only source of affection that I had ever known. But there was now another reason for me to be hated and despised.

The new reason for my misery was a German surname. I started school in September 1938. My named sound very much like a German maniac called Scheckelgruber. The other kids bullied me, called me names and beat. me. I had to run home from school several times a week and no one dared to be friends with me. This went on until the war turned around and the allies started to win. The trouble is that by then the bullies enjoyed picking on me so much that they kept it up the rest of the way through school. I had very few friends of either sex and did not know how to behave with the ones that I had.

I was so starved for love and attention that I fell completely in love with any female who looked in my direction and latched onto male friends with a strangling possessiveness. During this time, I molested any female relatives or neighbours who came within reach. I also started masturbating as soon as I learned how. I was also molested by a man who taught me the pleasures of receiving oral sex. I felt that I was the lowest form of life during this time. I tried to commit suicide for the first time at the age of 14 when a girl jilted me. I ate the jewels out of a piece of jewellery I had gotten for her, after smashing it to bits. I then lay down and waited for death.

I was no stranger to suicide. I had tuition from my mother. When I was seven, my mother married my step-father. He would gamble his wages away and come home and beat me regularly, using any excuse. Instead of protecting me, my mother would put her head in the oven and attempt to gas herself. I would have to pull her out and plead with her not to kill herself. Imagine the distress all of this caused me.

My mother would joke about 'sex education'. I wonder now if she was setting me up. I can remember vividly one incident that happened when I was about 12 years old. I had been molesting my cousin, who was my age and staying with us at that time. My mother, who had encouraged us to 'experiment', accidently walked in and raised the roof. I ran away, terrified, to my father's house. He lived in the same town, but I had never talked to him face-to-face before. I went to his door and knocked. He came to the door and I asked him if I could sleep in his basement overnight. All he could say was had I come to ask for more money for my mother. I was devastated. My fantasy had always been that he and my mother would get married (in spite of my hated stepfather being very much on the scene) and now when I asked him for help, all he could talk about was money.

In 1951, I left school, worked for a few years and then joined the Navy. A year or so later I met my wife and married her six months later. We have been married for 35 years and have two sons. During our married life, I have put her through hell. I molested young girls many times, though she was not aware of it then. I was not easy to live with and doubted that anyone could really care for someone as despicable as me. Certainly no one in my life had before. I set her up in situations that would prove to me that she didn't care. Our communication disintegrated. My sons rightly felt that I was not a fit person to either be married to their mother or to be a father to them. I was selfish, insecure, and impossible.

I did try to get help and finally turned myself in to an adult crisis home. They did not help me, but I was able to keep myself in control for a while. I managed to molest on only a few occasions for a period of twenty years. Then last year I abused a young girl and this time I was caught. I joined a well-known support group and have also been in therapy for about 2 years. Much of what I have learned in the past year has helped me to know the danger signals and ways that I can stop abusing. I cannot say that I will never molest again. I can't really be cured, but I can say that I feel better about myself than I ever have before. My wife and I were separated, but are going to counselling and are now back together. Incidentally my aunt, who started this cycle, is now in a convalescent hospital after suffering a stroke. I thought about sending a card to her, but just couldn't bring myself to do it.

I guess I will be in therapy for the rest of my life. I know that the experts say that female sexual abuse is rare. Don't believe it — there are many out there like me who were abused and who are now causing more abuse. In the support group of males I attend, 75 per cent of the molesters have been abused by women and some have been abused by both men and women. I sometimes wonder how different my life might have been, had my mother or someone else listened to the pain of a small boy instead of beating and blaming him for being abused.

Alan Long

Alan Long lives in the north of England and works in the arts.

Alan's story

I am 58 years old. During the war I was evacuated first to stay with my grandmother and then an aunt. My aunt whose name was 'Maggie' who would have been around 30 years of age, worked selling ice creams. She lived with a friend called Amy who had a daughter. Both of the women were in love with the same man (although I believe they had many other relationships), who came to the house every day. He was a cook in the American army. Amy's daughter was a year older than myself. Amy was in the habit of spanking her daughter over her knee and shortly after I was moved there she started spanking me. Once when over her knee she put her hand on my penis and said 'It's getting hard, come and look at this'. My aunt Maggie came in and they rubbed my penis until it was sore. I certainly don't remember having an erection. One day I was spanked in front of the American. I cannot remember what for and he suggested to the women that I be made to wear Amy's daughter's knickers as part of my punishment. I was 10 years old. From then until I was 13 I was constantly 'abused' by the two women usually with the man present and watching. I kissed and licked their nipples and vagina, they stroked my penis. I was always spanked, probably every day. (I hesitated to use the word abused because I soon began to like it, even being spanked. I also liked wearing the knickers, although on one occasion for swearing, I had to wear them every day for a week to school and I was frightened about being detected.) They were always very familiar with me, on entering the room for instance Amy often put her skirt over my head as a kind of greeting. Although the man was most often present he never touched me. On reflection, though, it was certainly done for his entertainment. Amy's daughter was also spanked every day, but was not present while the women touched me. Once when caught listening at the door she was whipped with a cane and tied to the toilet. Both of us were often spanked in front of visitors, who sometimes joined in. One of them was a fiancé of my uncle who was visiting. She became my aunt. She was extremely religious. She invited me for 'tea' at her own house, and while I was there spanked me for herself, nude. Afterwards she gave me a bath. I was introduced to another woman a friend of Amy's who was older than the two women. I should think she was around 40 — although I'm only guessing now at a much later date. This woman took me out once a week to her home and lifting her skirt put my head between her legs. She always kept her knickers on, pulling them to one side. She 'played' with my penis often for a whole afternoon and then would take me to the cinema, buying me sweets. Although it was never mentioned, it was obvious to me even then that Maggie and Amy had talked to the women about me before the outings. Although a 'friend' of Amy's she was not close and didn't ever visit the house except to pick me up and deliver me back.

When the war finished I was moved back to London. I was now 13. The abuse had taken place in Sussex. The woman (the 40 year old one) met me outside my house and we went to a room and then to the cinema. I never said anything to my mother. I met her once a week for another 2 years. She wasn't physically attractive, small and plump, whereas Amy was big and blonde (but probably not real).

When I was 15 I started going with girls and told the woman I wasn't going to meet her again. She didn't say anything. I don't know if she saw anyone else.

So where did it leave me? I'm not sure what effect it had. Obviously some. I have always been 'lucky' with women. Although I am not good looking, I have often had relationships (although sometimes short) with women that are usually called 'beautiful'. My taste has changed as I've got older. For many years I was attracted to 'cheap' women. I was bi-sexual from the age of 18 until around 45. I have never worked for anyone. I was an artist. Although not famous I have always done OK. I liked wearing women's underwear and spanking women and being spanked (by men). This has definitely affected me, for instance although I have had 4 children I have never once hit them or allowed the women I was with at the time to hit them. I have no doubt that this is because of my own experience.

I once appeared in a 'sex' magazine dressed in women's underwear, and from this I received over 200 letters from men. I wrote to all, and had sex with about 100 of them. One of the men I saw repeatedly until he was convicted of strangling a woman (strangely enough I have had several relationships with people who were convicted of murder or manslaughter, but this is almost certainly a coincidence).

With men I always played the passive part. I am sexually aggressive with women. I have lived with many women, my relationships generally last around a year and almost without exception the women have been masochistic. It's possible I attract this type of woman. As well as 'steady' relationships I have many more casual. Usually I get these from adverts in newspapers or magazines. At least three women I have been with have themselves 'abused' children. One was a headmistress, one a 'head of English' and the other a dance teacher. I have been married three times, and am married at present. of my four children, two were from the same woman who when she left took them with her. I was married to her. The other two have been left with me and live nearby. I have a good relationship with them all, but on reflection I don't show physical love. I never put them on my lap, etc., but we are all close. I have myself never been attracted to young people of either sex. I like women that are physically strong rather than intellectual although I always play the 'aggressive' role with women.

I think my own feelings about whether it was harmful to me or not are mixed. In the first instance I think it was wrong. My aunt Maggie, her friend and the American soldier combined sex with elements of violence and fetishism, which have remained with me, and probably wouldn't have if I'd never met them. With my Aunt Maggie and friends it was just an extension of their own sexual fun. With the woman I was passed on to, who took me to the cinema I think that, although she is the least memorable, it was probably OK, and there was certainly no lasting harm. She just felt more comfortable having sex with a boy.

Would I mind my own children having the same experiences? Hard to answer. Probably not. I think ideally sex should start with someone your own age. It seems to make more sense that it would be nicer for two 12/13 year olds to explore something together than, as in my case, to be initiated by a 'party' of adults for their own fun.

On the other hand I have always thought the greater damage is done by fuss surrounding 'abuse' than to actual action. I'm sure that if others didn't regard it as important, nor would the child. I don't see any harm with me and women who took me to the cinema. I have never felt the hatred that some people obviously do for people who sexually abuse children.

I have myself never been attracted to children. So it certainly didn't affect me that way. On the other hand, because my own 'abuse' was linked with spanking, I have never struck my children (although I've spanked women and men). So it's definitely affected how I express my sexual desires with adults.

I talk very easily to women, and get on in their company. This may be a plus. I don't think it's easy to say, what would 'I' be like if this, or that hadn't happened.

I suppose I'm a sort of sexual 'liberal' (in the 19th century sense). But I cannot say if that is good or bad.

George Woods

George is retired and lives in Scotland.

George's story

It would seem that only those who have been unfortunate enough to have been victims of violent sexual experiences come to the attention of researchers. No doubt this is because of the traumatic emotional effects that have followed.

However, the consequences of abuse are not always big. There must be, I'm sure, others like myself whose experiences were in fact completely the opposite. Who while being allegedly 'abused' knew only love, affection, kindness and, yes, considerable pleasure.

After all the publicity of recent years I believe it should be pointed out that there are two sides to every coin. And my own experience, I'm sure cannot be unique.

To begin with, a relationship which first began over 50 years ago between my sister and myself is still continuing today — albeit very spasmodically — because of the distance between us.

I suppose the 'abuse' — if that is the correct word for it in this case — began when I was about 7–8 years old. We lived in a small village. My father worked night shifts, and after he had gone to work, like most kids I went into my mother's bed for a cuddle. It is too far back now to recall how it began but I remember that my mother liked me to fondle and suck her breasts. I do have a distinct recollection of her taking my hand and pressing it between her thighs, as she fondled my penis. All of this was done with a good deal of kissing and affection. Somehow or other it all gradually progressed until it became a regular thing for me to go down under the bedclothes between her legs to give her oral sex, which, after a time, I must confess I rather liked. At no time can I ever remember my mother using any kind of pressure or coercion to persuade me. Everything was done with great love and kindness.

Looking back on it the first time we had sexual intercourse together was no great drama. It just seemed to happen naturally. I suppose my mother must have been the initiator but I can't say in all truth that I needed much encouragement. Even though I must have been only about 8 years old I seemed to need very little instruction and even less encouragement. With most of us under the right conditions, I have always believed, sex is as natural as breathing air. I was in my twenties the last time I had sexual intercourse with my mother.

Sexual contact with my sister began when I was about 10 and she was 12 years. If she ever suspected that there had been anything going on between mother and me, to this day she has never mentioned it. And if she had said anything, I'm sure I would have denied it. Just as I am sure my mother was aware of the sexual relationship between my sister and me, she never once mentioned a thing to either of us.

When the relationship between my sister and I began, it is difficult to say who was the most precocious between the two of us. It began when my parents started going out on Sunday nights together to nearby villages. My sister was left to bath me for school next day and put me to bed. After they had gone, when my sister had run the bath, we would both undress and get in the bath together. We still laugh about how she would stand up with one foot up on the side of the bath to pull the lips of her vagina open to show me the place 'where boys push their dickies', then it was my turn to stand up to let her play with my erection.

As can be well imagined, the scene was soon shifted to the bedroom for the ritual game of 'doctors and nurses' which was promptly followed by enthusiastically realistic games of 'mothers and fathers'. While naive adults would no doubt have blamed my sister, being the older, as the initiator of the so-called 'abuse', in reality from the beginning it was six-of-one and half-a-dozen of the other.

Yet, in spite of accepted wisdom, neither my sister nor I would seem to have suffered any of the feared mental or emotional after-effects — at least none that would seem to be overtly apparent. Both my sister and I eventually went on to grammar schools. My sister went on to train as a doctor. I went to university and studied chemistry then joined a major international corporation.

My sister and I both married successfully. I have three children and she has five. My wife and I are still together after more than thirty years; as are my sister and her husband. Neither my sister or myself have mentioned anything of our sexual relationship to our respective spouses. Off-and-on over the years, when the opportunity has presented itself, we have enjoyed the most passionate sexual intercourse. Once, some years back, when our joint families were together for a few days, we took every opportunity once and sometimes twice every day to steal away for our secret sessions of illicit loving.

Now both our families are grown up and married, without any of the problems and traumas one reads about that seem to beset so many others. My sister and I still sleep together, and our pleasure in each others' bodies, and the sexual satisfaction we give to each other, is as ardent and as fresh as it ever was. If the real truth was ever revealed, I feel certain that we are far from being alone.

I did not, however, have any sexual relationship with my own daughters.

Perhaps the nearest it ever came to a repetition of the relationship between my mother and me, was with my oldest daughter. It occurred when she was 15. My wife was away visiting a relative.

This particular evening I got home around 10pm from a dinner. When I entered the living room my daughter was lying stretched out on the sofa in her nightdress, as if asleep. The rest of the children were in bed. It was obvious that she was feigning sleep; what was significant was the way she was lying, with one knee raised exposing her bare genitals. I shook her shoulder to arouse her and tell her she should be in bed.

What happened after this, had I been a little bit inebriated, might well have turned out differently. After making us both coffee, she asked if she could sleep in the front bedroom with me. As tactfully as I could, I explained that I didn't think that would be wise; that she was now almost a young woman and that if in the night when I was half-asleep I mistook her for her Mum, then anything might happen.

Her reply to this was instructive. She, she said, didn't mind. If I wanted to, that was OK — she wouldn't tell anybody. Some of her friends at school, she said, were sleeping with their dads and had told her it was wonderful. It took some time to explain that it would not be fair on her Mum or me. If she and I became so close it would only create difficulties for everyone. I remember saying something like: Perhaps her schoolfriends didn't have any brothers or sisters, so they had to share all their love with their dads — but we were different. Although not entirely convinced she accepted this explanation.

Nevertheless, afterwards, I did begin to wonder what might have happened had she approached me differently. What would my reaction have been if, like myself, she had just come into the bedroom and got into bed with me for a hug and cuddle — as I had done with my own mother? What then would my response have been? The answer, quite frankly, is — I don't honestly know!

Certainly, neither my wife nor I would have actively encouraged such relationships between my own children. Though I sometimes wonder about my daughter and her younger brother. Nothing was actually ever seen but we strongly suspected that 'something was going on' between the two of them.

Neither my wife nor I — and not out of any cowardice — saw any compelling need to interfere in what both of us accepted as part of the natural process of sexual development and of growing up. This may not be a view shared by the majority of couples, I suspect, but I'm sure there are many more who — irrespective of their childhood sexual experiences — do.

One thing my personal experiences have convinced me of is that mutually agreed sexual relationships within families — especially between siblings — is far, far more common than the professional moralists would like to believe. Whether that is right or wrong, it is an indisputable fact of human nature after all the veneer of social morals is stripped away.

This is not to say incest is something I am advocating as some free-for-all panacea for everyone. Just to point out that, like most other things in life, there are exceptions to every rule!

William Banks

William was born in London to a widow who already had several children and couldn't cope with any more. He was adopted as a baby by his father, who was British born, but half-French, half-Jewish by blood and his mother, also British born, but of Spanish parent-age.

William's story

They had been married in their mid-twenties. He was conscripted into the army at the outbreak of War in 1939, and she followed him round Britain to his various postings. Despite wartime difficulties, she desperately wanted a family. She had been brought up in a Spanish Catholic environment and motherhood and housewifery were her be all and end all. But she had become a lapsed Catholic, was not at all religious, and believed in contraception. He was a communist atheist and very 'free-thinking'.

During the war years she had several pregnancies, but all resulted in miscarriages. She had been advised by medics that bringing a healthy baby into the world might be difficult for her because his and her blood groups were incompatible. But she has told me she was determined to have children.

However, after the trauma of the last failed pregnancy, she had an operation in a local hospital. She confided to a nurse her difficulty in having children and the nurse told her there was a woman in the hospital in great distress because she had an unwanted baby boy. That was me. My adoptive mother gave up becoming pregnant and I was adopted by her and her husband.

As far as I was concerned, we had a 'normal', happy, middle-class suburban life until he suddenly left us and home when I was about seven. Unknown to my mother he had been having an affair with his secretary and planned to live with her.

She and I were devastated. She had no idea he was discontented. He had been a very open and affectionate father to me. They had told me as soon as I was able to understand that I was adopted, and everything at home about bodily functions and sexuality had always been out in the open. They were quite modern for their day and didn't seem to have any hang-ups or taboos. I was never told any fibs if I asked what other parents would have considered a 'rude' question.

My adoption never bothered me, and still doesn't, because I was only two weeks old when they took me home and I never saw my natural mother again. I was so much part of them and their families that I always felt that I came from a Spanish/French/Jewish back-ground. I still do.

My mother, despite her grief at being abandoned, pulled herself up by her boot-straps, got a job, and kept us both quite comfortably, if on a shoe-string. She and I saw my father about once a month. He was still living and working in London; his girlfriend had ditched him. We never had a private address for him or knew exactly what he was up to but maintained contact through his office and by meeting in the West End for meals and outings.

When I was 10, he was involved in a shady financial deal (quite out of character because of his political and ethical stances), lost his job, and went to live abroad, leaving my mother with no financial support at all and a lot of debts. Unknown to us, he had remortgaged the house we were living in and couldn't keep up the repayments because he'd lost all his money in this shady deal. My mother worked even harder to keep a roof over our heads and even managed to pay the fees of a private school for me.

I was devoted to her and, looking back, I suppose she was over-doting, over-protective of me. In fact, she kept me wrapped in cotton-wool, so to speak. Every childhood ailment and accident was, in retrospect, treated like a major drama. And, indeed, I was often ill, and lost a lot of schooling through stays in hospital and being carted about to various specialists for this, that and the other thing. I was very much a mummy's boy, didn't relate much to other children, and much preferred the company of adults — mainly females among my mother's friends and family. There was no 'uncle' figure for me in her entourage. Her own brothers weren't at all avuncular or paternal, and of her many friends and neighbours it was the women — the 'aunties' — I was fondest of.

I played the piano, knitted, painted, attempted embroidery, loved dressing up in women's clothes, and shunned all what were supposed to be little boys' pursuits — sports, bikes, cars, guns, and so on.

I was regarded at school as a cissy and developed asthma and hay-fever. This made my mother even more protective of me. The teachers must have been really browned off with all her notes saying I was too frail for sport and must always put my blazer on to go out at playtime!

At the time, I didn't regard my mother as obsessive about me; but I do in retrospect. However, I did feel that we were rather special and used to boast about what a difficult life she had and how hard she worked and how clever she was, etc.

In order to help make ends meet, when I was about ten-and-a-half my mother let two rooms in our house to a bachelor tenant, who remained with us for 11 years. He was a shy, sexless kind of man and there was no trouble with him.

Very occasionally, a man would take a fancy to my mother, but it never got beyond the odd social occasion. The widowed father of a school-chum of mine took a fancy to her, and would sometimes take my mother out for a ride in his car or for a drink. His son occasionally stayed the night with us while his father was away on business. Because two bedrooms were let, on those occasions my mother slept in my single bed, and James and I slept together in her double bed. I fancied him something rotten (I was about 11) and wanted to cuddle him, but he wasn't interested. Some nitty-gritty!

Then my mother took pity on a friend who had three children and who'd been abandoned and rendered penniless by her husband. Two of her children were taken into care, and Rosemary and her baby came to live with us.

This meant I had to give up my own bedroom — which I did willingly and feeling very virtuous about it — so that Rosemary could have my bed and the baby's cot be squeezed in alongside it. I slept on a single bed in my mother's bedroom.

I must have been about 11 or slightly older and, despite my mother's openness about the human body, was beginning to become a bit shy about my own body. To give me some privacy while I was undressing and sleeping, a wardrobe door used to be pulled open to provide a sort of partial screen.

However, whenever anyone extra came to stay — a chum of mine, or one of my mother's female friends or relatives — they would sleep in my single bed, and I would sleep with my mother in her double bed at the other end of the room.

She used to ask me to cuddle up to her and would arrange herself so that her back was towards my front and she'd put my free left hand over her shoulder and on to her breasts.

I can remember not particularly wanting to do this because I thought I was too old for cuddles from Mum. I was also embarrassed because I was at the stage when developing boys have an erection at the slightest provocation, and certainly almost any kind of physical contact had that effect on me then.

But I never told her I was embarrassed, and she used to snuggle her buttocks against my erection. She must have felt it. Nothing more than that happened, and then only occasionally, except that it seemed to me she sought opportunities to see me naked. Motherly curiosity about her growing son? I wonder?!

I took to locking the bathroom and the loo door when I was in either, and she protested that I shouldn't 'in case you're taken ill in there'. On one occasion she caught me on my way to the loo in the night without my pyjama bottoms on and commented on how big my penis was growing. Despite our former openness, I nearly died and must have blushed all over, and I made every effort to ensure that she shouldn't see me naked again.

Once I was about 13, and her friend and the baby had been found a home of their own, I got my own bedroom back. But whenever there was an extra over-night guest, my mother always arranged it that the guest had my bed and I slept with her. This, it seems to me now, was unnecessary. There was a sofa downstairs, and camp or fold-away beds are not impossible to procure even on a limited budget. Indeed, in the case of the very occasional male guest, I would have much rather slept with him than my mother! But I was the quiet, obedient sort of boy, and never protested. I suppose she had done so much for me and had in many respects organised her work, housekeeping and helping others so well that I felt whatever she suggested was beyond argument or criticism or gain-saying.

I was, after my father left home, very much part of an almost all-female world. It's strange, and may be disappointing for female parents who've been 'correctly' open with their male children about sexuality and bodily functions, but I have to say that my mother's involving me in hers did embarrass and annoy me even, I think, slightly before I reached puberty. She always told me when she was menstruating and would sometimes send me to the shops to buy sanitary protection for her. As a wee boy I didn't mind, but later on I did, and when I said I didn't like to ask for what she wanted, she used to write the brand and size on a piece of paper so I could hand it over the counter without saying anything.

My mother was a very vibrant, attractive woman in a Spanish kind of way: long, thick dark hair, dark brown eyes, big busted and big hipped, but with used to be called 'a figure' — not a fat lump! She was always very well brassièred and corsetted and paid a great deal of attention to her appearance. She could make very attractive clothes for herself out of remnants and cast-offs, and was often the envy of other women because she had 'flair'. I suppose some suburban English women would have regarded her as a bit flashy, but would call how she used to look 'Continental' to be polite! In fact, she never looked cheap, but was always rather more daring with colour and hair-styles than the average Essex housewife of the 1940s and 1950s.

Men did fancy her. Two of them I remember well. But she made it quite plain to me that she wasn't interested in them. Of the father of a school-friend James who used to take her out occasionally, she once said to me: 'Would you like Uncle George (as I then called him) as a daddy?' I remember that I flew into a tantrum and made it perfectly clear that while I liked James as a 'brother' I most certainly didn't want Uncle George as a father. No doubt I was jealous, and later — in my late teens, perhaps — remember thinking how selfish I had been and that if I hadn't said that, something might have come of their relationship and she wouldn't have had to be having me cuddling her in bed.

I really did like Uncle George. But her suggestion frightened me, I suppose.

She always gave in to me. Despite the most awful financial contortions she had to get into to keep us and pay for my education, when I wanted a piano and piano lessons, she found the cash. When I said I was embarrassed because the other kids went on holidays but we couldn't afford to, she found the cash. In many ways I was an indulged, spoilt brat, and much prone to tantrums and illnesses which I now suspect were psychosomatic.

Now I'm a reasonably content homosexual in a stable relationship of 10 years' standing (a previous one lasted almost as long). My mother is in her eighties. She is frail and occasionally confused. Everything she scrimped and scraped for has had to be sold so she can be looked after in an old peoples' home and the tables have turned because I now subsidise her.

I love her dearly. She accepted my homosexuality almost without a qualm. There were a few initial tears (I would have been about 20 when I told her) and she at first blamed herself. But, again in retrospect, it almost seems to me that this was what she wanted and expected. While occasionally she says: 'Oh dear! I shall never have any grandchildren', on the other hand if I had been heterosexual and had girlfriends or wives, my goodness me, she would have been jealous!

I only now get cross with her when she does the usual old parent to middle-aged child stuff and tells me to comb my hair, or not stay out late at night in the dark, or says 'watch your chest' if I so much as clear my throat. Then I feel, and sometimes say, 'For God's sake stop suffocating me. You were always good at that!'

My lover and current life-partner and I have discussed much of this before. At the time my previous gay relationship broke up very nastily (curiously my previous lover treated me almost in the same way as my father treated my mother), I was very shaken up and went into analysis for a while. All the foregoing — and much else — came out then in what I regard as a very healthy way.

I was not wantonly abused. My mother could hardly have had any real sexual stimulation by having me lie behind her in bed. But it has left me with the feeling that, because she was a woman of the world and not some poor, ignorant waif, she in a way knew what she was doing. It was very much 'our private world' without anyone saying as much.

I was not given pleasure by it, but I certainly wasn't given any pain, just irritation and embarrassment.

Andrew Martin

Andrew Martin is 36 years old, married for the second time and has four children. His wife has been married twice before and was herself physically abused by her previous husbands. Andrew is a mature social work student studying in a university in England.

Andrew's story

My father died of a heart attack recently. My mother is alive and lives 400 miles away which suits me fine. I have not liked my mother for a long time, although I go through periods of faking an interest in her well-being. I do not think she is a very nice person, she is malicious and vindictive. She drove a wedge between my father and me, for which I cannot forgive her. I miss my dad even though I did not see him much when he was alive. I do not think it will be the same when mum dies.

Our family and mum's sister Ruth's family were close. Dad and her husband had been close friends, courted the two sisters and then married them. My cousin Mavie was 4 years older than me but spent more time with us on holiday, etc. and was like my big sister. She emigrated to South Africa 20 years ago and I miss her, but we are different people now.

I hated the transition from primary to Grammar school. My birthday is the end of August so I was the youngest in my year. I lived on a council estate and was also the only one going to the swot school, so quickly became alienated on the estate and also in school for coming from the 'slums'. Despite being tall and strong I was bullied a lot. Mum and Dad didn't know, and due to a job change had met lots of new friends, and had started going out a lot. My brother, who was young, and I were no problem. When left, we listened to records and caused no bother. My aunt and family had bought an off licence and lived above. This became a magnet for me. I hadn't started drinking yet, but free soda and crisps were good. They also had a colour TV, my cousin's record collection was excellent, and it was altogether a nicer place to be.

I started finding any excuse to be there — offering to help out in the shop at weekends, etc. and staying over when I could. I then discovered my uncle was heavily into porn magazines, the place was bursting at the seams with stuff: lots of what I would consider hardcore. He had been in the merchant navy and probably still had mates bringing stuff in. For an 11 year old this was heaven sent, I would smuggle magazines into school and quickly became popular.

Ruth had a reputation: mum and dad were forever talking about her having lots of affairs. She was always well-dressed, wore lots of make-up and tight-fitting clothes. She always smelled nice. I found myself noticing these things more and more, and feeling embarrassed when I was too close to her. This wouldn't stop me visiting. It made me want to spend more time there. She always seemed to have time to talk.

I had just turned 12 and was staying the weekend. John, Ruth's husband, was working nights. I was babysitting my younger cousin who was about 7. I remember Ruth getting ready to go out. I remember how she smelled and what she was wearing. She asked me if she looked good before she went out — I nearly choked. I thought she was gorgeous, but said she looked lovely. She kissed me on the cheek before she went and as she was going told me to put the magazines back when I finished. I wanted to die of embarrassment: in a few seconds I had just felt wonderful and then been gutted. She came in about one o'clock, drunk but not that drunk. I was still up and offered to make coffee. She wanted a drink and poured out a brandy for both of us. It was not unusual for me to drink by then, but I didn't like it much. She told me that she had gone back to some bloke's house after the club but it was a dump so she wouldn't stay. I said that if she had brought him here I wouldn't have told anyone. She laughed and started talking about how I should always keep secrets and then said that if I could promise never to tell anyone, then she would let me have a big secret. I said yes but felt a bit scared. I think I thought she would tell me she had murdered someone.

She called me on to the settee next to her but instead of whispering she told me to undo her denim waistcoat. I couldn't move. I was frozen and bright red and trembling I thought my heart was going to burst, I was shaking so much. She asked me if I fancied her, I nodded. She said she would soon settle my nerves and led me up to their bedroom. She switched out the light but it wasn't that dark. She undressed me. I wasn't saying or doing anything and just stood there being undressed like a child getting ready for bed. Then she took her top off and her skirt. I could see her in bra and knickers and I was terrified to move. She started saying that the pictures in the magazines were not as good as the real thing. She took off her underwear and I just sort of lunged at her burying my face in her breasts. I'm sure I cried or sobbed. She pushed me back to lie on the bed and started to call me baby. Don't cry baby. Come to Aunt Ruth baby. Slowly baby — all the time. I couldn't get an erection, which didn't seem to worry her. She got me to touch her, masturbate her, suck on her breasts. We rolled about, her giving instructions — me trying to do exactly what she asked. I was desperate to please her, trembling and constantly apologising for not getting an erection or not doing it right. I ejaculated without an erection. She tasted it and joked that it wasn't ripe: she made me taste it. I just did what I was told. She fell asleep I lay cuddling her for hours. Touching her skin, smelling her, pulling the covers back to look at her. She woke in the middle of the night and ordered me back to my own bed, very coldly. I obeyed but felt shunned. I lay thinking about her, praying I hadn't done anything to upset her and hoping she would let me touch her again. I could hear her in the bathroom having a shower. I decided I would never wash again.

The next morning it was like nothing had happened except, I felt as though I must have looked so guilty and bright red that it must be obvious to everyone. I went home before my uncle got up on purpose. She never said anything all morning, but as I was going she looked at me as if looks could kill. I felt gutted. I needn't have worried because it soon became obvious that Ruth was going to take any opportunity to play with her 'baby'. She would only call me that during or in connection with our times together, I wanted to be thought of as a man, but wouldn't protest for fear of upsetting her. It was always the same coldness afterwards though, with Ruth it had become all or nothing with her affections towards me. It upset and confused me, but I didn't argue. I kept secrets too, not only ours, but she started to bring men back when I was there. I would be listening to them at it wanting to burst in and order him out. They were always drunken slobs who didn't deserve her, but if I kept quiet then I would always get my turn, sometimes straight after they had left, which I hated. She would smell of them but I wasn't allowed to say no, was I?

I've never written about this before and even now am feeling all the emotions as I type. It's like I'm 12 again. Although I have told some people in different circumstances, it's like this is the first time I've said how it really was. Only I know the full details and I've been careful how much I divulge to people who know anything about it. I've been through the bravado bit in the pub with mates, I was fucking my Aunt when I was only 12. Even if I was believed, I was really lying because it is only fairly recently that I've begun to appreciate what was really going on. This year, being on a social work course and having my father dying, has been highly emotional. The other imminent factor is that purely coincidently Ruth and her new husband have moved to a village near us. My wife and I met them in town and I haven't felt so uncomfortable in years. I have obviously seen Ruth lots of times since we ceased our affair when I was 14, but now I feel different. It's as if my growing awareness has made me feel more guilty, more dirty. I looked at her and she is now 60, she looks like my gran. I felt sick when I thought that.

It's putting too many questions in my head, about why I hate my mother, why I was taking drugs and drinking myself into oblivion in my mid-teens, why both my wives are 11 years older than me? Am I blaming Ruth for everything that has happened to me since? Is that fair? I thought I was enjoying it, I admit I fancied her like mad.

There is more to tell but not now. It's the beginning that is vivid and relevant, and why it is probably more important than what followed. I don't know if typing this out has made me feel better. I think I expected to feel relieved that it was all out in the open. Somehow I don't because it isn't and too many people would get hurt if the truth were told.

John Daley

John is a 48 year old man who lives in London.

John's story

I would like to contribute an account of my own experiences and opinions of my own childhood, my relationship with my mother, and how this may have adversely affected my own sexuality.

It is difficult for me to evaluate objectively to what extent my mother's attitude towards me was abnormal, as opposed to merely having unfortunate results. Certainy, my mother never intentionally did anything to harm me, and certainly never did anything that could be classed as assault. My mother and I lived alone together for several years while my father was away in the merchant navy, and during this time suffered from severe and recurrent depression, leaving me to look after her physical needs and bear the brunt of her psychological state. She was excessively protective, and bathed me until I was about 12, on the grounds that she did not trust me to do it properly myself. While my father was away, she allowed me to take his place in her bed, although she never directly encouraged me to do so, and never attempted to touch me while I was there. She did, however, expect me to support her emotionally, and to offer her comfort when she broke down.

From my early teens, I seemed to find girls younger than myself most attractive, and when I was about 13 I repeatedly touched the private parts of a cousin, a girl who was then about five years old, and molested her in other ways. Since then, I have been sexually attracted towards little girls between about the ages of 9 and 14. I have never attempted to molest a child since the incident with my cousin, and firmly believe that I could not allow myself to do so at any time. However, I have recurring fantasies about sexual encounters with little girls, and am attracted towards photographs of little girls as pornography, especially those in underwear, leotards or swimwear. I do not seem to be so attracted towards the outright child pornography that I have occasionally seen, and find it quite offensive.

It may be that my image of women as being physically huge and threatening has contributed to my sexual fantasies and attraction to little girls. Although I am over 6 feet tall, I still feel that women can smother me if they embrace me, as my mother did when she demanded comfort and support from me when I was a child. This is not to excuse my previous offending behaviour, but to reflect that I am still only attracted to exceptionally small, very young women in their teens.

Although my account is very brief and simplified, it has been of some help to me to be able to write down and communicate all this. Perhaps, if nothing else, it might lead someone to try to understand why child abuse sometimes does happen and maybe that will prevent more children suffering from abuse.

Philip Marshall

Philip Marshall is in his fifties. He has been married twice and has children of his own. He lives and works in Wales.

Philip's story

It was only through all the media attention to child abuse over the past few years that I realised that I had been abused, I had pushed it that far down in my mind. I want to tell my mother that I know what she did and how she has ruined my life but I don't know how. If I go to see her, there will be a game of uproar and I shan't get it all out. The obvious answer is to write to her but when I put it all down on paper it looks so awful and I can imagine them all descending on me and causing trouble.

I came back home to my mother when I was about four years old, having been evacuated to my Grandmother's because of the war. My Mother used to trap me in her bedroom and get me to do things to her. When I was fourteen my mother used to come into my bed in the early hours of the morning, arouse me sexually, and sexual intercourse would take place. Until recently (I am now 52) I thought that I had dreamt these sessions, because I never fully woke up, but recently I have put two incidents together. She once made a remark about the size of my penis and I remember thinking, how does she know? Now I know that I was not 'dreaming' and that is how she knew the size of my penis. I can't tell you how I felt when this dawned on me.

One thing that puzzles me is that there were plenty of men available and willing. Why did she have to use me. When I was four we lived in Liverpool and during the war there were lots of Americans around. I can remember the 'Uncles' that I was not supposed to talk about. When I was fourteen there were also lots of men about so what was it; did she prefer boys?

I find it difficult to think about the sexual abuse. I have not evaluated as to how much damage it did. I do know a lot of damage was done by the emotional abuse — that really screwed me up. I recently went to a counsellor recommended by my GP and we worked out that the emotional abuse was used to rule me and keep me insecure so that I wouldn't tell about the sexual abuse; it worked! Until now.

It is very difficult to know where to start and just as difficult to know when to stop with these tales. It's a bit like pulling a thread on a jumper — if you keep pulling, the whole thing comes undone.

As I said before, I am now 52 and I am just beginning to understand myself. I feel that from now on my mistakes are my own but what a hard and rocky road to get here. I have been under psychiatrists on and off for 35 years. I have been on medication: anti-depressants, sleeping pills, 'nerve' pills for anxiety of all kinds. Apart from my own unhappiness I have caused unhappiness to a lot of other people. The cost to society — all those pills and medical treatment, broken marriages, etc., must be enormous.

I think that building a personality is like building a wall. You start off as a child building your wall and if it is not strong and straight it just keeps falling down.

I am so glad that you are doing something about this problem. It makes me feel less of a freak to know that I am not the only one this happened to. I guess as a child when you don't know what normality is, it is impossible to know how to deal with life.

To add to my confusion about normality, I was also sexually abused by my mother's boyfriends.

I have been a parent myself and as a parent you seem to develop a sixth sense as to what is going on with your kids, even if they are in the next room. This suggests to me that mothers whose boyfriends 'just go to say goodnight to little Jimmy' know or suspect what is going on and turn a blind eye. Isn't that also abuse by mothers, even though they are not physically there?

I have never felt better in my life than I do now but all this has left me with a deep, deep sadness. I know now how it should have been and I feel like the kid down the street who wasn't invited to the party. It's so very late and it's all gone and that in itself is hard to deal with. No doubt in other people, and perhaps with me in time, feelings will turn to bitterness and frustration. I hope not. However, unfortunately, I can quite understand why some men do things to women that no one can understand, and society picks up the bill for that too.

It isn't just my life that was screwed up. I have been married twice and have generally caused a lot of strife and unhappiness all along the way. If you don't know how to deal with yourself, you don't stand a chance in dealing with other people. I have been very lucky. I am just beginning to form a sound base for my personality: I suspect that some go on to the end of their days being 'funny beggars' and finding solace in a bottle — perhaps becoming abusers themselves to 'spite' the world.

Henry Bunbury

Henry is the middle-aged son of Iris. He is married. He speaks Chinese and other European languages. He is contactable through KIDSCAPE.

Henry's story

The story of Iris is remarkable in that it almost all comes from the memoires she told people in old age. But she sees the story as mostly idyllic, though sometimes marred by the war and other troubles of external origin, and it is only the occasional document or medical or other record that changes the complexion of the story to one of considerable horror.

One item that never appears in the idyll is that the domestic duties of Iris and her sister included servicing their father's sexual needs. Copulation would have led to loss of virginity and possible pregnancy — which would have provided evidence that he did not want; and possibly their father had some hesitation about this for other reasons. But Iris could do the job orally if she let his organ in far enough. She subsequently suffered from choking fits that he — a doctor — ascribed to asthma.

At 24 she got permission to leave home and study art. Her sister died of a failure of the cario-vascular system a couple of months after and a doctor friend of her father certified death from tuberculate aortal nephritis but, without post-mortem, this gives the same symptoms as any other choking. 60 years later, Iris has still not recovered from her sister's death. Possibly if Iris had stayed at home and helped with their sexual duties her sister would not have died. At least Iris could have supervised the sessions.

Iris does not appear to recall details well. She believes her sister really did die of unsuspected tuberculosis. She remembers her father 'annually' stripped the sisters bare for a 'medical examination' to 'see if they were developing properly'. She sees nothing odd in this (even in an English country town by a doctor trained in the reign of Victoria!), and frequently mentions the likelihood of having to strip naked when visiting doctors, although I doubt if any doctor has really ever asked her to do so. When, at a company medical the girls were told to 'take off their clothes' all the other girls stripped to their undies (substantial garments in those far-off days) as was intended by the doctor; but Iris — as though responding blindly to a Pavlovian stimulus — unhesitatingly stripped naked. And she made other public strips — superficially due to innocent misunderstandings in each case — all her life.

Iris always had odd views on nudity. She has always believed that people wanted to be publicly naked, but were prevented by an oppressive society. In the 1930s she was employed to survey children's height and weight. She reports that at 'progressive' boarding schools, where nudity was allowed, children would only volunteer for examination of their height and weight if told that this would involve taking off *all* their clothes. It does not occur to her that if nudity was allowed then they could do it any time — and that if it was only the *adult invitation* that made it attractive for the children to strip then this was a rather sinister situation.

Before Art College, she says, she rejected all young men as intellectually inadequate. She has never said anything about life at college — possibly she was emotionally paralysed, mourning the horrific death of her sister. As age 30 approached, her emotions appear to have awakened again. She joined a devout and ornate Anglo-Catholic church, with a strong concern for social issues. She met a man and married him, and immediately became pregnant by yet another man — she was not sure who. Her husband — too addicted to her to leave — appears to have made a treaty: he would accept this unwanted 'first born', but they would move to the country where she would be away from Bohemian temptations and he would realise his impracticable ambition to become a 'gentleman farmer'. And he imported a live-in mistress.

Possibly Iris was sexually neglected. Sex, she believed, was a pleasure — like that of a child eating a delicious cream-bun; something that felt nice — an improved masturbation, but cut off from affectionate and spiritual connotations. This accurately describes sex within the limits of what she had experienced. But, in reality, jealousy must have hurt her terribly.

In the country, she was socially isolated. The cottage where they lived was outside the village, and there were no telephones. She held the country women in contempt as politically unenlightened, and defied every social convention they had. They could not exactly put a name to it, but they felt she was 'weird'. Unsurprisingly, she had no friends at all and when the war cut off most visitors from London she had no company except her morose and alienated husband, exhausted by the physical and financial strain of avoiding bankruptcy.

She ascribed their financial and emotional problems to bad luck, the war, and almost to fate. But in fact they came from incompetence — adopting a way of life that could not be viable, letting dreams and short-run expediency take over from long-term realistic planning. But when current life is intolerable, humans do not give much thought to anything non-immediate. Neither she nor her husband had ever learnt a way to live, sexually or otherwise, and thus woolly Marxism and other fantasies had become the best they could do. Obscene human relations in childhood lead to incompetence in life-planning in adulthood.

There are hints she experimented with women. They would have provided physical stimulation and warm, often affectionate, bodies. But lesbian opportunities for a stranger in traditional rural England are largely limited to occasional visits by London friends. There are hints of three-in-a-bed, possibly with her husband and his mistress, trying to find a 'rational', cerebal, solution to the problem of sharing a man and the ignorance they all shared of the non-physical aspects of sex.

Someone reports two women and a child in a bed — the male child giving the faint touch of masculinity the women wanted, but without the full aura of horror that an adult male aroused in the womens' minds. Iris — and her female friend — may have been testing all possible solutions to the sexual spiritual barrenness arising from an unarticulated horror when males were near; a solution that would attract people whose emotion and instinct were too frozen in horror to act as a sexual guide.

As the third country Christmas approached, the child was playing by a dangerous window in Iris' bedroom and she beat him so hard his thigh was smashed. She had often injured him before, but this was the first attack to produce more than just scars. Under the conditions in which she was living, good tempers were not to be expected and wild outbursts are not surprising. She was now faced with a baby who was probably dead, or who soon would be. If she did not act fast, she would be hung for murder. She picked him up and threw him down the stairs — so creating an 'accident' on which to blame the injuries. How she cleaned up the blood in her room, I do not know.

People speculate as to why she was so violent to the child. She told her husband years later that if the child had died she would have been able to leave him; but her family was near-by and, at least after the death of her father in the coming year, she could have definitely returned to her own mother even with the child. But she did not. Others say he was a symbol of masculinity, or something that would grow up into a male — and as such to be hated. It seems to me more a case of mindless fury that had to find an outlet somewhere — like the traditional kicking of the cat if no other target is available.

I do not think either the hospital or her husband could have believed the story of how the child was injured — they would both have known it was anatomically impossible. But they pretended to believe it, because nothing could be proved, and there was nothing else to do. And, being human, they had only a limited capacity to think about really unpleasant problems. So the child returned home. But Iris believes the story; to this day, she warns small children about the dangers of stairs, and they look carefully around them, wondering how the stairs could be dangerous to children (or breakable by them). And, though she saw the scars every bath time, and his uneven walk in between, she still tells people that, fortunately, no permanent damage was done to the child.

The child believed the story for many years, and secretly feared he was becoming psychotic because of the conflict between the truth he had been told and believed, and his fragmented memories — especially of Iris's look of demonic fury when she looked down on him from the top of the stairs, and of the ride in the ambulance, while she swears she took him to hospital personally.

The village very likely suspected the truth about the broken leg. The village gossips had less interest in evading the truth, and very little wholly escapes the endless corporate fitting together of faint clues in every possible combination that occurs in any small village. And, likewise, they must have known about the sexual bizarrities that seem to have occurred — certainly Iris was terrified the child would say something, because he was endlessly forbidden to mention anything with the slightest sexual implications to the villagers 'in case they would be shocked'.

At first the child was taken 'to play with' the children of suitably upmarket neighbours. But such visits were never repeated and never returned; he was given to understand his behaviour had been unacceptable and must not be repeated. He disliked these visits and they gradually faded out as Iris's social ostracism became complete.

With respect to her son's upbringing, Iris had a problem. Obviously, she wanted her son to grow up as a civilised person. But, being male, his natural course was to grow up into a man — insensate, uncultured, violent and cruel. She resolved, like any parent, to train him in correct conduct and attitudes. She read him Grimm's and Andrew Lang's stories at bedtime, because they have great psychological archetypal value, she said. He gave the books away at school.

Iris's son was raped by other adults connected with his school but, although she could see his injuries, she refused to protect him by transferring him to a different school. Her son learned that mothers were not safe — they not only abused, but also colluded with others who abused. He was isolated and vulnerable.

At six, the child took an interest in electrical engineering and, inspired by the local rural electrification team, filled the garden with poles connected by strands of wool (he could not afford long bits of wire). He followed the domestic electrician everywhere. For a few weeks he had someone who respected him — who would let him watch, ask and learn and who respected his desire to learn and saw that as the child's valid position in society. He never forgot this man. Once he was genuinely able to help, making a hole from one side of the ceiling while the electrician waited with the wires on the other side.

He studied wiring diagrams (with Iris's constructive help, for once) before he could even read. Then he connected a bulb, by unorthodox but effective means, to a torch battery and found he could use this to switch it on and off. He had a feeling of triumph at finding he could be independent of the complicated, expensive and incomprehensible mechanism of the torch itself. He showed it to everyone. But the electrician had left now, and they were not impressed — it merely worked, and was clearly not a real torch because it did not have 'Marks and Spencer' stamped on the side of it. It was not official.

A new family moved nearby to set up a garage and he went to play with their six year old. The six year old came to his house and with Iris's great approval and generosity with materials they dressed up with her dresses and jewellery and garishly made up their faces. Iris was full of approval. Then they went back to the garage family for tea and told the mother there all about it. The adults looked doubtful and a bit giggly. They said nothing but after that the boys always played at the garage house. No child ever entered Iris's house again. In retrospect, it seems likely that more than just dressing up had occurred but there are no clues as to what.

The child was still almost Iris's only human companion. She now had an alleged friend in the next village (who was, or soon became, her husband's secret mistress, the live-in mistress had long gone) and another in her own village who she visited but who never came to see her. Her husband was cut-off and uncommunicable. She had a new baby who was not able to do things, to act out her fantasies or be instructed in her ideals for a man. Her child was the only communicating person who was wholly hers — that is, wholly under her control. But now he was becoming independent, developing masuline interests in electricity and more recently car engines, making his own friends, and was ceasing to be wholly hers. Much later, in her senility, when her son refused to see her naked and she complained to the District Nurse 'It's ridiculous. Men *are* silly. He's mine. I made him'. There is no more dramatic way of asserting ownership than to use someone sexually, and it seems possible that some hint of this at the dressing-up session was the reason why the garage family, like the rest of the village, refused after this to leave their child in Iris's care.

At some point, Iris's child began to feel unreal. He did not put it in these words, obviously, but everything he did was 'just a child playing at being an adult (real person)' and did not have any value in itself. Years later, it jarred on him when his granddaughter said she was doing something because she enjoyed it. He was pleased, and somehow he felt surprised at her feeling of continuing to exist between bouts of adult approval (sometimes informing her mother she did not have time to attend to lunch just now, having more pre-occupying things to attend to). As a child, he felt despairing at just being a child and being too young to be able to do things — like politics — that had real importance. One day, he destroyed all the poles and play electricity lines in the garden. Iris, alarmed at his distress, told him to stop and could not understand why they had been valued yesterday but today were hated reminders of just being a child. But he successfully insisted on destroying every trace. It was a first step to suicide, but also to independence — it was his own decision, a refusal to compromise.

He never felt the unreality when making clothes for the toy stuffed bear, or dressing up, doing any feminine activity. What he had picked up was Iris's underlying scorn — maybe even fear — for anything that was not part of her own dreamland Garden of Eden. As she had no respect for his mechanical activities, so he was unable to have respect for them. Pure enjoyment or learning to understand things had no role in either of their consciousness.

But just as she was not conscious of his masculine activities, so she was not conscious of his feelings. And thus she noticed nothing when he was raped. And was equally unaware of any possible effect on him when she used him sexually.

Peter Vaughan

Peter Vaughan is a 55 year old artist. He lives in England with his parents and brother. He is the father of two children and is divorced from his wife. He has been in therapy for three years and feels that talking about the formerly unspeakable abuse he suffered is helping him to find peace.

Peter's story

My mother owned and ran a boarding house. The people who came to the house, stayed and went at different times. There seemed to be no stability in my life. I never knew where I would be sleeping from one day to the next. If there were too many guests, I slept on the floor. When the wartime air raids happened, we would transfer in a panic to a bunk in the shelter in the garden.

In the boarding house, people quite often slept together in double beds or on bedsettees. I grew used to coming home from school and being told I would be sleeping in some room and that I wasn't to put on the light when I went in. There might be a person in bed with me or in another bed in the room. As I grew into puberty, sometimes this was a potentially exciting situation. On one occasion I remember being directed to sleep with an older woman, aged about 25. It was a narrow, single bed and the experience was warm and kindly. But whatever the combination of sleeping arrangements, the one I most dreaded was being made to sleep with Mother.

If I protested about sleeping with her, she humiliated me verbally — something she excelled in. I discovered weird compulsive rituals to protect myself from her. I could tolerate the blitz, the flying bombs, and even the V2 rockets. In fact, going to the air raid shelters gave me some protection from the thrashings, slappings and daily violence from Mother or seeing her with her knickers down to her knees poking into her blood during her period. A disgusting way for a young boy to find out about menstruation, if it was her normal periodic bleeding.

Gradually the message became clear. I was to kiss and hug her the way she liked or I would be punished yet again. When I slept with her, I would curl up, put my hands between my thighs and try to protect myself, both from the cold and from her. She would bring her right arm over my body and remove my hands, touching me on the thighs. She never allowed me to control my own body and I found it profoundly disturbing.

If I didn't do exactly as Mother said, it was always my fault. I vividly recall one night when she brought me a drink of hot milk. A skin had formed on the top, which I detested. It was also too hot to drink. When I told her this, she flew into a rage, and wooshed the hot milk in my face. My bed and pyjamas were soaked. My mother stalked from the room.

I became a whimpering, terrified wreck. I ran to the kitchen door, and begged to be allowed near the fire to dry myself off. I was shouting that I was sorry and pleading to be let in. I had wet myself out of shock and fear. Eventually I went back to the bed, wet and freezing. I lay there wondering what was in store. It might be a belt, or being locked into a tiny, dark room or perhaps I would be thrown out to wander the street. All had happened before. Time seemed to stand still. When the door finally did open, Mother walked in with a large, shiny steel knife. It was one of the worse moments of my life. Even Hitchcock could not have devised a more frightening scenario. She threw the knife onto the bed. I grabbed it and promptly fainted. When I came to, I thought she must want me to kill myself, or perhaps use it to protect myself from her. I was fourteen, confused and powerless in the face of this mad person who was my mother.

During my childhood, Mother also found reasons to stuff 'medicine' up my bottom and abused me in other ways. There were erotic consequences to many of her actions and to the physical punishments she meted out. This all became so entangled that I even began to consider myself lucky and 'good' if she only hit me with her opened hands and not her fists and if the soap put up my anus didn't contain carbolic acid. I am still recovering from some of her bizarre practices with 'medicines'.

My memories of my father are sad, as well. For reasons that were never clear to my brother and me, he would suddenly appear in our bedroom, drunkenly shouting at us. He would then yank off the bed covers, pull down our pyjamas and thrash us with a heavy leather belt until we lay bleeding and screaming in pain. We were only about 5 or 6 years old and had no way to anticipate when an attack would come or why. I know now that his mind was sick and that he was perverted. He may not have directly sexually abused us, but he must have used his attacks on us as a sexual stimulus because we would then hear of him raping our mother.

The abuse from all members of my family continued as my brother then would turn on me and beat me to vent his frustration. This went on from the time I was small until I was 16. Until I started my therapy, I would wake up screaming in terror, even as a grown man, reliving the horror of this wild man. When I became a father I realised how incredibly sick this man was. Thank God that my relationship with my children has been free from abuse. In fact, my daughter has taught me so much about being a good father and I am very proud of her and of our relationship. I cannot wait to be a grandfather.

How did I survive all these things, become a father and hold down a responsible job and get on with my life? I think it stems from the only time in my life that I was safe. It was 1939. We went to school one day and we suddenly, or so it seemed, found ourselves evacuees. We were moved in the clothes we came in, lock, stock and barrel. For some it was the worst experience of their lives. For me it was a chance to be loved, tolerated, given without question or punishment what it takes to make a child feel secure. Lost, but secure. Understood by people who shared their love and homes because they loved kids. It gave me an experience of security that I think set me up. I know that love or whatever the quality is, can be found and given even by total strangers and that really is what life is all about.

Peter Oxenburgh

Peter is a 38 year old poet and artist. He has recently and very painfully begun to come to terms with the abuse he suffered as a child from his mother, relatives and 'friends' of the family. To help himself survive, he has written a series of 26 prose poems concerning child abuse, incest and how the memories impinge on the present.

The poems are based on each letter of the alphabet, with a letter missing from each to accentuate his sense of loss and the inability abuse victims have to express themselves adequately. Here we share 14 of the poems.

A is for anal attitude action shaft abuse pleasure

Outside it is shining, the sun comes through the dust on the window. I being here such life in through new lungs, bright cheerful eyes, soft skin, unknowing, off the shelf, plus so trusting. In the void of light with sound, two big beings unlike children come smiling into the room. The bigger one comes to me picks my body up, I hope for big hugs with food. I so little full of joy gurgle this is fun! I being so trustful in his flesh in his flesh, while he puts me on the kitchen unit . . . he fingers me . . . I feel funny no words big enough, none I know of describe my being here. He mutters with liquid eyes, 'Oh look he's enjoying it'. I enjoy it not . . . but his story tells I do, so telling he puts his flesh into me. Not nice so I . . . me goes elsewhere, into the outside, through the window. I become the green me, red flowers plus sunshine. This picture turns through my now corpsed eyes. Soon he finishes, red not like my flowers but flushed. His flesh is wet, stinks of him inside me. Now crying she pulls me up to bring me out to run with her children. It's OK I'm no longer living, my bottom is icky, so I just sit rocking myself in the green sunshine. Smiling, thinking once gone, I need never return.

B is for bloody bum bowels broken nobody inhibit fumble limbs womb

Years passed since the last attack; so much time that all was seemingly forgotten. My mother and others spent the years hiding their shame, while encouraging the idea that I was always on the edge. And I made a pretty good act . . . so playing along, I turned it into an affirmation that directed my life towards the meanest edge. Though not all was stifling or limited, sometimes I cracked free and turned poison into medicine. One day it all fell apart and my skin felt as if it were peeled off with a craft knife. At last the corpse regained life and told the story of numerous attacks. Alone in a foreign land I found the scale of the torture shocking. For weeks I lay homeless, shaking in sleeping station or feeling sick while walking. I acted without seeing and hurt all around as I crashed. The hurt of rejection renewed meant the past had to change. Soon I will accept that people are what they are. And those who raped or tortured the childhood out of me are no longer here.

F is for fornicate ferocious fat fellow fuck father

He was a tall man, strong, surly and always out working. In my early years I have no memory other than a bad tempered shit who could not cope with parenthood. I was his child but a weakling that brought shame to his manhood. I was also stupid. Saturday, the worst day, he was stuck at home while my mother worked. Around the house he paced. Sighing and building up to a real hating rage. I would hear him, large steps coming towards my room. The door would burst open and a demon shouted words in pure venom. He then stood over me as I was made to clean up. He barked out orders and assured me that I would never see the day as it would take hours and hours to clean up. Then homework, his consistent attacks on my ability to cope. You should have seen the rages to know how mad he was. I still remember my mother saying pay no attention as his bark was worse than his bite.

G is for night lying god frigging strangely good gone hanging

In a sleepless bed, I hit my head on the wall to touch base. I am alive I feel pain. It soothes my mind like a hot bath, from ice to extreme heat within a second. From the warmth of plaster walls I can achieve some sense of order. Often my father would come into the room and ask if I was mad. At dawn I would hit my head on the cracked wall. In the day I would rock myself and murmur prayers for release. He never answered, years later I still wait. In the dark, I was seven I prayed. I asked that I be happy or famous. I wanted to have a life of hell, just like all the other men of history. Now I am here from one day to the next, I lack the certainty that he heard me correctly. Now I can't even bash my head on the wall for it hurts too much.

J is for joy joke major justice injure jape jerk

In days light, I think of seeking retribution. But there is no court in the land that will convict on a vision. I stretch this corpse out on the slab I call a bed and with the imagination of a fool, I hope to wake without screaming. When I feel real depressed I think that it is I who have been sentenced. For 34 years I have been in solitary. Sometimes as dawn's grey chorus bleaches the street lamps, I fantasise of confronting my parents. But then I am mad. As for their friends who raped me, I cannot even imagine finding them. Their son committed suicide, hanging himself from a tree. He took hours to die. Now I wonder if he suffered the same as I. In my dreams they shout at me, rape me, beat me and generally have never left me alone. I'm locked out of the house listening to the poltergeists breaking all that is sacred.

M is for remember mother mercy embrace empathy maternal man woman

To the bringer of life I give honour and love. Thirty-eight years have passed since I entered this world. The pain you felt has since strangled this adult every day. The trial of this birth was gentle contrasted to the initiation you had planned. I was a happy child full of joy and adventure. During this lull all was fine despite your insatiable needs. The pain you inflicted was too awful to bear alone. In love, I ask you to recognise, that pinching and punching was bad enough, but to be finger fucked? I know you hoped I would not recall this. I know you have suffered. But please do not say that this boy is crazy. It will not cover up your guilt, that ruse can not be used again. So do not forget the eyes of your abused child.

Do not forget the ginger haired boy banging his head at night. But do not forget that, when the bed was wet or the fear you created was too painful, I always called out for your love.

O is for school love orgasm psychotic move morning room dominate sodomy

He was eating the gristle with gagging neck. All the meals had been piled up on his plate. It shimmered in the summer heat, it stank. The dining hall was empty save the child and the gaggling prefects. Later I arrived in the headmaster's bureau. I tell him all that I have seen. I explain that this same child had asked that the abuse at night must be halted. The master rants at me and threatens a beating which brings intense feelings, of fear and sexual excitement. In the present I feel guilt that this child was left trembling and spent the time being their plaything, used by teacher and prefect alike.

Q is for queer question inquiry cheque liquor unique inquisition

When I first met my wife, I always had headaches. Whenever we went out for dinner, I would take pain killers and stuff for my stomach. As the evening progressed my neck stiffened and I started to feel ill. At night I dreamt of large growths covering my head. I would wake to a gentle hand and a whispered shush. It would take me many minutes to come out of shock. Fading into sleep I would start to scream again. For thirteen years I have tried not to see my friends as the enemy. Over the years my mood swings have mellowed, but the monsters still swim defying description and often scare the natives. In-between I phone my therapist. The cure for the disease of abuse seems more severe than any torture, as I am thrown from scalding bath to cold in an attempt to break this tormented fever.

S is for school sadism sex social class suck mess dress jest vest lust

Early one afternoon, when I be not that old and younger than eight, the teacher noticed I am not paying attention. I am rocking back and forth. The whole of the room of children turn round grinning wanting to hurt me. The teacher demanded that I come to the front and wait to be hit. The children wanting to maim me, to cry out for him to hit me with the ruler. He took a thick one and whacked the table hard. He nodded grinning taking my hand, and then waited for an age. When I urinated he hit me. Laughing he told the children I will probably crap my clothing next. I made a puddle on the floor. I am lucky. The children cried out with glee at the mad boy upright in a pool of urine. I cried no more but felt oddly excited, while my clothing clung to my groin. Part of me found the humiliation joyful. I returned to my chair feeling I had been perverted. Later the teacher fiddled too much with other children through their underwear. He had to leave early one winter evening, he had been caught on the bed of a young prefect. Now I am older, I think often of another time when to hurt daily became a way of life. I look at the dark river flowing, I hope to end it all. I never have enacted out wanting to end my life, not yet. It can not be that painful.

T is for tirade tough touch mother batterer father hospital visit spit

I had a shrink who spoke around me for many hours. She gave me drugs, which helped as I had nerves of acid. In sessions she would ask how I was feeling in regards my elders. I did feel odd while she fingered an area of me which was very fragile. You could hear snapping like ice in spring. She scared me and now when I look back, I know she knew more. Soon she was replaced by a man and cried no more. For years I lived alone as my lover had died during a seizure. I made my hair shorn and became too severe . . . no one came near. Many years have passed, now I pay for drugs, for a person who speaks and a person who prescribes. I walk in a daze, shocked how long I have been in pain and how crazy I am. I analyse every second and speaking, spend hours in recall. As leaves drop, I find solace in drink. Here and afar I speak among friends. I never really reveal how depressed I am. So dropping a pill in my face, I say how wonderful my life is . . . even if I have a few problems. When darkness falls I pray my drug is powerful and hope for deliverance. If I'm lucky I wake as dawn slips along Charles river's shore.

W is for wedding womb woman wrist watching wistful wailing witch

Seeing my parents makes me so sick, but then of course I am mad. They sit and listen as their eldest son turns green and deathly pale.

For years my spouse could never understand my illness. The symptoms of my pain rampaged through the landscape. Did my father have any idea? The first born must die, careful not to alert the police, she killed my young life. Day by day, Mum pinched, punched or pushed a finger hard up my arse, she ripped the life out of me. Soon her mad child moved around banging its head against floors or anything else. Years later I had visions and my brain stilled by drugs to stop the dreams coming into daylight hours. Later still trying to forget the memory of the family friend that raped me. I shaved off all my body hair. At my core lies a large cancer of rotting dead emotion.

X is for examination next Xray crux hoax Xmas transfixed

It was close to one of the main feast days of the year. I lay awake at night wishing snow clouds would fold over the stars and crisp ice might fall. One night near to Christmas, I heard a bellowing and roar from the deep. It was my father transformed three storeys below where I creaked in the wind of fear. My brother and I stood at the top of the stair. My father growled. My mother screamed freaking out. We stood as I remember for over an hour without a word. In a way I'm still trembling. Over breakfast, my mum hid her black eye with a silence that cut like a knife. At the dinner table it was my turn to receive the attention of my father. In dull winter light, he cursed my life, my birth. As he brooded over my inept mathematics. He looked at me with such hate that I wanted to piss myself, but instead with iron will, I cried. That night I lay as still as I could listening to my father's silent thunder. Knowing that if I moved the demons of the sleeping hours would act out my father's deepest desire.

Y is for youth brainy horny tricky lovely day play friendly folly enemy

Each night I sharpened the knife, oiled and keen it would be placed under the pillow. I would sleep with the knowledge that the attack was imminent. Clothing was placed to look casual but I could get dressed in seconds. I practised pulling the knife out from under the pillow. Besides I might be time warped into another dimension and a knife could be useful. I also carried a box of matches so that if I landed in pre-fire times I could keep warm. I landed in the battle zone after the bomb dropped. Now I have turned into an adult I can not remember much, but I now know a lot of how to damage and hurt a human life.

Z is for zip zest buzz stelazine breeze fizz daze Lazarus

I sat shivering on the Charles shore, huddled in a flurry of leaves.

Later two lamps burn as I hold a leaf, it's red. My hands tremble as I remember those days dreaming of death. In the tomb of a shed I placed a pink flower on a bicycle. As the summer faded away, I wished I could have shrivelled petal by petal. The rain stops and the cars rumble by on hissing rubber, I stick a small red leaf into a card. Two reading lamps burn softly like sentinels, champions in my court of attacking demons. I lay on my bed, fully clothed, wanting to sleep. But fearful of the ghosts. I play with myself to ease the tension. My body is not my own. At three I wake, stale mouthed, clothes wrinkled and damp. Aching, feeling the terror of those young hours, when face down in my cot I was turned and tortured beyond screaming, beyond memory. I am now the pervert that knows no boundaries. After the rapes, I live in the muck of their desires. As the clock ticks away I imagine slashing myself. In fear I smell myself and it is him, I get up and look in the mirror and see her looking back for forgiveness. I need a drink. Returning to the bed I stretch out like a corpse. In my forest all the birds have flown, as the creatures hid, the giants approach, snapping my soul underfoot.

Paul Thorrson

Paul is 38. He was born in Bristol and adopted at the age of 6. He is currently disabled with spinal problems and so is unable to work. He does write and paint. He is a local historian and interviews old people and compiles history from their memories. He is married and lives in Birmingham. Paul is interested in continuing research into the area of female sexual abuse. He can be contacted through KIDSCAPE.

Life twice

I am 38 years old and my name is Paul Thorrson. My adoptive mother was an abuser. She genitally interfered with me and tried to make me meet her overwhelming need for attention and love, which she had never had properly met as a child.

Her marriage to my adoptive father was unsuccessful sexually. I think I became her substitute penis, which she simultaneously hated because of her anger at her husband. She tried to suffocate me, used to beat me in frustrated rage at her life and she used to tie me up.

The most powerful abuse she had upon me, however, was the distortion of my identity. I was terribly insecure about losing my genetic mother, so I had a powerful need to bond to feel safe. She used this need by saying 'I will look after you, if you will look after me'. She made me into part of her. If she needed warmth and sexual gratification, I provided it.

My life was ruined by my adoptive mother. I spent 18 months in a mental hospital as a teenager. My fellow patients supported me, but the psychiatrists didn't have a clue about how to help. It was not until the age of 29 that I had the strength to go inside myself. In the 1980s I began primal therapy in Paris.

In order to survive the combined effects of several separations from my genetic mother, culminating in my adoption and subsequent child abuse, I had to 'black out' — 'shut down' on my feelings, myself and memory. In poetry I have often referred to this period as: 'The Valley of The Guillotine' or 'The Valley of Adoption'. Those images approximate how it begins to feel when re-travelling those personal zones.

Some events within personal trauma leave a key memory which must be unlocked in the future. Such an event for me was my adoptive mother's interference with my genitals. I was four or five years old and was sound asleep. It was not long after my genetic mother had left me to her care. I felt that something was crawling and invading me. I awoke with my adoptive mother's hand on my penis. She had been touching me with complete disregard. Thereafter she always insisted on 'cleaning' my penis. She said she was 'making sure I was clean'. She actually used to hurt me when she did this and I would cry my eyes out.

It's clear to me now that child abusers are most effective with those children who have a significant pool of unmet need. By the time I reached Birmingham in 1957 aged 3½ I certainly had a pool of unmet need for a mother. As an adult I discovered records of me being at a children's home. What accompanied those records were a number of letters written by my genetic parents. Although I was 2½ when I was admitted to the children's home, the letters flesh out my genetic parents' problematic marriage. They show how at 10 months old I was separated from my genetic mother for a year, and then when she returned to Bristol to try again with my father both of them contrived a plan to get a house by putting my sister aged 3½ and myself in a home for children.

My sister and I were in a children's home in Wales apparently without visits for 7 months. The effect it had upon me as an adult when I discovered the full records was dramatic. It floored me for a week and my wife stayed at home from work to nurse me while the knowledge I had uncovered simultaneously hurt and liberated me. That powerful emotional experience helped me to realise that I had experienced my adoption as the last in a long line of abandonments.

Experiences like this have helped me to understand that very desperate need I had to 'bond' to a mother in the face of ongoing deprivation. It is a terrible emotional paradox to have to bond to a child abuser, when she is the person you need to be rescued from.

I can remember a crucial turning point for me. One day in her bedroom I was crying on the bed. I was aged about 4. She was present and I was experiencing total anguish and screaming: 'I can't bear any more — no one loves me'.

As some of my grief relaxed I suddenly heard her crying too. I looked up and saw her face screwed up in total pain and she told me that: 'No one loved her either' and that 'Your daddy (adoptive father) does not love me either'. She then told me at this most vulnerable point that 'If you look after me I will look after you'. This singular moment was to develop into a perverse relationship that was to be the theme of our lives. What began there and then was her way of seeing me as a substitute husband and as a way she could satisfy herself. She saw me as a solution to her problem of 'absent husband/lover/ companion'. This attitude was reinforced by her behaviour in bed with me. Sometimes I would seek a comforting cuddle and then she would tell me it 'was her turn'. This meant that I had to hold her from the back and let her sit on my lap! It has also become clear to me through therapy that my child-needs provoked in her a little girl who was looking for the adult care she never had. There were several levels of perverted need in her.

Her relationship with me was completely unnurturing. If I had a need to be met, whatever it was, she would answer it with trying to get me to meet her need. For instance I had to 'appreciate' her I was told, if she had done something for me. It's clear she was asking me to make up for the love she never had in other parts of her life.

She was really good at disguising the way she was acting out her unmet needs. She seemed to be able to make herself and me believe that she had some legitimate reason for anything she did, however bizarre. An example of this came out in a therapy session I had as an adult.

I was having feelings that seemed full of tangles and knots. The knots seemed to change location in my body — my hands, then my stomach, then my genitals. Finally I was retching on the tangled feelings which had come up into my throat. I had memories of my adoptive mother tying me up with some washing line rope, on a chair when I was a little boy. She had said we were 'playing' and I remember that she even told my adoptive father after he had come home from work after one of the days when we had 'played' that: 'We played at him being tied up today — and he could get out of it.' My adoptive father did not seem to understand that there was something very wrong, but then he was a very unreactive man.

My adoptive mother had created a believable cover story for her need to act out her own fantasies on me. I did, however, find the strength to end this particular practice. One day she tied me up on the chair, I was aged about 5, and then she went out. Suddenly I was no longer the passive little boy, I became furious and I struggled but she had tied me up very firmly. The chair toppled and I hit my head on the floor. When she came home, I told her: 'If you do that again I will tell daddy'.

She never tied me up again, at least not physically.

I did discover that my adoptive mother's youngest brother had been tied up as a little boy and that he, too, was subjected to other humiliations and cruel treatment.

Through therapy I felt that this 'tying-up' behaviour was a way of saying: 'I am restricting your freedom and making you totally dependent on me'. On a deeper level it was a way of seizing a bond of love that she had never had. I did have some contact with her brothers and I felt that their mother was a tyrant who had constricted their lives. Their father had not been much better. Their parents in fact were born last century and were hardened Victorian Midlanders. I think they did not value the feelings of children.

I am sure that my adoptive mother's parents' influence under-pinned much of her attitude and behaviour towards me. She had little empathy toward me and little ability to address my emotional needs. She was devoted to her self and constructing fantasies of love or attention she had never achieved.

She was capable of great cruelty because as I was growing up I began to oppose her abusive rule over me. Control and dominance of me was very important to her and resistance was met with violence from beatings with canes to harsh verbal stabs. On one occasion after I had resisted 'cheeking her', she got astride me on the floor pinning my arms down with her knees and weight. She then put a pillow over my face which began to suffocate me. I was about 8 and I did not have the strength to oppose her. Tears just welled out of my eyes — I thought she was going to kill me. She saw my tears and she got off me and without remorse indicated 'she was in charge'.

My opposition to her grew more consistent at about the age of 11. It was met with persecution and beatings. One of the worst beatings is something I still re-experience; being cornered in the bedroom and being whipped with a fan belt from a washing machine until it produced cuts on my arms. In one such re-experience I can remember feeling acute stings on the inside of my abdomen and lungs. These 'stings' inside me began to make me feel absolutely tortured until I could no longer bear the pain. I lay on the bed eventually and began rolling around in agony giving way to the feelings of the stings and crying: 'Godstopper Godstopper Mom stop!'

My adoptive mother's invasion of me continued into my early teenage life in all sorts of ways. I found I could not have a private space for myself. She was mooching into my things, moving them. I drew some pictures of naked women and hid them but she discovered them and showed my adoptive father. He, as usual, did not react.

She convinced him that there was something wrong with me because she knew I was masturbating in my bedroom as a teenager. She knew because I caught her spying on me a few times. I was angry at her but she said she had the right to go anywhere in the house — it was hers.

She eventually consulted the doctor about my masturbating — but he said I would grow out of it. She was trying to stop me from being sexually independent. She was threatened by my growing sexuality because it would and did expose some of her sexual unhappiness.

She read my letters — took money out of my money box and generally showed no respect for my privacy. Paradoxically she demanded utter privacy and respect for her wishes. It was alright for her to walk into my room if I was masturbating, but no one could walk into her room.

Eventually I rejected her and created some fragile independence in my young life. I would go into some local fields alone, think my own thoughts and perhaps occasionally masturbate in a simultaneous need for love mixed with personal despair. It was in this period that I began to mourn for my genetic mother and long for the life I had never had. My genetic mother had in fact returned to Birmingham and was only living 2 miles away. It was torture because I knew it.

The abuse by my adoptive mother took place over years and it was a crazing process and was destined to affect my later life. When I was 16 it all began to surface and drive me mad. My adoptive mother had abused me by exacting a distorted and distorting compromise out of me as a child. I was to see and meet her 'needs' first before she met mine. This unreal scenario surfaced dramatically as a form of powerful internal sexual conflict in me as a teenager. Sometimes when I masturbated I would suddenly become overwhelmed by a need to become woman-like. Then I fantasised that I had to be fucked by a man before 'I' could get any sexual satisfaction. I was not quite sure which of the 'I's, I was in this crazy overwhelming feeling.

It's clear now that this was a product of my adoptive mother's child abuse. I cannot over-emphasise the effect it had upon me. It seemed every waking second was full of mental torment throughout my teenage life. Thoughts would come into my mind which hinted I was 'queer' and I felt terrorised by the fear that I would become homosexual. I suffered from a soul-destroying guilt. I wanted to tell my adoptive dad that I had a serious problem, but I knew he thought bum-boys were mental. I had no one to turn to. At the age of 17 on a Saturday in Autumn I decided to die. I took a mixture of painkillers and tranquillisers, went to a nearby motorway which was under construction. I found a tunnel. At the mouth of that tunnel I cried bitterly because I was laying my life down. In total desolation I looked up at the sky and looked around at the surrounding land of grass and trees. I walked into the tunnel and found a place to die. I thought I would be dead in a couple of hours, but time passed and I remained conscious. Eventually I did not want to die there — I did not like the thought of rats chewing my dead body — so I went home to die.

I went to my room and slept for 20 hours, then awoke from my 'death-sleep' and pissed Aspirin and drug smells for the following 3 days.

I survived.

I never told my adoptive parents that I survived my own suicide attempt. I did my best to glue myself together. I tried to work but could not hold jobs down for long because of my continual internal conflict. On New Year's Eve 1972 I had a nervous breakdown. I admitted myself to a local mental hospital in Birmingham. Inside the nervous breakdown I looked for my true self, the self I had lost, and that I kept feeling was full of distortions.

In therapy I have called this period of my life: 'The Holocaust Walk' because I felt I was living in my own destruction. Occasionally in therapy the Holocaust Walker returns (reactivated by stress) and there is a feeling in me of meeting a brother who has been through terrible things. He speaks shattering trauma, each statement is an emotional bomb of hurts. There is a destructive electric feel to it all but there is a fierce honesty in his eyes.

When I am fused completely to this part of me everything in me is screaming and quaking. The screams take the shape of one primal feeling: 'Help me'. The quality and the power of the voice is not shaped by a few events where help was needed. It is the voice of years of travelling through internal helpless darkness.

Here is a selection of verses from my personal life-poems book which describes the holocaust zone.

From 'Gone Galaxy Eyes'

Eyes watch alone on the sentient cliffs'
Acquainted so much with their own precipice
A legacy of the soul's earthquakes, and birth
At its own gambled and jagged edge

A coronal white disc steaming its edges
like the Sun's eclipsed serpented whips
Flickers behind this extraordinary figure
It is a chained holocaust ball and the
Promise of cancerous codes.

The Self dies to survive, granites its past
Cheat's history's hurt, but walks nearer its own
Fissible threshold
How many continental screams was it possible to store?

Ask this uncrushed Atlas with a lopsided walk

Sometimes his brother comes, stands by his side
Makes from his dumbness a shattering tongue
Screaming the million atomic divisions
He is called Holocaust Walker
'Life living destroyed . . .'

In a sense this poem strikes the central truths of my adoptive mother also — and it is with a great deal of compassion that I state that she fully became the last line. She denied so much of her own inner reality that she lost touch with all reality. She died without a mind in 1991.

It's very clear to me that through the years, my adoptive mother's child abuse prevented me from grieving for my genetic mother. My research forced me to conclude that there was no rational reason for my adoption — it was more a way of dumping her responsibility. I pined for my 'real' mother secretly and incompletely. My adoptive mother never encouraged this side of me. In fact she would go into a panic when I displayed pain and grief about my losses. This reality threatened her. In fact, under the conditions of my childhood, I effectively stored my early grief about the fact that I had another family in Bristol and that I had lost my mum, dad, sister and grandad. Can any reader imagine what it's like to be suddenly uprooted at 3½ and to lose contact with all former family?

I stored this grief for 30 years until in therapy I could finally deal with the feelings and some of my original identity. That's what I mean by my title 'Life twice'. For some years in therapy with the patient help of Hansjorg Messener, my therapist, I returned to the past to regain that part of my inner child. I 'told' my lost mother within this developing self-awareness that I had needed her — I had needed to be rescued but I had been forgotten. I told her I had to even forget myself, and that self-abandonment brought so much heavy water out of me from those early years. Feelings gradually returned with great difficulty. It was like I was joining with them and they were moving toward me through lands of tar.

Finally through art and poetry and research I built up an image of my genetic mother (as she had been when I was a child) and in my loss I iconised her. But slowly in therapy this icon broke into my own tragedy that had been emotionally delayed for 30 years. If my adoptive mother had not tried to distort me for herself then my life would obviously have been shaped quite differently. It's all been accompanied by feelings of helplessness, collapse and dizziness. At times it's been so bad that I have vomited with pain.

I do not expect to 'get over' my life of being abused after abandonment. Rather — through therapy, self-help, support from my wife and others, I expect to progressively integrate all those painful parts of my childhood. I see myself as doing a delayed job which parents should have accomplished. I cannot give myself back a childhood, but I can at least know I have put myself together. In a sense I do not mind being damaged so long as I know it's all of me and I have done my best to be all of me.

The great difficulty for those who are victims is the lack of real therapy or counselling that actually addresses the issues. There are so many people who want to help without having the real skills to do so. My own experience leads me to believe that people who have been abused as children must radically (in safe doses) re-experience their abuse so they can emotionally work through their unmet needs for a mother. Mourning becomes a progressive solution but one has to work through emotional defences which have usually been picked up from the abuser. It's tough work and there is a hell of a lot of pain on the trail.

One problem I have observed is professionals who 'treat' abused adults inadequately, but rather than admit their inadequacy they carry on a secondary form of mystification. The implication is the abused adult is being 'treated' when in fact nothing is happening that's therapeutic at all. Indeed, I feel that some professionals are downright dangerous. I have found that many have unresolved backgrounds of being abused in one form or another and some of them are in contact with children who have been abused. A social worker reported to me how, in one home, an abused child was marginalised because the child was so difficult to deal with. The same social worker had been shown by me some very simple techniques that are used in primal therapy — giving back the lost voice to the child, responding to the needs that lie just beneath angry behaviour. That social worker began to make progress. In one situation the social worker said to a child: 'You are missing your mother' and the child transformed from an angry delinquent to a mourning child. That's the kind of support a child needs.

In emotionally real counselling or therapy you know when you have gained a personal connection because emotional pain is expressed at last in its formerly repressed context. It often takes the form of deep crying followed by inch-by-inch acceptances that one did not have a good mother.

I will end by saying that being abused has shaped my life and destiny. I have tried to outline this briefly and powerfully. I have no doubt that primal therapy has extended my life beyond its 'suicide-date'. Others — friends and companions — found they were driven mad and have now perished: Alec, John, Mike and Barbara. Without the support and love of my wife, that none of you would be reading this is also clear to me. The last words should be those of the abused child inside me and I hope passionately that expressing them will help others:

'One day when I grow up I will try to remember this' (A vow at age 6).

Eventually he kept his word, through me, there was no other way but to live life twice.

12 Self-help for survivors

Val Young

Self-help is doing things you were unable to do for yourself when you were a powerless, dependent child. Reading this book is self-help. You may recognise some of your own feelings and responses in what other survivors say. Other ways of helping yourself include finding a therapist, asking for support and understanding from friends and family, talking to other people about your experiences and knowing you will be believed, saying 'no' to unwanted sexual advances, making yourself safe from punishment, and expressing the feelings that you have held back for so many years.

Self-help includes recognising that you were sexually abused, knowing it is OK to talk about being abused, knowing that it wasn't your fault, and knowing that you were powerless to stop it happening. Obviously, after several years of programming you can't change your beliefs overnight — self-help (and one-to-one therapy) is to support you while you gradually internalise the truth about what happened and define yourself in your own terms. It starts with the realisation that you are no longer responsible for hanging onto someone else's guilty secrets.

Self-help means that you are beginning to value yourself enough to believe that you deserve to recover from the effects of being abused. It also means that you have made a choice to regain some power over your life and become your own person — the meaning of 'self-empowering'.

Whether you choose to work alone, or with the help of a book, with a therapist or in a group, remember: *you're in charge*. You decide the pace, you decide what you do or don't say, and you decide the methods you want to use. No one can make you do or say anything you don't want to, and if you feel that your therapy, or your group, is pushing you, you are free to say so.

Survivors describe very different stages in healing from their abuse. Some have only a vague suspicion that the problems they are experiencing in their lives may stem from childhood sexual abuse. Others have such serious problems that these occupy all their energy, and have effectively buried any memory of abuse. Others remember the feelings only, and cannot connect them verbally or physically with abuse, only with what is happening to them in the present. Others remember most details and have kept them secret for decades, never knowing that other people share similar experiences. Some survivors feel that a part of themselves is missing, and years of childhood are forgotten.

Some say that their lives are wonderful, they should be happy, and yet nothing seems to work out for them. Relationships fail or become abusive, they lose their jobs, or travel around the world with no particular destination in mind, or live vague disjointed lives that seem to have no meaning or purpose. Many survivors do not recognise that what happened to them was sexual abuse, and this seems particularly true for those who were abused by women or older girls.

Recognising that what happened to you was abuse is in itself a painful realisation, because you may care deeply about the person who abused you, and you may still have some sort of relationship with them, especially if your abuser was your mother, and you are still trying to maintain close family ties. You may be what is known as 'the family scapegoat', the person everyone blames for all the family troubles, and are still having difficulty recognising your innocence. You may even believe that what happened was your fault, that you must have done something to encourage your abuser's sexual advances.

Any sexual experiences you had as a child, even if a part of you enjoyed them, were abusive if the woman was older than you, and using you for her own self-gratification. Children are naturally sensual, and pleasurable sexual feelings they may have are their own innocent feelings, and never connected with any sort of sexual relationship.

Abusers exploit these feelings, and encourage children to engage in sexual activities long before they are able to understand or explain what they want and what they feel. What abusers refuse to recognise is that sexual excitement in children — a natural physical response — is very different from adult sexual pleasure. To a child, this excitement, over which they have no control, can be frightening and, as it is over-stimulation against their will, is frequently painful. As they rely on older people to take care of them, and to explain the world to them, they believe what abusers tell them. This is why so many children are easily led to believe that they 'asked' to be sexually abused. In this way, the abuser knows that she is safe from discovery, as the child feels shock, bafflement and frequently shame.

At the time of puberty, young people often find their first rush of sexual feeling quite frightening; imagine how much more frightening these feelings are to a child. Abuse adds another factor — that these feelings are wrong. Abusers threaten children with punishment, with the break-up of the family, and the withdrawal of love or care. So the child believes that these painful and frightening feelings are immensely powerful and extremely dangerous. Is it any wonder, therefore, that being sexually abused by an older woman, perhaps a mother, sets up a lifetime of confusion, shame, and fear of relationships and leads to scores of other problems?

What type of self-help would you choose?

When choosing a method of self-help, it is important to know where you want to begin. You may, for instance, have problems with alcohol, drugs, medicines (such as tranquillisers) or food. Your main problem may be chronic depression, or perhaps relationships. You may be recovering from a breakdown, or perhaps you are, as an adult, in an abusive relationship and have just become aware of it.

Remember that sexual abuse isn't only 'sexual'; it is also physical, emotional and psychological. Many survivors describe abuse by their mothers (or primary carers) as 'spiritual', because they worshipped their mother, saw her as omnipotent, and truly believed that she could do no wrong.

Try and define the problem which you feel requires your most urgent attention. If it is an addiction or chemical dependency, you will need medical treatment for the detoxification process, and possibly support medication to help you through the withdrawal period. You will then be offered one-to-one counselling or therapy as well as membership of a facilitated group, that is, one led by an experienced professional whose job is to support group members until they feel able to join a self-help recovery group such as Alcoholics Anonymous, Tranx or Over-Eaters Anonymous. These groups usually follow the '12 Step' process.

If you are self-abusive or self-harming in any way, individual therapy with a specialist will help. Some hospitals have behavioural therapy attendance programmes, and your GP will know about facilities in your area.

If you are yourself sexually abusing someone you will need to stop doing this before you can work on your own problems. Again, seek specialist therapy and join a group such as Sex Addicts Anonymous. An initial step would be to phone a helpline.

If you feel your problems are with relationships, and how other people see you, a general therapy group would be valuable. This usually means committing yourself to one session a week for at least one year. Alternatively — and especially if you are very isolated — working as a volunteer in a supportive project where you will receive some training will build your self-esteem.

This would be particularly important if you are a lesbian or gay man; we have yet to reach any conclusions about the connection between childhood abuse and homosexuality. You may find that a heterosexual counsellor, or group, will have reached a conclusion about you before hearing what you have to say. Sexual abuse obviously affects the way you feel about your sexuality; however, lesbians or gay men do not choose partners solely because of being abused in childhood. On the contrary, some lesbian writers have stated that, if every girl who was sexually abused by a male became a lesbian in adulthood, one in four women in this country would be living as lesbians.

You may feel that you are unclear about the nature of your problems and feel unsafe in groups — this is especially the case for survivors with experiences of ritual abuse and multiple abuse (more than one abuser). Individual therapy would be the most beneficial — and you have the right to interview several therapists before making your decision on the one you feel will be good for you. Your therapist may later suggest that you also look for groups to join; no reputable therapist would let you believe that he or she is the only possible source of support.

Perhaps you feel unable to talk to anyone yet, and prefer to work on your problems alone. Or you may opt for an empowering type of group — a self-help group especially for incest survivors and, even better, one for survivors of female abuse.

The reason that these self-help groups are so empowering is because you are supporting each other equally in taking steps to heal yourself from past pain, and to change destructive patterns in your life, without a 'professional' guide or authority figure in charge of the process. Some people whose abusers were the most authoritarian figures in their lives find self-help groups a great relief. In addition, taking turns to be helper and helped offsets and balances the dynamics of one-to-one therapy, during which you may feel powerless.

Naturally, anyone who has no experience of any type of therapy and has avoided groups in the past will find the prospect of talking openly to strangers daunting. It takes courage, and perhaps several telephone conversations, to enable you to walk through that door, but remember: you will benefit in the long run and you have survived far, far worse experiences and are still here, determined to feel better about yourself.

Self-help has its limits, and there is no need to 'go it alone' if you don't feel confident in doing so. It is OK for you to share the responsibility — you've been struggling alone with your memories and problems ever since you were abused. It's OK to ask for help.

Working alone

You are already doing this. Reading this book, this chapter, recognising that what you experienced was abuse, and considering your options, means that you are half-way through the process of recovery. Yes — *half-way*. If you have previously felt like a victim, of either an abusive relationship, an addiction, depression, or any other problem that dominated your life, the fact that you are beginning your self-help process means that you are already in the next phase; you are a *survivor*, and you are *in recovery*. The next months or even years will not be easy, and reading this and other books is probably bringing to the surface some very painful memories, and feelings that you may believe are uncontrollable and dangerous.

You do not need to work entirely alone if this is too difficult. There are helplines you can ring when you feel desperate, networks you can contact if you want to talk to someone who has similar experiences, other books you can read, and several excellent 'workbooks' which will give you a structure for your personal recovery plan (see Part 3 Resources).

If you have a sensitive partner or close friends, you can ask for help, or at the very least, tolerance, time alone, and understanding, without intrusive questions, of what you are trying to achieve. You may feel that at this time, sexual relationships are out. This is difficult for partners to accept, but if this is what you need to do, then ask your partner to help you by not insisting on sex. If this is impossible, ask for an appointment at a relationship counselling organisation, or make an appointment for family therapy. If your partner is unsympathetic, or downright unco-operative, then your first self-help step is to consider whether or not you want this relationship to continue. If you have children, this may of course be extremely difficult, and you will then need to join some sort of support group who can help you with your recovery process while you continue to manage your domestic arrangements.

It may prove easier for you to maintain some privacy about your memories and what you are trying to do. As few people are willing to understand that women can sexually abuse, it is, sadly, often the case that survivors have to keep their own counsel.

Whatever happens, whatever the effects on your domestic life, keep telling yourself that you are a *survivor*, and that you have been through much, much worse than this, and that you are still here. All the memories which are beginning to flood back are simply that — memories. Your emotional feelings are about something that isn't happening any more; the uncomfortable sensations in your body, perhaps making you sick, panicky, sleepless, or giving you thumping headaches are the reactions your body has been 'storing up' for many years, and is now discharging. You may feel guilty and miserable, even agonised, much of the time, so keep telling yourself *this phase will pass*. If you are a mother or carer, you may find that you start worrying about your behaviour with your own children. Try and be realistic about this. If you feel you have been abusive, it could be helpful to find ways of talking to your children. You might want to seek help with ways of doing this.

Sexual abuse is an attack on all levels: psychological, emotional, physical, sexual and spiritual. Healing, therefore, also needs to deal with all these levels too. You will be changing your ideas about yourself, learning what your emotional reactions mean for you, taking better care of your body, and redefining your sexuality. And, hopefully, finding a sense of spirituality and meaning in your life.

Survivors use a variety of techniques for self-help. These techniques are for you to choose whichever one you feel most comfortable with. What you do depends on the type of person you are. You may prefer simply to read on your own. You may like to tape or write down what you remember; thousands of survivors, including those who have contributed to this book, have found this very helpful. You may find that working through exercises designed with sexual abuse survivors in mind is the most helpful — a 'getting to know yourself' process which is reassuring because the exercises and questions were devised by people like you.

Find ways that you enjoy of expressing yourself. Deep down inside you is a creative, curious, loving and happy child wanting to relate to the world, who could never let go and enjoy the simple pleasures of life. Find outlets for this spontaneity, however childish they may seem. Have fun, take up a team sport, go to funfairs, write ditties, learn a musical instrument, go dancing, build sandcastles, go swimming, and indulge yourself with more adult pursuits such as being massaged. You may experience powerful surges of complex mixtures of emotion that you may never have felt before, including anxiety or fear, sadness, anger, grief, remorse, hate, wanting to be violent, shame, jealousy or resentment. Alternatively, you might fall in love, or have inexplicable surges of exhilaration, bursts of laughter, or a painful tenderness or compassion for small animals or tiny children. All these feelings, especially if there is no apparent reason for them, can be alarming. You might even feel you are going mad. You're not. Be careful of any relationships you form during this phase — they may not be real.

One survivor said that she felt immense relief and happiness on discovering, after 30 years, that other people had been abused by women and that she was no longer doomed to suffer alone in silence. All the hate and rage she also felt was balanced by her joy in rediscovering herself and making important changes in her life.

Other survivors report new and persistent thoughts entering their heads, usually self-abusive, or 'voices' telling them they are dirty, disgusting or liars, and should be locked up. These are, of course, the deeply buried memories of the abusers' voice and attitudes coming to the surface. Acknowledge them, identify them, and tell them to shut up and go away. If the voices sound very much like people you know now, read a book on assertion, or join an assertion training class. Voices and the language of threats play an enormous part in abuse and were the abusers' most powerful weapon in silencing you. Some survivors find that learning another language, including signing, joining an amateur dramatic group, or learning to sing or chant is very helpful.

The target of self-help is eventually to disconnect your normal and natural feelings from the experiences of abuse, and to disconnect the psychological and physical memories of your abuse from the feelings that accompany them. This is a slow process, of course, as you cannot unlock decades of association overnight. It may be helpful repeating to yourself, as often as you like, corrective statements such as: 'When people tell me to shut up it doesn't mean they are going to abuse me'. Or: 'I'm feeling angry, someone must have said something that reminded me of my abuser'. What are known as affirmations are also valuable, and cannot be repeated often enough. Think up some for yourself, such as 'I am a worthwhile person, I am loveable, and deserve to be happy' or 'The abuse wasn't my fault, it shouldn't have happened, I didn't do anything wrong, and it's OK to talk about it'.

Everyone's reaction is different, so don't worry if your own recovery process doesn't fit in which what you read in books. One thing that seems to happen with many survivors is that they begin to feel that deep inside them is another person that seems to be in charge of the healing process. Many people describe this as spirituality, or being in touch with their higher selves. Often people seek out some form of religious group, traditional or New Age, and find the meditation and chanting under guidance cleansing and relaxing, and the philosophies valuable, because they offer hope. Avoid any philosophy or religious group which insists that you are responsible for negative events in your life, and that it is 'karma'. Whether this is true or not, it is the last thing you need to hear right now. The abuse was not your fault, nor was it your responsibility.

An extremely important factor in recovery from sexual abuse is making friends with your body. This could mean a healthier diet, regular exercise that you enjoy, different clothes, taking better care of your health, relaxation exercises to help you sleep, and being in control of who touches you and in what ways.

Sexuality is a complex concept and especially difficult for abuse survivors. What you felt during abuse was a sexual *response* to an activity being imposed upon you. The difference between these feelings and your own sexuality is that you yourself create the feelings when it is appropriate for you to do so, and the outcome is that of your own choosing. Sexuality isn't the same as sensuality, and one of the things you may need to relearn is how to enjoy natural sensual pleasures without immediately feeling that sexual activity must follow. If this is the area of greatest difficulty for you, you may find consultations with a psychosexual counsellor valuable. If memories of abuse are affecting your sexual relationship, and you want to keep it going, partners should try to seek sexual counselling together. Tell your partner that sex makes you feel vulnerable, and try and identify what you need to make yourself feel safer. This could include you making the choices about when you have sex, having the room the way you like it, being allowed plenty of time, asking your partner to talk gently and reassuringly to you rather than being demanding, keeping to foreplay only for a while, or having sex in a place unconnected with your memories of abuse — for instance, the living room instead of the bedroom. Obviously, it is hard for partners to change their habits, which is where sexual counselling helps.

Ultimately, you will want to separate guilt and shame from your sexual feelings. They are yours, and feeling sexual doesn't require you to be vulnerable to unwanted advances from anyone.

The most important thing to remember is to *put yourself first* whenever you can. Your entire young life was spent focusing on your abuser, and much of your adult life will have been spent in trying to puzzle out why she did such dreadful things to you. Though some survivors find it helpful to work out what abusers' motives were, or to find reasons for their behaviour (such as being abused themselves, or being addicts or mentally disturbed) an essential of recovery is to *take the focus off your abuser and turn it on yourself.*

Allow yourself to have needs, and to try and find out how these can be met. Understand that your emotions are important signals for you, both in telling what you do and do not want, and in helping you to identify your needs.

Your healing process may start with self-forgiveness. Since you will have probably been told that the abuse was your fault, you will need to release yourself from the shame this induces. Whatever you have done in your life — perhaps becoming an addict or behaving compulsively in some way, or suffering from depression or panic attacks — can all be thought of as coping skills which you developed in order to deal with being abused.

Abuse survivors are often unusually gifted: the need for them to remain attentive, to try and predict their abusers' needs or moods, to attempt to placate her, or endeavour to get some form of care and love in order to make it through life, frequently results in the development of sensitivity to others, powerful intuition, and creativity.

At your lowest point — and everyone has low points — remember these skills and talents you developed, the greatest of which was courage. It is this courage you can now use in your own healing process.

The twelve steps

This process, originated in AA (Alcoholics Anonymous) has been successfully used in numerous other 'recovery groups' and adapted for self-help incest survivor groups, as it provides a clear, proven and well-documented plan.

It is also useful if you are working alone, and gives you some goals to set for yourself. The twelve steps are only a basis, you may want to adapt them to your own circumstances. AA also uses the famous motto 'one day at a time', and the promise to yourself that 'just for today' you will try and be happy; adjust to what is, rather than trying to control the world, strengthen your mind by study or reading; have a programme to save yourself from hurry and indecision; take a half hour or so for yourself; and try to be unafraid. Here are some of the twelve steps, rewritten to be more relevant to abuse survivors.

1. Accept that you were powerless over your abuse and acknowledge the problems you have which control your life.
2. Believe that you have a powerful inner self, or spiritual core, which is taking charge of your healing process. Trust your personal growth process: it will not let you down.
3. Get to know yourself, honestly and realistically, including knowing your limits.
4. Openly admit any wrongs you have done to others and decide to make amends to them.

5. Acknowledge any harm you are doing to yourself, and decide to find ways to stop doing this, however difficult it may seem.
6. Forgive yourself for anything you feel you may have done to contribute to your abuse — you were powerless to stop it. Forgive yourself for loving your abuser: all children are born loving and giving and are naturally attached to adults who give them attention.
7. Allow the child in you expression in whatever ways you enjoy.
8. Take care of your body and make friends with it.
9. Tell yourself that you, and you alone, are now in charge of your sexuality.
10. Look for ways in which you can focus on yourself and treat yourself with love and respect, and make a commitment to tell someone about your experiences of abuse, and to ask for help and support wherever you can find it.
11. Identify ways in which people are abusive to you now, and tell them their behaviour is unacceptable.
12. Understand that taking responsibility for your own healing also means taking responsibility for your behaviour towards others, including your sexual behaviour. Make a commitment to stop talking or behaving in abusive ways to anyone — no one but your abuser is to blame for abusing you.

Setting up a self-help group

Knowing that others have been through similar experiences to your own is a great relief. You are not peculiar or crazy, and you are no longer isolated from people who believe and understand what you are saying.

The support of your peers in a group allows for safe feelings of dependency, by moving away from the hierarchical social structures we are used to, and so eliminating any potential abuse of this power. As mentioned previously, being in a group means that you take turns to help and be helped, which balances out feelings of power/powerlessness.

The shared group purpose is, broadly, healing, though a more realistic target would be coming to terms with your childhood experiences of sexual abuse, and finding ways of making your life better.

If you want to join an existing group, you will need to find out if there is an 'open' group in your area. Though there are very few groups for survivors of female abuse, there are networks of incest survivor groups throughout the UK, Canada, Australia and the USA.

Some long-running groups have time set aside or 'sub groups' for newcomers, and the remainder for the core group. Others welcome new members, and one or more people take turns to talk to potential members, or even meet them, to explain how the group works. Most use first-names only, and there are strict rules about confidentiality.

Joining a group

If you are looking for an existing group to join, see the resources list in Part 3 of this book, or contact KIDSCAPE, ChildLine, the NSPCC or lesbian and gay helplines, or your nearest women's centre, for a list of contacts and networks.

Contact organisations such as the Citizens' Advice Bureau, or health, community, neighbourhood and women's centres, the public library, local or community radio help lines, relevant charity or advisory service, personal growth and health magazines, and listings magazines which have 'therapy' or 'growth' sections. Most of these organisations will have lists of incest survivor group networks. If you are uncomfortable doing this, phone one of the helplines referred to above.

If you identify with a minority group, your enquiries would start in your minority community; if you are isolated, local councils and national organisations, which operate equal opportunities policies, will be able to direct you to contacts or resources in your area of interest. Public libraries may carry directories of local self-help support networks. If not, The National Self-Help Support Centre (see resources list) can direct you to your local Council for Voluntary Services, and has a data base of organisations which can help you find a group or to start one of your own, or put you in touch with a therapist or self-help group support workers who could advise and, if required, facilitate your group (that is, act as a counsellor or group leader, in the short term if necessary).

Setting up your own group

If you want to start your own group, you could begin by seeing what rooms are available locally and start thinking about how and where to advertise your proposed group. The organisations referred to in the above paragraph will guide you to the appropriate resource.

Find out about the availability of cheap or free rooms which are quiet, comfortable and *secure*. If you are in a rural area, try your adult education centre or church hall. Local council lists of halls and rooms to hire are usually available in public libraries. If 'official' premises do not appeal to you, you could start in your own living room, perhaps agreeing to rotate meetings between the members' homes. If the group always meets in your home you will find yourself doing all the administration — and this will affect the essential equality and shared responsibility, important self-help group ethics.

Contacting other potential members

Survivors of sexual abuse are, understandably, reluctant about advertising publicly the existence of groups and meeting places. If you want to contact members for your new group, start by letting the right people know about you: the main incest survivor help agencies and networks, the helplines mentioned above, rape crisis centres, women's centres, women's listings magazines, gay and lesbian publications and helplines, selected community centres, and your Social Services Child Protection department, which is often contacted by adult survivors. Also tell the clinical psychology department at your local hospital, or a psychiatric social worker.

Many groups have been set up by word of mouth, or through individual therapists contacting each other for information. If you have a therapist, it is therefore best to start by asking him or her.

Other self-help networks are often willing to pass on details of new groups. You could contact your local Alcoholics Anonymous or Over-Eaters Anonymous, for instance.

If you are a member of a religious group, this could be a good starting place. Some, though certainly not all, churches have their own counselling centres, or contact with a local centre. You could have some notices photocopied and put them up free in public libraries, community/women's/health/youth centres or colleges. Your local radio or community radio help-line (if there is one) could pass on your details to callers, or even give out details on air.

Be clear about how widely and openly you want to publicise the group and, in particular, whether you want to use your own telephone number or address at this stage. If you are still living in the same area as your abuser, you may want to keep your group a secret from her. This is particularly the case if your experience has been of ritual or multiple abuse. If it is at all possible, move out of the area. If you are still living with your abuser, some local councils have schemes to rehouse you; alternatively, contact Women's Aid (if you are a woman) or your local hostel, housing association, or housing co-ops.

Protect yourself

Local newspaper or specialist magazine advertising, though not free, means you can use a box number, and only contact the genuine enquirers. Self-protection is an important issue, so box numbers are a good idea. If you are prepared to wait a while, the quarterly personal growth magazines, and newsletters of the various holistic organisations, mean that you know you will be reaching an interested readership. The same applies if you want to contact a specific minority membership, you will only want to advertise in specific publications. If yours is a permanent group, you can also rent a post office mail box.

What sort of people do you want in your group?

Between six and eight is usually a good number, though many groups have started with two or three determined people and grown from there. Ten or more strangers can seem threatening and cumbersome, unless enough of the members are familiar with group processes. If 20 or more people reply, consider forming two or even three groups. You may also consider inviting a therapist, or experienced group facilitator, to start you off for, say, six meetings.

Do you want your group to be same-sex or mixed? Gay or lesbian? Over 40s only? Singles? Black women/men only? Working class? Do you want people who have some experience of group work? You need a mixture of people with different abilities for a group to work well.

Do you want to be a little original, and perhaps devote your group to writing about your experiences? If so, you need to make this clear in your advertising.

Establishing group rules and boundaries

A self-help group, theoretically, 'runs' itself. However, you do all need to agree on some basic rules.

People who were sexually abused as children experienced a complete invasion of all their personal boundaries and basic human rights. As adults, you can expect to feel anxious about talking to other people until you know them well; some group members report concerns about voyeurism, and it is always possible that one of the women will remind you of your abuser in some way. Some rules are therefore essential, while others are renegotiable as the group members come to know each other. The ony way to create an atmosphere of safety in the group is to insist on *total confidentiality*, first-names only, and no contact between group members outside meetings – unless you formally set up co-sponsorship, which other members will know about.

You will need an 'open evening' to discuss setting up the group, the essential rules, and the way it is going to run.

Though as an abuse survivor you may resent the imposition of rules, they are necessary to provide safety, boundaries, and a purposeful structure, and, sometimes, specific group goals. And they can, of course, be changed.

Breaking new ground, finding a format which suits six or eight individuals, letting a group go its own way, is obviously more empowering. However, no one will come to the second meeting unless the boundaries are clearly defined.

The chosen room must provide privacy, quietness and comfort. A closed door, with a 'Do Not Disturb' notice which will be respected, is essential. Set firm meeting times, and agree on the frequency of meetings and the period the group will run — say, one year. People cannot make a commitment unless they know what that commitment is. Other practical rules include those about note-taking and private conversations. The former can feel threatening if the note-taker doesn't explain she is merely recording her own feelings, and the latter is distracting and irritating to other members.

Your group may be unable to meet regularly, and may decide to form pairs for cocounselling; if this is the case, you need an agreement on whether the content of these 'mini-groups' is to be shared at meetings.

Once all this is agreed, this open session can be used for each person in turn saying why they want to join, what they hope to gain, and what their personal targets are — such as learning to deal with anger, stopping bingeing, expressing pain and sadness, finding creative ways to live, or forming better relationships. And, of course, one or two may decide that this is the wrong group for them: people who have been very isolated, or who have had dreadful experiences with their familes, will find group work threatening; others, who have perhaps just got in touch with the pain of being abused, find other people's pain intolerable.

It is unrealistic in the beginning to expect people to be able to identify their feelings or to know what their needs are, or how they prefer to 'work', or even what type of support they are looking for, unless they have a good knowledge of therapy processes and a reasonable level of self-awareness.

So rather than 'work' or follow targets, you may like to discuss topics, such as personal responsibility (also referred to as boundaries), All members are responsible for their own feelings, and for taking care of themselves outside meetings. However, since the group is for support, it is sensible to mention if someone appears to be under too much stress to manage in the group, or appears not to be eating at all, or is drinking too much, or is not strong enough to be able to give their attention to others. You could suggest that they find a facilitated group, or seek individual therapy, or join a problem-oriented group.

No one will say a word unless there are basic rules about time-sharing and listening, so you need to decide if the group will be free-flowing, or whether you will have ten minutes each to talk; whether people will talk without any response from the others except attentive listening, or whether dialogues are acceptable. You may decide that it is the individuals' responsibility to negotiate for time each week. The group dynamics which will emerge are the responsibility of the whole group.

Acceptance is essential for healing, so you will want some rules about judgemental comments (for instance, that it is OK to point these out) and expressions of prejudice. Clearly, verbal abuse is unacceptable (unless you like 'Encounter' techniques) and obviously physical abuse has to be ruled out. You could agree that anyone being verbally abusive (after all, none of us is perfect) must agree to 'work' on it immediately.

For some members this may be the first time they have spoken of their abuse, so patience is necessary and feedback may be helpful, as it is so important to be heard and believed, and be 'given permission' to be 'selfish'. In addition, the whole point of being in a group, and its value, is that we learn an enormous amount from listening to others, and from how we react to what others are saying or doing. This is known as 'active listening'.

Some people may prefer, and ask for, complete silence, or interventions, or supportive comments, empathic comments or insights, all of which can be helpful to someone struggling to express themselves. 'Interpretations' are usually unhelpful because they are subjective. That said, they may still raise someone's awareness — as talking about things that may have happened before the child had enough vocabulary is almost impossible. The speaker may need recognition of this if they are feeling stupid or inarticulate, and help in expressing what is going on in another way — acting it out, perhaps or moving around the room, kicking cushions, or being wrapped up in a blanket.

Interruptions and interventions are distracting and confusing, as are claims that you understand when you clearly do not. Sincerity is more valuable than trying to find answers for someone, and it is usually unhelpful to say you feel the same way — no one can ever feel exactly the same thing as someone else in the same way. Even though you may all be angry or sad, for each person it will be a different feeling. Everyone needs support in feeling whatever they are feeling.

Experiencing oneself is the only way to self-awareness and therefore growth; that said, sharing ways of dealing with anger or grief (for example) followed by a group exercise, is helpful for everyone.

We all have unique ways of expressing ourselves. People who join a group because they are unable to deal with powerful feelings will not be helped if the only accepted form of expression is bashing cushions or shouting at the abuser. There are hundreds of methods to choose from. Art, movement, sound, body work, writing, dream work and many other forms of expression can be used.

Many groups now use personal growth methods such as the I Ching, Medicine Cards, Angel Cards or similar. Perhaps you could agree that there are no 'boundaries' about ways of expression. Body work and techniques such as psychodrama have powerful results, however, and you need to be sure you can all support the person 'working' and have had some experience and/or training.

There will need to be rules about touching, hugging and holding. Support is important; however, sexual abuse survivors are the only people who can make decisions about who may touch them. 'Comforting' people can actually squash their feelings and interfere with their attempts at expressing themselves, as well as giving the impression that the 'comforter' does not want to hear about the feeling, or does not want to experience his/her own reaction to whatever is going on. Being unable to accept others means we are unable to accept ourselves (or a part of ourselves). If someone's anger frightens you, then it is most likely you are afraid of your own anger (as well as your abuser's). In other words, no one else can 'make' you feel anything. If someone always feels squashed in the group, you could surround her and encourage her to 'fight' her way out — as long as you and she are able to deal with the results of her newly discovered power.

Some groups like to hold hands at the beginning and end of meetings; others do not. All these, and many other points, are areas to negotiate.

One of the most wonderful things about the healing process is beginning to find out about different parts of yourself, or seeing in others behaviour or attitudes that you previously undervalued. You start to think, 'Oh, other people do that too — it must be OK'.

Any form of therapy is also permission to be yourself, the unique individual that you are.

Staying together

There is no 'right' way to run a group, and many evolve naturally, allowing the group energy to lead the members. If you can remain aware that what happens in groups tends to reflect what happens or happened outside or in your family, you can gain insight into why other people irritate, frighten, or attract you, and what you need to do about changing the dynamics, becoming more assertive, and hopefully, getting your needs met.

A good rule is to be sincere and avoid sentimentality.

Invariably attractions will develop, including sexual attractions — and this is one of the difficulties of keeping a group of abuse survivors together. It is *essential* that sexual relationships are not allowed to form between group members; one of the most important things to learn is non-sexual behaviour and non-sexual love, something survivors never had as children. To be able to experience free, non-sexual relationships is a very important part of the healing process. This is worth discussing early on in the group, since the members will be experiencing various levels of sexual confusion.

People may begin to adopt the 'roles' they were forced to develop as children in order to cope with the abuse. Some of these are: seducer, counsellor, 'parent', negotiator, coper, scapegoat or 'doormat', actor, rescuer, story-teller, intellectual, martyr, tantrum-thrower, dreamer, hard worker, sobber, or joker, or they may find themselves withdrawing, getting depressed, getting illnesses, backaches or headaches, arguing with people, having panic attacks, getting obsessional, or experiencing being out of their bodies.

From the beginning, it is good to open up discussions on these possibilities, and ask people to say if they are aware of the sort of things they did as a child to deal with the abuse. Everything that happens in the group is a learning experience. Some members may want to leave, perhaps to join a more suitable group, such as an addiction recovery group, or to go into individual therapy.

A group being what it is, power structures will emerge, people will clash, some will rarely speak while others are always ready to share — and group members do drop out.

What to do every week

There are thousands of therapy techniques as well as those already mentioned (such as the twelve steps, or agreeing on weekly topics). Unless several members have a good understanding of these techniques (also called tools) there is no point in using them. Some can actually be damaging.

The first thing to do every week is to make sure that everyone is breathing fully. Then each member could take it in turn to say whether or not they want to talk or just listen for today, or whether they want to try and express a feeling, or deal with a problem that has come up for them, or share an insight.

If you know you are all paralysed with fear by other people's anger, crying, or panic attacks, then make this the focus of group attention. You could use the gentler means of expression referred to or explore their opposites. All feelings have opposites, such as loss/love, shame/pride, fear/courage, happiness/sadness, anxiety/confidence, pain/healing. To diminish painful feelings, you could start by looking at the opposite, and finding one thing that creates that opposite feeling in you, and get in touch with it. Crying, as well as being a sign of pain, is a natural way of healing, and so is laughter.

You may all be uncomfortable with any form of group ritual, or rules about limiting expressions of feeling, so before exploring feelings of pain, rage, or shame, you could look at valuing or developing positive things, like work skills, talents, love, creativity, self-nurturing, loving your bodies. Other positive ideas are finding a safe space within yourselves, being grounded, and using visualisations, relaxation tapes or centering meditations.

Groups often use 'Gestalt' techniques as there are so many books available giving details of how they work. However, if anyone in the group has experienced feeling 'split' or 'out of their bodies' during sexual abuse, talking to another 'part' of themselves supposedly inhabiting a chair or a cushion could be very threatening. Other forms of 'Gestalt' (which are not by any means exclusive to this therapy) such as 'owning' your feelings, being in the 'now', and being aware of needs, are central to any group. Care is needed in using these and any other therapy techniques.

One of the side-effects of the self-help group movement is the proliferation of 'work books' now available. These are usually editions of other books written on the same subject, either by therapists or people who have gone through the experience (or both). If there is not a good bookshop near you, you can buy them mail-order either from magazines or specialist firms.

Whatever you decide to do, a rule for the early weeks is 'keep it simple'. It takes time to build trust in yourself and others, so don't look for instant 'results'. The process of taking it in turns to organise meetings and buy refreshments, books or cushions is in itself a process of self-help and sharing. Your group may in fact spend many weeks exploring how to relate to small groups under the theme of 'recreating a family'.

If your group is floundering, or you are all fighting for time to express powerful feelings, or if you all feel you are 'stuck', you may wish to invite a therapist or group facilitator along to feed back what appears to be happening (this could be a quarterly occurrence, for example). Or you could devote a session to exploring the 'stuck' feelings. Are you 'down a well', bored, scared, feeling it's not worth the effort/you're not worth the effort? Is being 'stuck' merely a natural process of resisting an extremely painful memory that you're not yet ready to deal with? Trust your own process, and don't allow yourselves to be pushed.

Do you dislike each other? What does this mean in terms of your other relationships? Devise ways either of moving forward, or, alternatively, accept that you need to be 'stuck' right now. Maybe you need to feel stronger before moving on, so relaxation and energising exercises would be beneficial. You could join hands to feel more like a group, or look at roles members may have fallen into — simply changing places can change the dynamics.

Remember always to *be kind to yourselves*. If you all arrive loaded with the day's stress, start by 'shaking off' some of it; another good way of doing this is to have a good laugh. If that's inappropriate, try breathing exercises, and tense/relax movements.

Stages of group development

Studies have shown that all groups follow similar processes as the members get to know each other and the group develops and strengthens. It is helpful for self-help groups to understand the format so that they can identify what is going on.

Some of the stages are obvious, such as the first one, in which members are wary of each other, feel unsafe in the group and are reluctant to speak. A way to defuse this is to keep the first meeting to general talk — in turn — about what people hope to get out of the group, without needing to give personal details. In the next stage, people may talk more, though not about themselves; or they may be silent and withdrawn rather than listening. This is usually followed by people starting to express what they have felt about other 'groups' (including their families), then projecting these feelings onto the group, perhaps saying that they don't want to be in it any more, or it's a waste of time, or not trusting one or more members. This is actually resistance to talking about personal feelings. Instead of saying to someone 'I hate you', you can be helped through this by saying, 'I'm experiencing feelings of hatred towards women'. You will probably find that other members are going through a similar stage.

From this stage, people gradually begin to talk about themselves, what they are feeling, what the group means to them, and what insights they are gaining. Then they will begin to share what they feel about each other and why. It is at this point that the roles members have adopted become most apparent. If this is pointed out, the group begins to work as a whole and help each other through the healing process. This is followed by self-acceptance, acceptance of each other's differences, and recognition of individuality. This may be a good time for people to give each other helpful feedback, including feedback on the effects on others of people's behaviour.

As you work through your memories of abuse, you will get in touch with a sense of yourself as a victim. You may find that awful things keep 'happening' to you. The reality is that life is problematic, difficult and frequently irritating; people are hostile and critical and concerned with their own lives. These things do not mean that people (or life) is singling you out for attack. It means that you are being presented with challenges and problems, so ask the group for help in finding creative solutions.

You may express this 'victim-consciousness' directly, however, what often happens is that you start to identify with other victims — injured animals, war wounded, refugees, or deprived people in other countries. Take care that you do not abandon your healing process by giving your attention to other causes, though this can, of course, be a route to healing yourself — as long as you are aware of what is going on.

Also be wary of any feelings of self-sacrifice, also known as 'martyr-consciousness'. This might be expressed as always saying you don't need time, or that other people's problems are more important than yours, or always being the one who opens up, locks up, buys the supplies and washes the mugs. The other one to watch out for is 'abuser-consciousness'. You may find yourself unable to say anything to people in the group because you have no wish to criticise or attack them — even expressing a need may feel to you like attacking someone else. Monitor what is really going on for you, and whether you are truly being (or wanting to be) abusive or not. You could say 'I want to give you some constructive feedback, and I'm finding it difficult because I don't want you to think I'm being abusive or invading your privacy in any way'.

In groups you can share the responsibility for what goes on — you don't have to carry it all alone any more.

Training in group skills

Invaluable to any group — whether starting out, or being 'stuck', is attendance at a weekend (or longer) workshop, for instance, body work, meditation, creative visualisation, or co-counselling (the latter is said to be the ultimate in self-help therapy, as it is based on equality between counselling 'partners', whether in pairs or groups.) There are several introductory counselling and group skills courses at adult education centres.

Training for self-help group members and support workers is available from organisations in the resource list. If there is a self-help support network in your area, they will have information on training — and possibly even funding. Alternatively, contact your local branch of *Mind*.

Part 3

Resources

13 Female child molesters: a review of the literature

Kathryn T. Jennings

Child molestation is a serious problem in Canada. It is a topic which has been examined in considerable depth in recent years (Badgley 1984, Finkelor 1984, 1986, Groth 1979). According to the findings of the Badgley Committee on Sexual Offences Against Children (Badgley 1984), approximately one in two women and one in three men has experienced unwanted sexual acts at some point in their lives. Moreover, the survey showed that some four out of five of these incidents occurred when these persons were children or youths.

Further, Finkelor (1986) reports that the victimisation rates for child molestation derived from various North American studies range from 6 per cent to 62 per cent for females and from 3 per cent to 31 per cent for males. Similarly, Badgley and King (1990) report the prevalence rates of child sexual victimisation studies carried out since 1979 involving 9000 persons from Canada, Britain and the United States. Their findings suggest that between 11 per cent and 45 per cent of females and 3 per cent and 9 per cent of males reported at least one instance of sexual abuse before the ages of approximately 16 to 18 years old. Taken together, this information suggests that child molestation is fairly common, and for some, a bitter reality.

A review of the literature on sexual offences committed against children points out that relatively little research has been done on female sex offenders (Finkelor 1984, Groth 1979, Mathews 1989).

Given that the majority of reported child molestations are committed by men (studies demonstrate approximately 80 to 95 per cent), the issue of the female sex offender has been virtually ignored.

The literature on female sex offenders is sparse. The majority of publications and research on the topic have appeared since 1987. Prior to that, relatively little attention was paid to the female offender in the main body of literature on sex offenders. Consequently, the existing knowledge and data on this topic is somewhat preliminary and conflicting.

With respect to the victims of female child molesters, there is a dearth of literature available to them on their unique experiences. The overwhelming majority of books for survivors of child sexual abuse address those individuals who were abused by a male. For example, one of the primary healing books that is presently on the market, *The Courage To Heal* by Bass and Davis (1988) devotes 3 out of 495 pages to the specific issue of female child molesters. Although they concede, 'Since much of the literature has focused on father–daughter incest, or solely on abuse with a male perpetrator, those survivors who were abused by women have felt even more isolated than those abused by men' (Bass and Davis 1988, p. 96), they do not provide any major contribution to the literature that survivors could utilise in their healing process that would specifically address the unique circumstances and consequences of being abused by a female.

However, the issue of female child molesters is being raised. At a conference given in 1991 in Toronto, Dr Fred Mathews, a community psychologist, gave some interesting statistics on female sex offending that are worthy of attention. He states:

> [he assumes that approximately 10 per cent of child molesters are female] . . . if one in seven Canadian men and one in four women were sexually abused as a child, as a study has indicated, that works out to about five million people. Ten per cent of that figure would mean *500,000 Canadians have been abused by girls or women*; 1 per cent would mean about 50,000. I don't know about you, but that doesn't seem like a minor number, he said (*The Globe and Mail* 30 October 1991, A1–A2).

With respect to the incidence of female child molesters, the literature is problematic. The definitions for what is considered child sexual abuse by a female are inconsistent and the population samples from which the data are drawn vary and are often unrepresentative. Moreover, given the grossly under-reported incidence of child sexual abuse, caution needs to be exercised when examining this data. In Canada, the Badgely Commission found that 1.1 per cent (8) of the 727 convicted sexual offenders who were interviewed reported to have experienced sexual abuse by a female when they were children

(Badgley 1984). Conversely, Groth maintains that 60 per cent of a sample of sex offenders he interviewed had been victimised sexually when they were young and of these 20 per cent had been victimised by a female (Groth 1979). Similarly, Burgess states that 56 per cent of a sample population of serial rapists disclosed having being abused sexually as children; and of that percentage, 40 per cent were identified as female perpetrators (Burgess, Groth, Holmstrom and Sgroi, 1987).

Finkelhor and Russell (1984) attempted to isolate data on female sex offenders that was collected by the American Humane Association study (1978) and arrived at a figure of females being the perpetrators in 14 per cent of the cases against boys and 6 per cent of the cases against girl victims. Further, they looked at statistics gathered from the National Incidence Study (1981) which reported that 13 per cent of the female sexual abuse victims and 24 per cent of the male sexual abuse victims stated that they had been abused by a female. However, owing to some of the methodological and definitional problems, the authors assert that the numbers may be somewhat high. According to Home Office Criminal Statistics (1975–1984), data were collected over a ten year period (1975–1984) on sexual offences committed by both sexes and it was found that women committed 0.95 per cent of the sex offences. Discrepancies over the incidence of female sex offending cause enormous difficulties in determining the extent to which women perpetrators are involved in sexually offending against children. However, one thing is clear; the incidence of reported female committed child molestation is quite low in comparison to the reported abuse of their male counterparts.

This has led researchers to ask why it is that women commit fewer sexual offences than men do. Some argue that the incidence of female offending is quite low due to serious under-reporting of their offences (Groth 1979, Justice and Justice 1979). Krug (1989) offers some possible explanations as to why males in particular who were abused as children may not report the offence. He states:

1 Males do not get pregnant, and the evidence of sexual abuse has not been present.
2 A double standard in belief systems has existed in which fathers have the potential for evil and mothers are 'all good'.
3 Adult males have been too embarrassed to reveal their sexual activity with and arousal by their mothers.
4 Male children have been presumed to be unaffected by sexual abuse, and reports by sons have been ignored.
5 Patients and therapists alike have been unaware of the connection between the sexual abuse of males by mothers and later interpersonal relationship problems (pp. 117–118).

Information such as this is helpful in increasing the understanding of why male survivors are reluctant to come forward and report that their abuser was a female. However, it ignores possible explanations that a female survivor may hold for not disclosing her abuse from a female child molester. Mathew and Speltz maintain that:

> Viewing females as perpetrators of sexual abuse, perhaps parallel to viewing males as victims, challenges traditional cultural stereotypes. Females are thought of as mothers, nurturers, those who provide care for others; not as people who harm or abuse them. Since, historically, females have been viewed as non-initiators, limit-setters, and anatomically the receivers of sexuality, it is difficult for some to imagine a female sexually abusing others (Unpublished manuscript, 1987).

Stereotypical views of women such as those mentioned above are further substantiated in a study conducted by Sylvia Broussard and her colleagues (1991). They asked 180 female and 180 male undergraduate students about their perceptions of child sexual abuse on the victim. The results revealed that the participants tended to view the interaction of a male victim with a female perpetrator as less representative of child sexual abuse. In addition, they also thought that male victims of this interactional pattern would experience less harm than would victims of other interactional types (e.g. female victim–male perpetrator) (Broussard, Wagner and Kazelskis 1991). Societal attitudes such as those displayed in this study demonstrate the difficulties male victims may have in reporting sexual abuse and why women perpetrators continue to remain undetected and under-reported.

A study done by Fischer (1990) demonstrated similar results with subjects who were themselves victims. The author found that males who were sexually victimised by a female when they were children retrospectively reported having liked the experience and maintained that they did not have any stress or emotional problems because of it. It should be noted that the males who were abused by an adult rated their stress from the abuse as less when it was heterosexual than homosexual. It seems that, not only do a certain percentage of the victims (mostly male), but also a proportion of the population in general continue to subscribe to the traditional view that women are harmless individuals who could not possibly commit such a crime. From what we know, women commit a much smaller proportion of criminal offences in general, and an even smaller number of sexual offences against children. Ignoring their crimes though, is analogous to trying to put a puzzle together with pieces missing.

We need to recognise that women do molest children, and given their traditional role as caretakers, they are considerably more able to hide their crimes. It is not disputed that women have been given the primary responsibilities of raising children, and with that comes not only a lot of responsibility but a great deal of control over their dependents. Women are charged with bathing and changing children, putting them to bed, breast-feeding, changing nappies and many other intimate activities surrounding the care of the child. Many of these are done in private, thus providing the mother (or any other caretaker) with a space that allows her to commit the sexual act under the guise of child care. Justice and Justice (1979) maintain that mothers more frequently engage in types of sexual activities that are less likely to get reported such as fondling, sleeping with their son, caressing him in a sexual way, and keeping him tied to her in an emotional way with implied promises of a sexual payoff.

Further, in certain cultures where there is excessive closeness between the mother and her son, the chances that an incestuous relationship will develop are high. Katahara (1989) notes that Japanese mothers typically initiate the sexual acts with their sons. Usually this occurs when she witnesses her son masturbate for the first time. She uses this as an opportunity to teach him about sex. Other common incidents that lead to an incestuous relationship are when the son sleeps with his mother or they are bathing together. It appears then, that in Japan, the mother regards the sexual aspect of her son as 'another biological phenomenon like eating, sleeping, or eliminating. As a result, she deals with it as if she were letting a three-year-old son urinate' (Katahara 1989, p. 449). Clearly the implications of this behaviour on the son could potentially be quite damaging. To try to understand what motivates certain women to cross that line and commit sexual acts against their own as well as other children, researchers of child sexual abuse have begun to explore the aetiology (if there is one) behind female child molestation.

Various theoretical approaches have been advanced in an effort to understand the male child molester; however, it is not clear whether such approaches could be applied to women sex offenders. Finkelhor and Araji (1986) argue that theories of child molestation tend to fall into one of four categories: emotional congruence, sexual arousal, block age and disinhibition. Theories that can be classified under emotional congruence centre on concepts such as arrested psychosexual development, low self-esteem, and narcissism. There is an effort to understand the emotional motivations behind sex offending. Theories examining sexual arousal rely on early sexual experiences in the offenders' childhood, whether or not they have an unusual heighened sexual arousal to children. The emphasis is on atypical indicators of sexual arousal in the child molester. Many of the popular theories about child sexual abuse focus on blockage as an explanatory factor. Such theories rely on the idea that individuals are blocked in their ability to get their sexual and emotional needs met in normal adult-oriented relationships and so turn to children for gratification. Examples of blockages can range from a lack of social skills to a breakdown of the marital relationship.

Finally, theories that concentrate on disinhibition take into account factors that work to remove or weaken restraints so that persons can become sexually involved with a child. Psychosis, mental retardation, lack of impulse control and substance abuse are examples of disinhibiting factors that allow the child molester to abuse a child sexually. This four-factor model helps make it possible to understand why it is difficult to draw unambiguous conclusions about what factors lead to child molestation. Through the utilisation of Finkelhor and Araji's model, it becomes possible to discern the various theoretical approaches that exist in the literature with respect to female child molesters. It should be noted though, that the theoretical views are not necessarily mutually exclusive; rather, females who sexually abuse children may have a host of motivations that underly their behaviour. For example, O'Connor (1987) describes some of the motives given by a sample of female child molesters:

> boredom after a broken marriage complicated by sedative and alcohol abuse [. . .] sex with a 13-year-old boy as revenge against her husband for being unfaithful; punishment of a 13-year-old boy for breaking into her house by taking his trousers off and interfering with him (aided and abetted by her husband); fear of being beaten by her boyfriend if she did not aid and abet him in indecently assaulting a 9-year-old boy (O'Connor 1987, p. 617).

Some women focus on one factor that they feel was the major contributing factor to their molestations. A common explanation for sex offending cited frequently throughout the literature is that the offenders themselves were once victims of child sexual abuse. This is noted in case studies:

> I was sexually abused as a child from quite young on up, until I was a teenager. Some of the same things that I did to my children, some of the inappropriate boundaries, of growing up, of thinking, came from the family (Irene) (Mathews 1989, p. 27).

and in larger samples:

> Six (21.4 per cent) of the subjects (sexual offenders) reported a history of being physically abused; 14 (50 per cent) were reported to have been sexually abused (Fehrenbach 1988, p. 150).

Clearly, one must be cautious when interpreting this information. It is well known that the majority of reported victims of sexual abuse are women; and the majority of reported sex offenders in our society are men. It seems that women tend to deal with past abuse in a different manner from men, i.e. through repression, denial, substance abuse, depression or by working it through in a therapeutic environment. Therefore, when looking for possible explanations of female child molesters, other factors need to be taken into consideration. In fact, if the popular theory that being abused as a child leads one to go on and abuse others were correct then the majority of our child molesters would be female! It is therefore important to examine other areas and motivations that underlie the behaviour of these women.

Therapists and researchers tend to agree that female offenders differ from their male counterparts in a number of areas. These differing characteristics can be useful not only theoretically but also on a more practical level such as in the creation of treatment programmes and offender typologies. Some of the more striking differences between male and female sex offenders are, firstly, many more females than males sexually abuse in consort with another person (usually male). In contrast, it is very rare for men to commit their offence with another person (Mathews 1989). In a study of twelve female offenders, Wolfe remarks:

> Perhaps one of the findings of this material which demarks this female offender population most sharply from male offenders is that fact that half this sample offended in concert with another adult, in all cases the other adult was male (1985, p. 3).

When women do participate in the abuse with another person, they generally play an adjunctive, rather than primary initiating role. Usually, women who abuse with a man are doing so in order to please their partner (many times out of fear). It is important to recognise however, that a proportion of female child abusers do act alone. For example, Fehrenbach (1988) collected descriptive data on a population of female adolescent sexual offenders and he points out that all of the subjects in his study acted independently of another person when committing their offence. Information like this has implications for the construction of a typology for female offenders. This will be discussed later on in the chapter.

Secondly, females tend to use violence less frequently than men do during the course of their offending behaviour (Krug 1989). This may simply be attributable to the differential socialisation process of males and females in our society. Thirdly, given the relative proximity that women have traditionally had with children, they are more likely than males to know their victims. Availability is a key factor in victim selection; and given that women are generally the nurturers in our society, it stands to reason that they would have greater access to children. Finally, the duration and frequency of the molestation appears to be less for females as a group than for males. Moreover, the number of victims per female offender seems to be less than for their male counterparts (Wolfe 1985).

The importance of collecting data on the characteristics of female child molesters cannot be underestimated. The literature is new and lacking in some of the basic information necessary to the development of research in this area. To date, there have only been a handful of studies documenting background and offence characteristics of female sex offenders. The following studies have attempted to provide data on these women. From what we know about female sex offenders, they appear to be somewhat of a heterogeneous group. However, generally speaking, one can identify particular factors that are pertinent to all of them. This review will endeavour to examine them. To speak of the 'typical' female child molester would be next to impossible as she simply does not exist. What one can do, however, is to construct typologies composed of the various similarities and differences among the women themselves. This will be examined later on. With respect to the characteristics of female child molesters, many different data are collected in an effort to gain a better understanding of the background and identity of the women themselves.

Firstly, the age range of female sex offenders lies somewhere between approximately 16 and 36 with a mean age of 26 years (Johnson 1987, Wolfe 1985, O'Connor 1987). To some extent, these women differ from their male counterparts in that the latter offend up to a later age in life than women do (Johnson 1987). In addition, pre-adolescent females under sixteen also commit sexual offences against children for which they remain undetected. Their behaviour usually occurs while they are trusted to look after a child (Knopp and Lackey 1987).

Comparatively speaking, female molesters as a group are more likely to know their victims, whereas more of their male counterparts will molest not only children they know but strangers as well. Briefly, Faller (1987) identifies the perpetrator–victim relationship in her sample:

Because the women in this sample frequently sexually maltreated more than one child, they could have different relationships with different victims. Thirty-four of the women (85 per cent) were mothers to at least one of their victims. Twenty-two (55 per cent) sexually abused only their own children, and the other 12 (30 per cent) abused their own children and others. In three instances, the women also abused nieces and/or nephews. Two abused their children and stepchildren and two their boyfriend's children as well as their own. Two who sexually abused their children also victimised their grandchildren. Three sexually abusive mothers

maltreated neighbour children or those of friends as well . . .
(Faller 1987, p. 265).

Generally speaking, female sexual offenders are usually acquaintances
of their victims (if the victims are not their own children), most
notably a neighbour, babysitter, or other trusted adult or adolescent
(Johnson 1987).

With regard to the actual sexual acts that these women commit
against children, the molestations involve a variety of sexual acts.
They include fondling, mutual masturbation, oral, anal, and genital
activities, pornography and sexual games (Johnson 1987, Knopp and
Lackey 1987). The vast majority of female sex offenders used
persuasion on their victims rather than physical force or threats.
Aggressive behaviour appears to be more prevalent with male child
molesters (Wolfe 1985).

With regards to the sex of the victim, the data are somewhat
confusing. Given that sexual molestation is grossly under-reported, it
is impossible to generate accurate figures of this phenomenon. Is it the
case that male victims are less likely to report being victimised by a
woman due to societal norms that endorse and even glorify 'older
woman/young boy' relationships and fantasies? (Hunter 1990).
Clearly, issues like this need to be taken into account when attempting
to determine the sex of the victim (as well as other data on female sex
offenders). In a study conducted by Knopp and Lackey (1987), they
found that out of 646 offences committed by female abusers, 329 of
them were against male victims while 317 were against females. These
figures show an almost even split between male and female victims. A
sample of female molesters studied by Falkler (1987) revealed that
approximately two-thirds of the victims were female and one-third
male. Similarly, Fehrenbach's study on female sexual offenders found
that 35.7 per cent of his sample abused males while 57.1 per cent had
abused female children. It appears from the above findings that girls
are more likely than boys to be molested by females; however,
conclusions such as this should be made with caution due to the severe
under-reporting of child molestation in general and the possible
additional under-reporting from male victims for the reasons discussed above.

In attempting to understand the motivations of female sexual
offenders, many researchers examine whether these women were ever
themselves the victims of child sexual abuse. It is not clear if this belief
in the association between past abuse and offending behaviour has a
lot of credence given that most child abuse victims are female, yet
most sex offenders are male. Nevertheless, such a possible factor
needs to be taken into consideration. In Mathews' (1989) sample of 16
female sex offenders, she found that all of the women except one were

abused sexually when they were children. In a study by Fehrenbach 50 per cent of his subjects reported to have been sexually abused in their past (1988). Similarly, Wolfe (1985) reported that 58 per cent of her sample of female offenders stated that they had been molested during childhood. Conversely, in Johnson's study (1989) 100 per cent of her sample of female sex offenders were abused themselves as children; however, it is not clear whether this contributes to these women offending later on in life. More research in this area is seriously needed.

Another factor characteristic of female sex offenders appears to be their extreme dependency on or rejection by males (Mathews 1989). These women have a very low level of self-esteem and are dependent on men for not only their survival but for their sense of self as well. They are easily manipulated or coerced by their male partner to engage in inappropriate sexual acts against their own or other children. It is important to note that not all female child molesters have these characteristics; but, it is likely that those who do, generally abuse because they were coerced by another person (usually a male).

Finally, other considerations relevant to sexually abusive women are substance abuse and mental health. The literature points out that many female child molesters abuse drugs and/or alcohol. This is a good example of what Finkelhor refers to in his four-factor model as a disinhibiting factor that the women may use in order to weaken or remove cognitive and emotional restraints and allow them to become sexually involved with a child (Finkelhor 1986). In terms of prevalence, Faller (1987) found in her study that 55 per cent of her subjects reported substance abuse. Further, in Wolfe's study of twelve female sexual offenders, she found that five of these subjects had a history of substantial substance abuse, primarily alcoholism (1985). Clearly, in treating female child abusers, one needs to address the issue of substance abuse in an effort to prevent these women from engaging in disinhibiting activities that may contribute to their molesting patterns.

With respect to the mental health of female sexual offenders, the literature is somewhat confusing and contradictory. Society has this view of women that they are innocent and pure individuals who could not possibly be capable of committing deviant acts. There seems to be an underlying belief that, if a woman commits a crime, she must be unstable and in need of psychological help. As Wolfe remarks, 'A societal myth maintains that any woman who would commit an act of paedophilia has to be crazy' (1985, p. 7). It is unclear if in fact these women are unstable or if they are determined to be unstable by the mental health profession who test them rigorously in order to confirm their biased belief that women who commit deviant acts are 'mad' and not 'bad'. It is hard to tell as the literature is in disagreement. For example, in O'Connor's study, he states that 48 per cent of the female molesters in his sample had a psychiatric diagnosis and a history of previous treatment (1987). Conversely, Krug (1989) maintains that, in his study of mothers who sexually abused their sons, there were no cases where the mother was psychologically ill. Similarly, Mathews comments in her study that:

> none of the women was classified as severely emotionally disturbed or psychotic. Emotional problems abounded, but the reality contact of all of the women was satisfactory; none of them manifested a chronic history of psychiatric dysfunction (1989, p. 88).

With discrepancies in the literature over the mental health and stability of female child molesters, it becomes clear that there needs to be more research conducted in this area. By looking at some of the motivations that underlie the behaviour of female sexual offenders, one can recognise that they are not necessarily the same as male child molesters; these men tend to molest for reasons such as power and control. However, despite the current information available, we need to recognise that some women may molest children for similar reasons as their male counterparts; we have simply not discovered this information yet. This could be for a host of various reasons such as the cultural blinkers that we wear against women and their association to power and control. It is therefore important when examining this issue not to discount any areas that may be crucial to increasing our understanding of these women.

Through an examination of the characteristics of female child sexual abusers, one begins to see distinct categories emerge. Specifically, researchers are beginning to create typological schemes that will allow them to characterise specific types of female sex offenders. This information is also useful for the treatment of these women as it provides therapists with specific information that will assist them in making effective therapy and case management decisions. Faller (1987) has created a classification scheme of female molesters where the women fall into one of five case types:

1 *Polyincestuous abuse* where there are at least two perpetrators and generally two or more victims.
2 *Single-parent abuse* where the mother abuses her own child.
3 *Psychotic abusers* are those whom she maintains are psychotic and who suffer from out-of-control libidinal impulses.
4 *The adolescent perpetrator* generally has access to children in a babysitting situation and their sexual behaviour was meant to gratify themselves rather than pleasure their victim.

5. *The non-custodial abuser* does not have custodial rights to her
    child and·sexually abuses during visitation times.

Mathews (1989) has created a classification scheme somewhat
different from Faller's. Her types emerged from the types of abuse
perpetrated, the perceptions the women hold about their victims, the
involvement of co-offenders, and the psychological similarities and
differences of the women themselves. The first type is the teacher/
lover offender. This molester does not believe that her behaviour is
wrong; in fact, she frequently sees the child as her partner and the
sexual behaviour as a positive experience for both individuals.
Mathews second type is the predisposed (intergenerational) offender.
These women acted alone while offending and they generally abused
their own family members. The majority of these women were
sexually abused themselves at a very young age. The third type that
the author discusses is the male-coerced offender. These women are
passive and feel powerless in interpersonal relationships. They
endorse a traditional lifestyle where the husband is the breadwinner
and in control of the family. Generally, these women were coerced
into the sexual abuse by their husbands or partners. They feared
abandonment and violence if they did not participate in the abuse. It
appears, from what we know, that this group of women comprise a
large percentage of the overall population of female child molesters
(see Chapter 5).

It is important to critically examine the way in which a particular
typology is constructed. Specifically, are these categories mutually
exclusive? On what basis have they been constructed? Would a
continuum be more useful for understanding these women? Finally,
if such tools as typologies are being utilised in the treatment of these
women, it is crucial that an appropriate method is adopted in order to
evaluate them in such a manner so as to determine how effective and
useful they are in increasing our understanding of female child
molesters.

There are many questions that arise out of the literature on female
child molesters. It is a relatively new area in need of further
exploration. From what we know, women comprise a very small
percentage of child abusers; however, despite their small numbers, it
is crucial that their behaviour is not ignored. This issue has just begun
to become unearthed from a research perspective and is slowly being
given attention by the media. For example, in Canada, the *Toronto
Star* newspaper printed two articles on 14 and 15 March 1991 entitled,
'When mothers sexually abuse their sons' which describe the stories of
two men who are adult survivors of incest by their mothers. They
trace the lives of these men and how they coped with the buried

memories, conflicting emotions, and other consequences of being abused by a trusted female.

In addition, in November 1990, a Canadian daytime talk show named, 'Shirley' aired a show that specifically addressed the issue of female sex offenders. Researchers and survivors on the panel highlighted some of the issues associated with this unique and newly exposed phenomenon. The public is slowly learning more about an area that was once thought to be fully understood only with reference to male sex offenders. This is in no way to be under-estimated as it is clear from the literature that men do comprise the overwhelming majority of sex offenders and that women are their primary targets; however, one also needs to realise that females also abuse. Moreover, females are not always the victims of sexual abuse, some are males. Despite current evidence that females do abuse; researchers are still somewhat reluctant to accept this reality. For instance, an article on the front page of the *Globe and Mail* 30 October 1991 written by Sean Fine and entitled, 'Sex abuse by women ignored, psychologist tells conference' alluded to some of the problems that contribute to the disbelief that women abuse. Dr Fred Mathews, a psychologist who spoke at a child abuse conference that was recently put on in Toronto stated:

> Politically [he said], there is resistance to identifying the problem for fear that this will divert attention from male sex offenders. Also, to some extent women have been in control of the discourse on child abuse in Canada and the United States. Culturally, he said, women are seen as passive receptacles of sex rather than as aggressors (A1–A2).

There are some interesting questions left unanswered by the current literature but worthy of attention. Firstly, does being sexually abused by a female have different effects and consequences for the victim than if the perpetrator were a male? Clearly, on a general level, the effects that child sexual abuse have on both males and females are fairly similar; however, it was alluded to earlier on that society has this sacred and pure view of women that regards them as incapable of committing any deviant acts, especially child molestation. Women are the primary caretakers of children and entrusted with their care. Although we would all like to feel that our mothers, aunts, grandmothers and babysitters are trustworthy of our children, it needs to be acknowledged that a small proportion of the female population do in fact molest children.

Given that we as a society generally regard women as nurturing asexual individuals, will victims suffer any additional effects by being abused by the one group of people that they thought they could trust? This is not to say that children are less trustworthy of the primary male caretakers in their lives; rather, that women (especially mothers) have traditionally been regarded as more 'virtuous' in nature. If indeed there are differences between being abused by a female compared to a male, this information may have implications on the focus and direction of therapy and treatment programmes provided to survivors of child sexual abuse. Further research in this area is needed.

Another area of inquiry worth investigating is with respect to the changing role of women in our society. Specifically, has the changing role of women had any appreciable effect on the extent to which women sexually abuse children? As more and more women leave their traditional roles as homemaker and caregiver in order to join the labour force, will there be a decline in the incidence of their offending behaviour? Further, will we witness an increase in the extent to which children are abused in daycare centres, by babysitters or other caretakers? Conversely, will the added pressures of working in the labour force along with still being expected to be responsible for the home and childcare contribute to an increase in women sexually abusing their own as well as others' children? Moreover, as women strive to be given the same rights, privileges and freedoms as men, will their sexual crimes against children become more similar to those of their male counterparts? Specifically, will women offend for some of the same reasons that men do, i.e. power and control rather than for reasons that are particular and unique to women, i.e. being coerced by another person.

It is difficult to predict the nature and direction that female child sexual abuse will take in the future given the difficulties involved in forecasting behaviour. However, it is my belief that it is unlikely that one will witness any real changes in the behaviour of female child molesters due to the differences in the socialisation process of males and females in our society. Males are generally socialised to be more sexual and aggressive than women are, and for this reason among others, it is doubtful that the incidence and nature of female sex offending will alter to any great extent over the next few years. Nevertheless, these questions remain important ones worthy of exploration.

In conclusion, the topic of female child molesters remains a relatively unexplored phenomenon. Researchers have only in the last five years begun to gather data on these women and only within the last couple of years have the Canadian media paid some attention to this issue. Clearly, women do molest children; however, from what we know they comprise a small minority of the total number of sex offenders (approximateliy 1–20 per cent). Despite the apparent infrequency of their offending behaviour, it is still a bitter reality that cannot be ignored. Women are in a far greater position to sexually abuse children given their traditional roles as caregivers in our society. Moreover, their behaviour is less likely to be detected owing to the relative privacy that goes along with taking care of children. It is therefore quite difficult to determine the extent to which women are actually committing these offences.

This literature review was conducted in an effort to highlight some of the current research being done on female child molesters and to allow better understanding of some of the issues surrounding these women. The information in this paper represents a selective rather than a comprehensive review of the literature. Information was provided on some of the characteristics of female sex offenders, and typological schemes were discussed with the intent to demonstrate some of the similarities and differences among the female offenders themselves. It seems clear from this review that increased attention needs to be paid to the behaviour of female child sexual abusers. As Finkelhor asserts:

> Certainly in the past some people have assumed that sexual abuse at the hands of females never occurred. If this is how people have interpreted past research, then it is wrong and does require correction in the direction that some of the current commentators indicate (Finkelhor 1984, p. 184).

There are many holes within the existing research that are in need of exploration. The solution to the widespread problem of child molestation cannot be fully understood by ignoring a certain percentage of the offenders themselves. It is only through an examination of *all* types of child sexual abuse that we may increase our awareness of the dynamics that occur between perpetrators and victims, whether they are male or female in our society.

References

Badgley, R. F. (Chairman) (1984) *Sexual Offences Against Children. Report of the Committee on Sexual Offences Against Children and Youths* Ottawa: National Health and Welfare.

Bagley, C. and King, K. (1990) *Child Sexual Abuse: The Search for Healing* London: Routledge.

Banning, Anne (1989) 'Mother–son incest: confronting a prejudice' in *Child Abuse and Neglect* **13**, 563–570.

Bass, E. and Davis L. (1988) *The Courage to Heal: A Guide for Women Survivors of Child Sexual Abuse* London: Harper and Row.

Broussard, Sylvia, Wagner N. G. and Kazelskis, R. (1991) 'Undergraduate students' perceptions of child sexual abuse: the impact of victim sex, perpetrator sex, respondent sex, and victim response' in *The Journal of Family Violence* **6**, 267–278.

Burgess, A. W., Groth, A. N., Holmstrom, L. L. and Sgroi, S. M. (1987) *Sexual Assault of Children and Adolescents* Mass & Toronto: Lexington Books.

Condy, Sylvia (1987) 'Parameters of sexual contact of boys with women' in *Archives of Sexual Behaviour* **16**, 379–394.

Cooper, A. J. (1990) 'A female sex offender with multiple paraphilias: a psychologic, physiologic and endocrine case study' in *The Canadian Journal of Psychiatry* 35, 334–337.

Faller, Kathleen (1987) 'Women who sexually abuse children' in *Violence and Victims* 2, 263–276.

Fehrenbach, Peter (1988) 'Characteristics of female adolescent sexual offenders' in *The American Journal of Orthopsychiatry* 58, 148–151.

Fine, Sean (1991) 'Sex abuse by women ignored, psychologist tells conference' in *The Globe and Mail* 30 October 1991, A1–A2.

Finkelhor, D. (1979) *Sexually Victimized Children* New York: The Free Press.

Finkelhor, David (1984) *Child Sexual Abuse. New Theory and Research* New York: The Free Press.

Finkelhor, D. and Araji, S. (1986) 'Explanations of pedophilia: a four factor model' in *The Journal of Sex Research* 22, 145–161.

Finkelhor, D. and Russell, D. (1984) 'Women as perpetrators' in Finkelhor, D. (Ed.) *Child Sexual Abuse, New Theory and Research* New York: Free Press.

Finkelhor, David et al. (1986) *A Sourcebook on Child Sexual Abuse* California: Sage Publications.

Fischer, Gloria (1990) Why more males than females report retrospectively positive feelings about and/or regard as inconsequential child sexual abuse experiences. Paper presented at the Ninth Annual Conference on the Treatment of Sexual Abusers, Their Families and Victims, 4, 5, 6 October 1990, Toronto.

Goldstein, Seth L. (1987) *The Sexual Exploitation Of Children* New York: Elsevier.

Grayson, Joanne (1989) 'Female sex offenders' in *Interchange. A Cooperative Newsletter of the Adolescent Perpetrator network* The C. Henry Kempe National Center for the Prevention and Treatment of Child Abuse and Neglect, Denver, Colorado.

Groth, Nicholas (1979) *Men Who Rape* New York: Plenum Press.

Hunter, Mic. (1990) *Abused Boys. The Neglected Victims of Sexual Abuse.* Lexington: D. C. Heath and Company.

Johnson, Robert (1987) 'Past sexual victimization by females of male patients in an adolescent medicine clinic population' in *The American Journal of Psychiatry* 144, 650–652.

Johnson, Toni (1989) 'Female child perpetrators: children who molest other children' in *Child Abuse and Neglect* 13, 571–585.

Justice, D. and Justice, R. (1979) *The Broken Taboo* New York: Human Sciences Press.

Katahara, Michio (1989) 'Incest — Japanese style' in *The Journal of Psychohistory* 16, 445–450.

Knopp, F. H. and Lackey, L. B. (1987) *Female Sexual Abusers: A Summary of Data From 44 Treatment Providers* Orwell, VT: The Safer Society Program.

Krug, Ronald (1989) 'Adult male report of childhood sexual abuse by mothers: case descriptions, motivations and long-term consequences' in *Child Abuse and Neglect* 13, 111–119.

Mannarino, A. P. (1986) 'A clinical demographic study of sexually abused children' in *Child Abuse and Neglect* 13, 111–119.

Mannarino, A. P. (1986) 'A clinical demographic study of sexually abused children' in *Child Abuse and Neglect* 10, 17–23.

Margolis, Marvin (1984) 'A case of mother–adolescent son incest: a follow-up study' in *Psychoanalytic Quarterly* 53, 355–385.

Marvasti, Jamshid (1986) 'Incestuous mothers' in *The American Journal of Forensic Psychiatry* 7, 63–69.

Mathews, Ruth (1989) *Female Sexual Offenders. An Exploratory Study* Orwell, VT: The Safer Society Press.

McCarty, Loretta (1986) 'Mother–child incest: characteristics of the offender' in *Child Welfare* 65, 447–458.

O'Connor, Art (1987) 'Female sex offenders' in *The British Journal of Psychiatry* **150**, 615–620.

Pierce, L. (1987) 'Incestuous victimization by juvenile sex offenders' in *Journal of Family Violence* **2**, 351–364.

Russell, D. (1983) 'The incidence and prevalence of intrafamilial and extrafamilial sexual abuse of female children' in *Child Abuse And Neglect* **7**, 133–146.

Sarrel, Philip (1982) 'Sexual molestation of men by women' in *Archives of Sexual Behavior* **11**, 117–131.

Steed, Judy (1991) 'When mothers sexually abuse their sons' in *The Toronto Star* 14, 15 March 1991.

Wolfe, Florence (1985) *Twelve Female Sexual Offenders* Presented at Next Steps in Research on the Assessment and Treatment of Sexually Aggressive Persons Conference, St Louis, MO.

14 Books

Self-help books

Allies in Healing: When the Person You Love was Sexually Abused as a Child Laura Davis, Harper Perennial, 1991.
Encouragement and specific, practical advice for those trying to help someone who was abused, while at the same time coping with their own emotions and needs.

The Courage to Heal: A Guide for Women Survivors Ellen Bass and Laura Davis, Mandarin, 1988.
For women who have survived childhood sexual abuse, this book gives positive, practical help and advice.

The Courage to Heal Workbook, For Women and Men Survivors of Child Sexual Abuse Laura Davis, Harper & Row, 1990.
This workbook acknowledges abuse by women and has exercises to help survivors cope and come to terms with having been sexually abused by a man or woman.

Out in the Open, A Guide for Young People Who Have Been Sexually Abused Ouaine Bain and Maureen Sanders, Virago Upstairs, 1991.
A sympathetic, easily read book which talks about the range of feelings experienced by young people who have been sexually abused.

Outgrowing the Pain, A Book For and About Adults Abused as Children Eliana Gil, Dell, 1983.
An easily read book with many positive messages. This is a good first book when people are beginning to deal with the abuse they suffered as children.

Victims No Longer, Men Recovering from Incest and Other Sexual Child Abuse, Mike Lew, Harper & Row, 1990.
The author states that female abuse is far more widespread than previously thought. The book gives both survivors and therapists essential advice for healing.

When You're Ready, A Woman's Healing from Childhood Physical and Sexual Abuse by her Mother Kathy Evert and Inie Bijkerk, Launch Press, 1987.
The first book written by a survivor of physical and sexual abuse by her mother, with input from her therapist.

Books for professionals

Beyond Sexual Abuse, Therapy with Women who were Childhood Victims Derek Jehu, Wiley, 1989.

Female Sexual Offenders, An Exploratory Study, Ruth Mathews, Jane Kinder Matthews, Kathleen Speltz, The Safer Society Press, 1989.

Handbook of Clinical Intervention in Child Sexual Abuse (revised) Suzanne M. Sgroi, Lexington Books, 1993.

Males At Risk, The Other Side of Child Sexual Abuse Frank Bolton, Larry Morris, Ann MacEachron, Sage Publications, 1989.

Mother, Madonna, Whore, The Idealization and Denigration of Motherhood Estella V. Welldon, The Guilford Press, 1988.

Nursery Crimes David Finklehor, Sage, 1988.

Treating the Sexual Offender Barry M. Maletzky, Sage, 1991.

Treating the Young Male Victim of Sexual Assault Eugene Porter, The Safer Society Press, 1986.

Vulnerable Populations Volumes 1 and 2, Suzanne M. Sgroi, Lexington Books, 1988/89.

Women and Men Who Sexually Abuse Children, A Comparative Analysis Craig Allen, The Safer Society Press, 1991.

15 National help organisations

United Kingdom

AWARE, c/o KIDSCAPE, 152 Buckingham Palace Road, London SW1W 9TR
AWARE (Awareness of Women as Abusers, Recognition and Education) supports survivors of sexual abuse by women, and gives advice and training to professionals about this issue. Send a large self-addressed stamped envelope for more information.

British Association of Counselling, 1 Regent Place, Rugby, Warks CV21 2PJ Tel: (0788) 550899
Send a self-addressed stamped envelope for a list of counsellors in your local area.

ChildLine, Freepost 1111 Tel: (0800) 1111
24-hour free phone counselling and advice service for children in trouble or danger.

KIDSCAPE, 152 Buckingham Palace Road, London SW1W 9TR
Tel: (071) 730 3300
Send a self-addressed, stamped envelope for a list of help organisations.

National Society for the Prevention of Cruelty to Children (NSPCC), Child Protection Helpline, 67 Saffron Hill, London EC1N 8RS Tel: (0800) 800500
The Helpline is a 24-hour nationwide counselling and referral service.

Royal Scottish Society for the Prevention of Cruelty to Children, (RSSPCC) Melville House, 41 Polwarth Terrace, Edinburgh EH11 1NU Tel: (031) 337 8539
RSSPCC gives advice and practical help, and referral information.

Samaritans, see your local directory
24-hour help lines for anyone who wishes to talk in confidence. Some
areas have drop-in centres.

Youth Access, Magazine Business Centre, 11 Newark Street, Leicester LE1 5SS Tel: (0533) 558763
Gives information, advice and counselling.

Ireland

Irish Society for the Prevention of Cruelty to Children (ISPCC), 20
Molesworth Street, Dublin 2, Irish Republic Tel: (01) 6794944
ISPCC will give referral information about local help organisations.

ISPCC Childline Tel: (1800) 666666
Freephone helpline for children, open from 10am to 10pm.

United States

The following organisations will give you information about counselling and self-help groups in your local area:

Adults Molested as Children United, 213 East Gish Rd, San José, CA
95112 Tel: (408) 453 7617

National Center of Child Abuse and Neglect (NCCAN), 330 C Street
SW, Room 2064, Switzer Building, Washington, DC 20201 Tel:
(202) 205 8586

National Committee for Prevention of Child Abuse, 332 South
Michigan Avenue, Suite 1600, Chicago, IL 60604-4357 Tel: (312) 663
3520

C. Henry Kempe National Center for the Prevention of Child Abuse
and Neglect, 1205 Oneida Street, Denver, CO 80220 Tel: (303) 321
3963